ARE
YOU
DAVE
GORMAN?

Dave Gorman & Danny Wallace

EBURY PRESS

First published in Great Britain in 2001

1 3 5 7 9 10 8 6 4 2

Ebury Press
Random House, 20 Vauxhall Bridge Road, London SW1V 2SA

Random House Australia Pty Limited
20 Alfred Street, Milsons Point, Sydney, New South Wales 2061, Australia

Random House New Zealand Limited
18 Poland Road, Glenfield, Auckland 10, New Zealand

Random House Africa (Pty) Limited
Endulini, 5A Jubilee Road, Parktown 2193, South Africa

The Random House Group. Limited Reg. No. 954009

A CIP catalogue record for this book is available from the British Library

ISBN   0 09 187964 7

Photography by Danny Wallace and Hanne Knudsen
Cover and plate section design by Push
Text design by Textype, Cambridge
Printed and bound in UK by Mackays of Chatham plc, Chatham, Kent

Papers used by Ebury Press are natural, recyclable products made from wood grown in sustainable forests.

About the authors

Dave Gorman is a Perrier Award-nominated comedian, a storyteller and a writer. His television work has earned him two BAFTAs, as well as his own series on BBC2. He has taken his live shows to cities as far afield as Melbourne, Aspen, Montreal and Aberdeen.

www.davegorman.com

Danny Wallace is a writer, producer and award-winning journalist, whose work has appeared in numerous newspapers and magazines, including *The Guardian, The Independent* and *Melody Maker*.

www.dannywallace.com

This is their first book, but not their first adventure.

Dave and Danny would like to thank. . .

Our parents, for letting us get away with stuff like this as kids.

Rob Aslett and all at Avalon, Jake Lingwood at Ebury Press, Robert Cogo-Fawcett, Sonia Friedman and The Comedy Theatre, Robin & Alison Mitchell, Christopher Richardson, Piers Torday and The Pleasance, Felix Schoien, Jaakko & Yoko Anttonen, Simon Streeting, The Riverside Studios, Myfanwy Moore, Andrew Wiltshire, Claire Teasdale, Kate Holdsworth, Pati Marr, Ian Collins, John Pidgeon, Espen Tårnesvik, Victoria Cameron and Nick Watts, for letting us get away with stuff like this as adults.

Very special thanks to the very patient Hanne Langeland Knudsen (sorry), to Dave's bank manager (sorry) and, of course, to Dave Gormans everywhere.

PROLOGUE

Hello. My name's Dave Gorman.

Throughout this book, I'll be writing in this bold, rather confident typeface.

Hello. My name's Danny Wallace. And I'll be writing in this relaxed, more elegant font.

Now, Danny Wallace isn't really a name you're going to see all that much in this book, so if I were you, I'd go back and read it again.

A little while ago, Danny and I. . .

That's me.

. . . set off on a journey that should never really have happened. It was something that would take us tens of thousands of miles around the world, meeting dozens of strangers, all of whom have one vital thing in common.

But I'm sure you'll work out what that is as you read on. . .

The most worrying thing about the book you are about to read is that it is true. Entirely, painfully true.

Read the book. Pity us. And then pray that it never happens to you.

Or, follow in our footsteps and do it for yourself.

No, don't do that.

Thank you.

Dave Gorman & Danny Wallace, St. Tropez, 2001

Chapter 1

HARROW BOYS. . .

If I'm to be regarded as an authority on anything – and I hope that one day I am – I would guess it would be on the subject of flatmates. I've had my fair share, and probably yours, too.

Ranging from the freakish to the unutterably dull, more people have bought me a pint of milk than they have a pint of lager, and that's the way I like it.

There was Tony the Greek, for example; a man whose nickname stemmed not from a shady gangster background but from the fact that his name was Tony and he came from Greece. I'm quite proud of the fact that it was me who came up with the name. Before then, he'd just been Tony, which, to be honest, made him sound a bit common.

Tony would buy fishburgers from the chip shop down the street and fill every spare shelf in the fridge with them. He was a fan of what I believe polite society might term 'comical cigarettes' and would often emerge from his room surrounded by a haze of smoke and an exotic smell, take a fishburger from the fridge, and then head back to his room where he would sleep for most of the day and night. When occasionally he would leave the flat, he'd only go as far as *Tesco*, where he would prove their perfect customer and fall for each and every multibuy deal they had going. We might be two boys sharing a flat, but as far as Tony the Greek was concerned, as long as you were saving a fiver in the process, you could never have enough tampons.

I didn't stay in that flat for long.

I have lived in a house full of Norwegians and a man called Janush who would often be mistaken for George from *Seinfeld*. I have shared a flat with eight musicians, with two fashion designers, with a bouncer called Big Al, and, variously, three dogs, a stoat and six fish.

Now, let's not draw any conclusions from this. Let's not start thinking that I must have some kind of anti-social tendencies that might cause flatmates to drop their belongings and flee the minute they walk in the door. I don't look like a serial killer, a born again Christian, or a children's entertainer. My hygiene is second-to-none. The stoat didn't belong to me. And when it's my turn to buy the milk, I treat my responsibility with all the gravitas it deserves.

But it was when I was living in a converted hotel in Harrow-on-the-Hill with a Finnish musician called Jaakko and a Polish 'visual poet' called Marcin that I found true flatmate happiness.

Jaakko was a kind and gentle Finn, who'd make proper coffee in the mornings. Marcin was wise – almost mystical – and statements of astounding profundity would often fall from his lips. 'I have noticed,' he once said, 'that items made from stainless steel have "stainless steel" written on them . . . I wonder if it would not be sensible to extend this practice to other materials also, for the sake of clarity. . .?'.

The day Marcin revealed that he was being kicked out of the country just because he was living here illegally, we were drinking Jaakko's proper coffee in the kitchen as usual. Of course, the fact that Marcin couldn't afford his ticket home, had nowhere to store his stuff, and had to say goodbye to his pretty new girlfriend wasn't great news, but the fact that Jaakko and I now had to find a new flatmate really was the straw that broke the camel's back.

For a while we did nothing. We tried to ride it out. But now that there were only two of us, it seemed like *every other night* it was my turn to do the dishes.

Jaakko felt the same. And so one night, after taking the last of Marcin's stuff to the tip, it was decided.

We would take out an ad for a new flatmate.

If there's one thing I knew about myself it was that I didn't want to live with other people. I lived alone in a one bedroom flat, overlooking the canal basin in the centre of Manchester and I loved it that way.

I had spent most of my life sharing with other people. For the first ten years of my life I had shared a room with my brother, Nick. For nine months before that we had shared a womb – he's my *twin* brother. Since leaving home I had lived with first seven people, then five people, then four people, then three people, then two people, then one person, then one-person-I-was-sleeping-with who turned out to be one-person-I-wasn't-the-only-person-sleeping-with and so, finally, I lived alone. And I was convinced that each of these arrangements had been better than the last. (Although, obviously, I missed the sex).

It's not that I don't like other people. It's just that with fewer people there's less compromise. And with no people there is none. I was happy this way: just me, my music, my choice of TV channel, my furniture and my sleep pattern.

Living alone means never having to say you're sorry. Living alone means you can use the toilet without shutting the door. If that isn't the very definition of personal freedom, I don't know what is. And when I look back at that flat, that flat so full of good memories, I am unable to tell you whether or not the bathroom even had a door.

The only problem with living alone was having a mortgage. Apparently, there's something in the small print that means you have to pay all that money back. Crazy, isn't it? So, the mortgage needed paying, which meant that *I* needed paying, which in turn meant I would have to involve myself in the grubby world of work.

There was an offer and it left me on the horns of a dilemma. A TV company had asked me if I might like to work for them. The contract would last for nearly four months, the wage would more than adequately cover my mortgage, but – and here comes the particularly tricky horn – the job was in London.

Manchester had been home for ten years, I lived alone in a flat that I adored but in order to pay for it I would have to spend four months not living there. Worse . . . the cost of living in London *and* paying the mortgage in Manchester meant I would have to, gulp, live with other people.

With a heavy heart I bought a copy of *Loot* and started making my way through the small ads.

I was looking for a payphone in Budapest Central Station. Yes, I know it's a little early in the story to suddenly confuse you with tales of Eastern Europe, but it's the truth, that's where I was, and it seems a little silly to lie to you and tell you I was in Bournemouth when Budapest is far more glamorous and makes you feel your buying this book has already been a little worthwhile.

Anyway, it was midnight, it was freezing, it was Hungary, and my only concern was whether or not Jaakko had managed to find us someone new to live with. I dreaded not being in on the big decision. Jaakko had wanted to wait until I got back from Hungary, but I was insistent; I trusted him to find the right person for the flat. And anyway, I was going to be late for my plane and I hadn't changed any money yet. A few people were coming round to look at the flat that night, but I was sure, as is the way, that none of them would be suitable candidates for our very metropolitan way of life.

I'd been asked to go to Hungary to write an article for a magazine, but it was a last minute thing and they needed me to go out there as soon as possible. Before I left for the airport, I'd tutored Jaakko on what to look out for in a potential flatmate. I gave him a few pointers, a few questions he might like to throw in. I warned him of women who look like they might just have split up with their boyfriends and would simply love two male flatmates to spend twelve hours a day pouring her heart out to, and then the other twelve hours screaming at for all the Bad Things Men Do. I warned him of men who look like they might be about to bring an unnecessary amount of computer equipment to the flat and then never leave their room. And I warned him about the people who look like they might very well take an active interest in live folk music and all that that entails (I have, over the years, come to realise that there is nothing more terrifying than discovering your new flatmate has brought an acoustic guitar and some bongos with them).

On the plane to Budapest, though, I began to have my doubts. It's a big thing, deciding on who should move into your flat with you. A lot of issues come into play. I couldn't put my finger on any of them, but I knew they existed, and that was enough to fluster me. I now dreaded coming back from Hungary and meeting whoever Jaakko had decided should move into the flat. I became convinced that he would almost certainly have taken leave of his senses, or panicked because he couldn't answer a potential flatmate's question about the water rates. Or perhaps he would buckle under the pressure and simply offer the room to the first bucktoothed simpleton with a set of bongos to walk through our door. . .

I couldn't stand it. I needed to be in on the decision. I asked a man in a hat where the nearest payphone was.

'Where are you coming from?' he asked.

'London', I said, and regretted it instantly. The man asked me whether I knew that in 1953, Hungary beat England at Wembley 6-3.

I said I did know that, actually, although I neglected to mention that it was only because I'd been told exactly that three times already since our plane landed, each time by an eager Hungarian stranger. The man smiled at me. I smiled back. I asked him again if he knew where the nearest payphone was, and he said yes, and pointed at the most obvious-looking payphone I had ever seen, surrounded by fluorescent yellow arrows and big signs saying *Telefon* (which I have since discovered is the Hungarian word for 'telephone').

I used it to wake Jaakko up.

'Hi Jaakko.'

'Hey Danny.'

'Listen, I think we should wait with the flatmate thing until I get back...'

'Ah...'

'It's not fair me putting all the responsibility on you...'

'That's okay, 'cos...'

'I think we should both be in on the decision, so that we get someone we're both happy with...'

'Yeah, absolutely...'

'Cool.'

'But a man called Dave is going to move in this weekend. He's coming down from Manchester with all his things on Friday.'

I weighed the situation up, deciding how much anger and annoyance to show.

'Okay then.'

I'd had a list of fifteen places to look at and two days in which to do it. Number 44a was the first place I checked. It was in the heart of Harrow, which seemed an awfully long way out of town – but it was only a five-minute walk to the tube and, from there, a twenty-minute journey into central London. The house had been fairly grand in its day – although that was clearly some time ago. Since then it had been converted first into a hotel, then into two flats, with 44a being the first and second floors. The man who showed me round was called Jaakko (pronounced Yah-co). He was Finnish.

'I'm Jaakko', he said with a broad grin and a faint accent, 'I am from Finland.'

We shook hands.

'I'll show you the spare room. It *was* Marcin's room. He is from Poland. He's a very interesting guy – he is a visual poet.'

'A *visual* poet? What does that mean?'

'I have absolutely no idea. But he's a very interesting guy.'

'So, was it just the two of you?'

'No. . . there is Danny also. I'm sorry he's not here. He's in Budapest.'

'It all sounds very international. Where's *he* from?'

'Bath.'

'Oh.'

Jaakko seemed like a laid-back enough guy.

'Do you have any house rules?' I asked.

'No,' he said. 'It is very much a house of convenience. Especially convenience foods.'

At the end of the tour, I made a rash decision. I decided to take the room. There were two thought processes at work here. First, I figured that a flat full of globetrotters would be as close as I could get to living alone. You can't trot the globe *and* be in the living room arguing over the remote control at the same time. Second, I was meant to visit fourteen more properties before the next day was done and I just couldn't be arsed. Jaakko and I shook hands once more and the deal was done. On Monday I would move in.

On Tuesday I returned from my Eastern European jaunt with a working knowledge of Hungarian, a few facts about the country to pepper around my article (apparently, in 1953, Hungary beat England 6-3 at Wembley), and a furry white hat which I planned to give to Jaakko to make up for the fact that I hadn't done any hoovering since about Christmas 1971.

The fact that Jaakko had already done the deal and decided who was to move into 44a had taken a weight off my mind. There was now nothing I could do about it. If this Dave fella turned out to be a semi-professional wrestler who just loved to involve his friends in practising his new moves, I'd just have to grin and bear the inevitable headlocks.

But when I arrived at the tube station I began the five-minute walk to the house with my head low and my bags heavy. I started to feel slightly awkward about walking into my own house. Presumably this 'Dave' would now be there. He would already have unpacked his wrestling gear and found a quiet corner for his many bongos.

Jaakko would have shown him how to operate the needlessly complicated shower. He would have shown him which button on the needlessly complicated remote turns on the video without turning off the stereo at the same time. He would have demonstrated how to use the various kitchen appliances – each of them needlessly complicated, and each of them usually shunned in favour of the microwave. Which would actually have taken some explaining before use, being one of the few things in our house that was deceptively simple.

Dave would probably have been hungry after moving his stuff into the flat – as semi-professional-wrestlers-cum-folk-musicians often are – which meant that he would have probably done his first shop. He'd have to have chosen between the *Tesco* down the road or the *Spar* two minutes away. He'd then have to have chosen which of our spare shelves was to be his.

I turned my key as quietly as I could and walked into the house. I looked around the hallway. Nothing too different. He'd clearly not had time to make his mark yet, but I bet he had plans. Oh yes. I bet he had *all kinds of plans* for that hallway. He probably already wanted me and Jaakko out, based on those hallway plans of his alone.

I walked into the kitchen. I was right about the shopping. Dave had chosen the *Spar* two minutes away. The cheap bastard. He'd also decided on the shelves right opposite the kitchen door . . . no, not the ones you're thinking of, not the ones in the cupboard, but the ones out in the open and in full view of any visiting dignitaries! The sheer arrogance! His tastes, it seemed, were for canned goods – beans, tuna chunks and soup with bits in. Not the fresh fruit, fresh vegetables and garden herbs that Jaakko and I often talked about buying but never did – oh, *no. Convenience* foods! How would this man fit in?

An inspection of the fridge revealed that Dave had bought a new, two-litre bottle of semi-skimmed milk, presumably to try and win his new flatmates over. This desperate attempt to curry favour was too much for me, and I became instantly convinced that Jaakko had made the gravest of errors. How could he not have seen that this cheap, arrogant and lazy new flatmate of ours was in no way the kind of man that I would willingly know?

And then Dave walked into the kitchen.

And I realised that I already did.

I'd first met Danny – the man whose kitchen I now found myself in – at the Edinburgh Festival four years earlier, in 1996.

I was there performing a one-man show – which meant that I

was working for one hour a night but that I was away from home for four weeks. By the time the festival was nearly four days old I'd started to get a little bored. I'd gone out to one of the many parties and I was in the mood to get drunk.

At the party, the bar was so crowded and I was responsible for getting in such a big round that every order became rather a time-consuming exercise. So to help me acheive my goal that evening (getting drunk) I had taken to the unsavoury habit of bookending. That is, I was ordering my own drink twice – once at either end of the order.

'I'll have a rum and coke, two pints of Guinness,' (at which point the rum arrives and I start to drink) '. . . two pints of lager, a vodka tonic, a vodka lime and soda, a whiskey no ice, three Jack Daniels and coke . . .' (I finish the rum) '. . . oh and another rum and coke please. Oh. And a tray. Thanks.'

On ordering one round, the barman was at the till and I found myself trying to work out how best to negotiate my way out of the crowded bar area. I tried to half-turn so that I would still be able to collect my change but also be ready to sidle through the throng. Amateurishly, I dropped my shoulder, and I knocked the elbow of the man next to me and spilt the pint that was attached to it. I looked at the spillee. His forlorn face convinced me that I should do the decent thing. The barman offered me my change, and I risked the wrath of the queuing drinkers . . .

'Sorry . . . er . . . could I have *another* pint of lager, please. Thanks.'

I turned to the forlorn one and offered my hand, 'I'm Dave.'

He shook my hand. 'Danny.'

I turned back to the bar.

'. . . And another rum and coke. Ta.'

Usually, when someone spills my pint in a pub, I break their nose. Or, at least, I do it with my eyes. But I hide it behind quite a pleasant glance, an 'oops', and more often than not, I apologise to save them having to. But I think we both walk away knowing who the victor was.

On this occasion, I had been talking to my two friends Adam and Steve, fellow writers, also covering the festival, who'd been roped in to doing all the coverage for *The Daily Star* – not a paper that normally plumbs the depths of arts coverage . . . *arse* coverage is a far more likely subject – but who nevertheless had decided that this would be the year the *Star* went upmarket. Shows were awarded not *points* out of five, but *pints*. You get the idea.

When Dave nudged my elbow and made my knees wet, Adam and Steve had just spotted Scottish belle Gail Porter – then just an obscure kids' TV presenter – and were trying to work out how to get through the crowded bar to try and speak to her.

I, however, had just been bought a pint by a stranger, and it would've been rude not to talk to him for at least a while.

Now, there are certain situations that seem to disable proper conversation. For example, during the first seven days of anyone's time at university it is impossible to have a conversation without discussing each other's A-level results, even though they are no longer relevant and were never interesting. Well, the Edinburgh Fringe is like that. No conversation can occur without discussing the Fringe itself and your place in it. All conversation must centre on why you have decamped to Edinburgh for the month. What you do/what you've seen/what you *should* see . . . these are the accepted subjects of conversation, those are the rules.

Well, that night, Danny and I *broke* those rules. We talked about all sorts of things – we worked out that if an aircraft were to take off vertically and then wait for the earth to rotate before descending it would only take five hours to travel to New York; we established that a slinky on an up escalator would be in a state of perpetual motion; we decided that the introduction of 'Uncle Albert' had damaged the sitcom *Only Fools and Horses* almost as much as the introduction of 'Scrappy Doo' had damaged the cartoon *Scooby Doo*; and we invented *Travel Twister*. We didn't discuss the festival once. And that was why I liked him. In a city obsessed with self I had found someone with something else on his mind.

I was working as a features writer and reviewer for *The Scotsman* that year – a paper with integrity and independence high on its list of priorities – and *The Scotsman's* reviewers are generally highly discouraged from making friends with performers.

Bizarrely, it's seen as just one step away from moving in with them.

The next day I discovered an alarming fact about Danny Wallace. He was a journalist. Worse, he was a reviewer. I knew then that any potential friendship that might have grown out of the drunkenness of the night before was illicit. Performers and reviewers just don't mix. Seeing the two together is like seeing a Premiership footballer wining and dining next Saturday's referee; it just isn't done. So that was that. Neither of us mentioned it, we just shrugged our shoulders and got on with things while making sure not to get on with each other. He was a Montague and I was a Capulet and that was that. Over the next couple of years we occasionally crossed paths in the course of our work, but while we would nod at each other in acknowledgement, there was never any conversation.

But now here he was, standing in front of me once again, in Harrow, looking shocked. Surely it would be okay to talk to him now that we shared a kitchen?

I'd been upstairs trying to work out where to put my bongos. Then I figured they might look quite decorative on the mantelpiece in the living room. It occurred to me that it would be a nice conciliatory gesture on my first proper day in a new flat to donate something like that to the shared rooms of the house, so I'd taken my bongos downstairs. While doing so I heard the front door shut. I got downstairs and there was a suitcase in the hallway. I walked into the kitchen and there was Danny. The man I'd met four years ago in Edinburgh was now standing in my kitchen. Or rather I was standing in his kitchen. Or rather, we were standing in what was now *our* kitchen.

There was a big pause. Eventually, Danny spoke.

'Do you want a rum and coke?'

Alcohol seemed like the sensible option in this situation, given that a) that bloke Dave had moved in, and b) he'd brought some bloody bongos with him.

And that was how we started talking. And from there we talked, and drank, and talked some more into the early hours of the next morning.

As time moved on I realised I was actually enjoying living with Danny and Jaakko. I wasn't just tolerating it. It was an actual pleasure. The compromise I'd so wanted to avoid just wasn't there. They were, but the compromise wasn't. In the months we shared, I don't think there was ever an argument or even a discussion about what should be on the TV. We all made each other cups of tea, we kicked a football around together, we put a dartboard up in the hall, and there was always a cocktail being mixed in the kitchen.

The toilet door remained closed, but apart from that, life at 44a was close to perfect.

I rented out my flat in Manchester to a young professional couple who were only too pleased to pay me more money in rent than I needed to cover my mortgage, and I decided to stay in London.

Dave and I became firm friends almost immediately. Our strange sleep patterns and willingness to brew up at the drop of a hat only served to strengthen that. And there was a real synchronicity to our lives. If I decided, at 3 o'clock in the morning, that what I really wanted to do was watch *Karaoke Challenge* on cable TV, you could bet I'd bump into Dave in the hallway. And more often than not, he'd have two cups of tea in his hands.

The nature of our jobs meant that our hours were our own to keep. We didn't have bosses. We had only the lightest of responsibilities. We could stay up all night, and sleep in all day. It was like being unemployed, but without the hassle of looking for work. We were perhaps the only two people in the country to watch more than one episode of *3-2-1* in a week, beginning, as they did, halfway between when most people go to bed and when they get up. We became avid viewers of Harrow's local cable TV channel, eagerly awaiting each new programme recorded on home videocameras by the town's surly fifteen-year-old schoolchildren.

In short, we had a lot of time and not much work to do.

Jaakko wasn't so lucky. He was working every hour of every day in a soulless telemarketing job, researching things that really didn't need to be researched, so that he could save up enough money to visit his fiancée, Yoko. As is the fashion with many Japanese people these days, Yoko lived in Japan, and what with her busy job in banking and her various hobbies, some evenings it just didn't make sense for her to make the trip over to Harrow.

But Jaakko and Yoko remained in love thanks to frequent phone calls and infinitely more frequent e-mails. In addition, they must have known they were in with a chance of making a go of it; it's usually couples with rhyming names that stay together the longest. Who knows how different things could have been if Prince Charles had only changed his name to Guyana? It may also, I think, be the real reason why William of Orange never found true happiness.

But one morning, doubtless as Dave and I were sleeping off the tea-soaked night before, Jaakko received some happy news. I knew this because my room was nearest the kitchen, and I could smell bacon, coffee and all manner of other smells guaranteed to rouse his flatmates. It was clear he had something to say.

He did. Yoko had been offered a job in London, and would soon be joining her husband-to-be in the upstairs bedroom. This was great news. Their patience, loyalty and love had paid off. They would marry. They would live together in bliss. They would live together in love. More importantly, they would live together in a converted hotel with me (and Dave).

I sensed the possibility of change in the air.

Jaakko and Yoko were married at the Finnish Church in London one sunny summer's day.

The bride and groom were swamped by their families – the Finns unable to speak Japanese, the Japanese unable to speak Finnish, and no-one able to speak English. This made Danny's best man speech quite a tough gig, all told.

The reception was on a canal boat in London's Little Venice, and it was there, on the deck, champagne in hand, that Danny and I began to talk about Jaakko, about Yoko, and about 44a. We now had to consider the possibility that Jaakko and Yoko might not want to live with us any more.

We'd ignored the thought before, of course. How could marital bliss possibly compare with a scruffy houseshare with two scruffy men? But as the day came to an end, and Jaakko and Yoko prepared for their honeymoon, Danny and I reached a virtually unspoken agreement. The days of 44a, of long afternoons in the sun-trap garden, of darts and cable TV, of cocktails and tea, were coming to an end.

We would need somewhere new to live. And we had a fair idea where it would be.

The East End of London in general is a wonderful place. And trendy, apparently. Shoreditch is where it's all happening this week, but next week it'll be Bethnal Green, and in a fortnight, the clever money and all the new bars will be opening up in Aldgate. There's Bow, as well, which apparently some circles now refer to as 'Bow-ho' but as far as I can work out contains nothing more than a *Costcutters* shop, a long and busy road, and a police station that the Kray twins used to visit quite regularly. The part of town we chose, though, was authentically *un*trendy. In fact, it was shit.

Our new flat was opposite a number of convenient amenities. A genuine East End pub, as rough as any you'd ever seen. A genuine East End cafe, as greasy as any you could imagine. A chip shop, a newsagent, an off licence. The type of barber's shop you really had to be careful while passing should any accidentally lopped-off ears bloody your shoes. Each of these places we would come to know intimately in the next few months, but most of all the pub.

This pub was the type of place you really wouldn't visit if you didn't live opposite it, and even then you wouldn't really visit it unless you were two twentysomething men with time on your hands and a penchant for darts. Or a man named Graham whose quest for a free pint was only slightly stronger than the smell of his deodorant.

Every minute we spent in that pub probably took five off our lives. It remains a place which, to our continued amazement, somehow escapes the knowledge of the Environmental Health department – I would say it's no coincidence that the urinals are located directly above where the beer barrels are kept. Nevertheless, it's a pub that seems to *glow* at night, and whatever the weather, that's a tempting sight.

A few weeks into our new flatshare, it was Danny's birthday. Well, no, actually, it wasn't. His birthday had been about six months before, but his present – a shiny new video camera – had only just arrived. And the rule in our house is, if you get your present, it's your birthday.

We got a few friends together and decamped to the pub. The landlord had promised us the day before that if we turned up late enough, he'd officially allow us an illegal East End lock-in . . . and at 11.30 that night, the revelry began. . .

Danny had his video camera out and Graham, as usual, was buzzing around trying to blag a free pint. We bought him one –

well, it *was* a birthday celebration after all – and amazingly, he instantly reciprocated with a round of tequilas.

Now, tequila is not a drink that Danny or I would ever willingly get involved with. It is an evil drink, put on this earth to make us do stupid things, and as such is best avoided. But this was the first time Graham had bought anyone anything at all, and provided us with yet another reason to celebrate. The tequila was gratefully downed, and slowly began to edge its way towards becoming that evening's official drink of choice.

Now, when I'm drunk, I like to tell stories. When Danny's drunk, he likes to not believe me. I had a feeling tonight would be no different. I'd had an e-mail that day, and tucked away in a PS at the bottom was a fact that made me all but forget what the rest of the letter was about . . . apparently, in the 1970s, East Fife Football Club had had a goalkeeper by the name of Dave Gorman. He was, it went on, still working at the club to this day, now in the capacity of Assistant Manager. I found this news of a Scottish namesake fascinating. Dan, of course, didn't. In fact, as usual, he didn't even believe me.

This wasn't the first time I'd heard of another Dave Gorman. One time, in a pub in Manchester, a taxi driver had come in and shouted 'taxi for Gorman?'. I stood up. *So did another man.* The taxi driver looked at us both, then at the scrap of paper in his hand, before saying '*Dave* Gorman'? We both remained standing. There was confusion, we showed each other some ID. We were indeed both Dave Gormans. There was a small argument about who should take the taxi but I graciously stepped down. Mainly because I remembered that I lived 200 yards away and hadn't ordered one. But it was a true story. A true story that Danny once again refused to believe.

I ploughed on. On another occasion, a friend of mine had rung me up to ask why on earth I was applying for a job with their company. I hadn't applied for *any* job – to do so wouldn't be like me at all – and I told her so. There was a confused silence, then she read the application form back to me as if to jog my memory. It was indeed an application from a Dave Gorman, but it wasn't this one. The confusion was further compounded by the fact that he lived only ten doors away from me. And that is a true story. And Danny didn't believe it.

I brought another round of tequila to the table and placed Danny's in front of him.

'All I'm saying, Dan,' I slurred, 'is that there must be hundreds of people in the world called Dave Gorman, or I wouldn't have heard of *three* of them.'

'It doesn't mean that there are hundreds, Dave,' he said, 'it means that there are at least three others, that's all. If they even exist, which I very much doubt.'

'I'll show you the e-mail later.'

'And what does that prove?'

'Well, that proves that my friend has found out about another Dave Gorman.'

'Doesn't prove he's *real*, though, does it? Doesn't prove he *exists*. For all you know, you might be the only person in the *world* with your name.'

The thought chilled me. Maybe I was all alone. I downed my tequila.

'Bollocks, Dan. There are *plenty* of Gormans in the world, some of them *must* be Davids.' I was getting angry now. 'It stands to reason, doesn't it? There have to be *hundreds* of Dave Gormans in the world.'

'Not *hundreds*, Dave. . .'

'*Hundreds!*'

'No. Sorry. I'm pretty sure you could go your whole life without ever meeting another one. In fact, I don't think you ever will.'

Sometimes, certain phrases are so ingrained in your consciousness that they're a little too easy to say without thinking. I was about to say one of them.

'D'you wanna bet?'

And I did.

He called my bluff. This was good. This was interesting.

He seemed to be taking this very seriously. This wasn't good. This was frightening.

We now found ourselves in a very difficult position; neither wanting to back down, both insisting the other was wrong, each brain surfing a wave of rum and tequila.

'Well, prove it, then,' I said, my eyes nervous but my voice steady.

'I *will* prove it, then' Dave replied, his voice just as steady but his eyes twice as nervous. 'I . . . er . . . just have to make a phone call'.

And with that, Dave legged it out of the pub, chickening out of the bet and running home, where, in the morning he would probably claim to have forgotten about the whole thing.

I'd won. That had been easy enough. I laughed with the others and joined them in a victory round.

But twenty minutes later Dave was banging on the door of the pub. He had a small bag with him, and his phone was in his hand.

'Taxi's here, Dan.'

I looked at him, confused. 'What do you mean the taxi's here?'

'Are you coming, then? He's waiting.'

I peered over his shoulder, and sure enough, parked outside the door, was a red car, engine running.

So Dave had called a taxi. At . . . I looked at my watch . . . 10 past 5 in the morning. So what? That didn't mean he was going to beat me. He was just trying to make me back down, to scare me into some kind of submission. He'd probably pay him off and send him on his way when I did so.

'And where are we supposed to go?' I said.

'East Fife. You think the assistant manager of East Fife Football Club *isn't* called Dave Gorman, I'm telling you he *is*. You bet me you *wouldn't* find any more Dave Gormans, I'm betting you we *will*'.

So I looked Dave in the eye. 'Okay, then. Let's go.'

For a split second I'd seen a look of panic flash across his face – enough to convince me he was bluffing. I told the others I'd see them in a little while, and strode purposefully past Dave, into the cold night air, and into the warm red taxi. We'd be gone ten minutes, maximum, I was sure.

Dave clambered in behind me. 'King's Cross Train Station, please,' he said, and I regarded him with pity. He was going a long way with this – making my imminent victory all the sweeter – but all credit to him for it. I didn't care. This was a free ride in a bright red car as far as I was concerned and, being a boy, this was the kind of thing that I lived for. With a confident, drunken grin on my face, I settled back into my seat, waiting to see just how close to King's Cross we'd get before Dave snapped and told the driver to turn back and head for home.

We pulled in at King's Cross train station and I got my wallet out to pay. Danny looked slightly nervous about this. Perhaps this

would be the moment he snapped and ordered the driver to take us home?

Instead, he got out of the taxi, and I followed. King's Cross was all but deserted, much as you'd expect on a Saturday morning at whatever ungodly hour it was. With the commuters fast asleep and the prostitutes tucked up safe and warm in someone else's bed, we walked – lit by orange lights beneath a dark blue sky – towards the entrance.

'This is stupid,' said Danny, stopping.

'No, *you're* stupid,' I replied. 'Stupid for not believing me.'

'How am I supposed to believe you when you're wrong?'

'I'm not wrong.'

'Yes you are. You're wrong and you know it.'

'We'll see.'

'Yes, we *will* see, yes . . . where are you going?'

'To buy the tickets.'

I left Danny shivering by the entrance and weaved – clearly still suffering from the effects of the tequila – towards the only booth open for business.

'Hello,' I said. 'My friend and I would very much like to go to East Fife. How on earth would we go about doing that?'

Dave returned to me after a few brief words with a man in a cubicle and a credit card transaction.

'Here you are, then,' he beamed, proudly handing me my two orange tickets. 'Your passport to East Fife and the world of Dave Gormans.'

Oh my God. Our tickets had a combined cost of £170. Dave had just spent £170 on this piece of drunken whimsy. £170!

I stared at Dave, mouth wide open, and he matched my gaze with a look of steely determination. He smiled, a glint in his eye.

It was then that a worrying thought struck me . . . had I been tricked? Had Dave led me a merry dance all the way to King's Cross, and was he now hoping to make me dance all the way to East Fife?

The big digital clock on the departures board reads 6:08am. Our train, Dave informs me, leaves at 6:15.

I was forced to think fast. I would bluff him and then not go! No, I would *double*-bluff him, by pretending I wasn't going, and then go anyway. No, I'd go *on my own*.

No.

I was drunk and this kind of thought process very nearly caused me to pass out.

'Come on, Dan, platform five' said Dave, walking away from me.

I started to feel sick. A mixture of too much drink but not enough in the last hour, meant that I was in that strange netherworld of hazy vision and only very basic decision-making skills.

Which is why, I think, I followed him and we boarded the train.

'Dave, now look, what's going on here?' I wasn't slurring any more. Panic was sobering me up. 'I don't like this at all.'

'It's fine, Dan. You made the mistake of calling me a liar.'

'We were drunk! We still *are* drunk! I'm not sure that this is a good idea at all.'

'Relax. Have a nap. We've got a long day ahead of us.'

The train began to move.

'Dave. . .'

'Look, we're going to meet Dave Gorman, and I'm going to win this bet.'

Well. The arrogance.

'You're bloody well not.' The anger was taking over where the desperation had left off. 'You're bloody well not at *all*.'

And this is how – terrified, drunk, and cold – I sat on a train and watched London get smaller and smaller until it disappeared.

Only later would I discover that the very same thing was happening to any plans or ambitions I may have had for the next six months of my life. . .

This was going to be fun.

Chapter 2

MAKE MINE A DOUBLE

I watched Danny drift in and out of consciousness with some degree of fascination. Every so often he would wake, take a terrified moment or two to fully appreciate where he was and what he was doing, and then seemingly pass out again.

Of course I was tired too, but *I* was *excited*. This certainly wasn't something I was used to doing, but it seemed to somehow make sense. Why *shouldn't* I travel the length of the country to meet a man with my name? I already had much more in common with *him* than I did with most strangers up in Scotland. At least enough for a quick chat.

The man in the booth at King's Cross had told me we needed to alight at Edinburgh – not a word I often use, 'alight', but one that it seems almost churlish *not* to use when discussing railway matters – and find our way onto another train, this one bound for Glenrothes. As for how to get from Glenrothes to the football stadium, the London ticket seller displayed an alarming lack of local East Fife knowledge, and suggested we simply phone for a taxi. That was, so far, the plan.

As we neared Newcastle, Danny wiped the sleep from his eyes.

'What the hell are we doing, Dave?' he said.

'Morning, pal. Here's your tea.'

'I don't want any bloody tea.'

As a rule, Danny finds tea hard to turn down.

'Yes you do.'

'Okay, thanks, but listen – this is stupid. We're . . . *where* are we?'

'Nearly at Newcastle.'

'We're nearly at Newcastle, on our way to. . .'

'Scotland.'
'And remind me why?'
'To meet a man with my name.'
'Yes. Exactly. Now tell me if that sounds like it makes sense.'
'Aw, c'mon. It's . . . you know. Lads. Drink. Bets. Wahey!'
'No, Dave. Forget the waheys. It's Idiots. Drink. Bets.
Ohmygodwe'reonatraintoScotland.'
'Danny, I think you're taking this a *bit* seriously.'

Maybe I *was* taking it a bit seriously. Maybe I should have just relaxed into the journey and resigned myself to a lost weekend of idiocy on trains. But as I sipped at my tea – which was unpleasantly hot – I couldn't shake off the feeling that this wasn't a situation I could very well relax into. That morning at quarter past six we had got on a train to Scotland, to *perhaps* meet a man who shared my flatmate's name. No, this definitely *wasn't* something I could relax into, I'm afraid.

My brain began to thump-*thump* in time with my heartbeat. I had a headache.

'Well. . . what are we going to do, Dave?'

'We've got tickets which will get us to Glenrothes and from there we get a taxi.'

'A taxi to where?'

'To the East Fife Football Club stadium. It's Saturday, remember. Matchday. Dave Gorman will be there. They'll be playing.'

'Yes . . . but . . . will they be playing at home?'

Dave's smile crumbled instantly. Oh my God. He didn't even know if they were playing at home today. They could be battling away in Alloa, or Midlothian, or bloody *Munich* for all we knew. Depending on their league, obviously.

'Oh, God, I don't know' said Dave.

'Well, what are we going to do?'

'Find out when we get there?'

I tried a smile. Danny remained stoney-faced, then turned his head to look out of the window.

I reckon it's unlikely that many people travel at 6.15 in the morning from London in order to watch East Fife play football that afternoon. In fact I think we can safely assume that we are probably the *only* two Londoners in history to have made such an effort, so it probably wouldn't have been much use wandering the carriages and asking random people if they were also going to the match. I stayed where I was, crossed my fingers and sipped my tea.

Danny turned back to look at me. I tried another smile. He said 'tsk' and looked back out of the window. I *really* hoped they were playing at home.

At around 11 o'clock our train pulled in to Edinburgh's Waverley Station and we stood up – realising for the first time exactly how badly we smelled. We were pretty much entirely sobered up by now – our basic senses having begrudgingly settled back into place. I smelled bad. I couldn't tell if I smelled worse than Danny, but if I looked worse than he did, I'd have been clinically dead.

Our hair was sticky. We were pale. We had bags under our eyes. Our clothes reeked of booze, of our friend's cigarettes and, of course, of sweat. If the cliché is that most of London's tramps are from Edinburgh, then anyone seeing us get off that train must have thought that London was finally returning the favour.

I'd had an idea while our train shot through Berwick-upon-Tweed. If we were going to do this, then it'd be a real shame not to record it somehow for posterity. I mean, granted: I'd shoved Danny's video camera in my bag when we were in the taxi to King's Cross and so I knew *he'd* have a record . . . but what about *me?*

I told Dan to wait two minutes while I dashed out of Waverley Station and across into Princes Street, where for £20 I bought myself a polaroid camera with which to take a picture of my football managing namesake. Well, it seemed only right.

A train journey to Glenrothes and one taxi ride later and we were at the stadium where we discovered a wonderful thing. East Fife were playing at home.

We were going to meet a Dave Gorman.

Now, I'm not what you would call a huge football fan. Being born in Dundee, I will gladly cheer on Scotland when they are playing and, having lived most of my life in Bath, I will certainly always shout for England . . . so long as it's not Scotland that they're up against. And I have various other allegiances that I try to stick rigorously to when the opportunity arises . . . I will lend my cheers to Norway, because my girlfriend, Hanne, is Norwegian, but not if they're playing Switzerland, as to do so would offend my Swiss mother. I have even been known to feign excitement at a Carlisle United game, at the insistence of my dad, but the experience was so traumatic that for a very brief time I felt like writing someone a letter.

But each of these games is at least an international footballing event and as such an acceptable way to spend my time. Apart from the Carlisle United example, obviously, which wasn't international, was hardly an event, and could only very loosely be termed 'football'.

So the fact that I now found myself sitting in the freezing cold in a stadium which appeared to be only half-built watching two teams I'd never really heard of try and kick a ball that the wind was determined to keep well away from them, didn't make for the ideal start to my weekend.

We'd arrived at Bayview Stadium after a worrying taxi journey in which the driver had had to stop twice to ask for directions. You've got to worry about a football club when that's happening.

We bought our tickets and joined a small crowd of supporters as they tried to get excited about standing in the cold, being battered by a chilly wind, and watching an empty pitch. Eventually, 22 shivering men had made their way onto the field, but by that time my feet had already decided that they really didn't need to bother with all that blood circulation nonsense, and had formed an independent state of their own.

East Fife were playing Brechin City, and both sides seemed to be big fans of making the other practise their throw-ins. This was all the crowd had to work with, thrill-wise – throw-in after throw-in after throw-in – but to their credit, they faked their excitement brilliantly. I, however, was cold and hungover and not even from Fife. Or Brechin City.

'I'm going to get some tea,' I told Dave, because tea, as we already know, solves everything. 'Do you want a cup?'

'Yeah,' he replied, his eyes searching the sidelines for anyone who looked like he might be an assistant manager, 'Ta'.

'Have you spotted him yet? Can we get this over with?'

'Not yet, no, but I will.'

Bayview Stadium turned out not to be half-built at all; it's got just the one stand and, from the attendance that day, it appeared to be ample for its needs. Bayview's name gives it a more picturesque image than perhaps it deserves, though. 'Big Ugly Factoryview' might have been a more appropriate moniker.

I turned the corner and found the tea-seller, who handed me two polystyrene cups of grey, foamy tea and, because I can go a bit crazy sometimes, two pies filled with unidentifiable meat. I took my change and was about to say 'thank you', before I realised that 'thank you' seemed somehow too much given what I was now holding. And anyway, I was distracted by the light drizzle that began as I negotiated my way back to my seat, which was *perfect*, because who likes to be freezing cold without being *wet,* too?

'Here you go,' I said to Dave, who took his tea and now slightly damp meat pie.

'Thanks'. Again, a little over the top, considering.

'I bought a programme off that lad down there,' he said. 'Dave Gorman *is* the assistant manager, look'.

And, sure enough, in tiny writing, there was his name. I'd lost. I was very upset. Okay! Let's go home!

'He used to be the goalkeeper, too, apparently.'

'You said. Great. Finish your tea, then, we're off.'

'Eh? What're you on about, there's another hour yet.'

'Another hour of this? C'mon, mate. He exists. Dave Gorman the assistant manager of East Fife FC exists. We've proved it. Good. We don't have to stick around any more. We can get a train back to Edinburgh and then go home.'

'No. We've travelled all this way . . . too far to go *not* to meet a man. We're going to wait 'til the match is over and then at least shake his hand and confirm his name. And anyway, *I've* got the train tickets home. . .'.

My head began to thump in double-time, half anger, half hangover. But Dave was right. He had a point. He *did* have the tickets.

'My money's on it being that fella there,' he said, pointing at one of three men standing on the sidelines making wild gestures with their arms. The man he was pointing at was wearing one of those manager's jackets that covers the wearer's entire body, and the only thing I could see peeping out the top was the back of his head. I say 'his'. It really could have been *anything* in that jacket. How could he even tell it was a man, let alone a man that looked like another Dave Gorman? Dave can be quite softly-spoken, but that doesn't qualify him for female intuition.

My concentration was momentarily broken by a goal at the other end of the pitch. At which point I realised that in my foggy, inefficient state, I didn't know which team was which.

'Who scored?' I asked Dave.

'The Fifers.'

'"*The Fifers*"?'

'It's what we call them.'

'Who's we?'

'Fifers.'

'So you're a 'Fifer' all of a sudden?'

'You've got to stick up for your own.'

'But you're from *Stafford*!'

'I don't mean Fifers, I mean Dave Gormans. Look! Look at Dave Gorman!'

If that really *was* Dave Gorman, he was suddenly looking very happy with himself – far happier than he'd looked when all you could see was the back of his head. As he faced the small crowd and clapped for his team, he appeared to be in his mid-fifties, and had sandy hair, and rather a loud voice when he was shouting.

He was altogether more subdued when Brechin City equalised moments later.

The match drew to a close just as the clouds opened up properly and a dozen umbrellas in the stands appeared from nowhere. By the time the teams had jogged back through the tunnel, the same clouds had decided to try and properly soak us through, and as I watched the small crowd of fans scuttle away for cover I realised I'd lost sight of the man we'd come all this way to meet.

'Uh-oh,'

'What?' said Dan, his shirt pulled right up in an attempt to keep dry but succeeding only in making his midriff as wet as his head would have been. 'What d'you mean "uh-oh"?'

'I can't see Dave Gorman. He must have gone in already. We'll need to blag our way into the clubhouse. . . '

'That doesn't sound too bad,' says Dan. 'Are clubhouses warm? Do they serve *warm* things? Will I be warm?'

'Yes. On all counts.'

We walked around the side of a large grey building, letting the steady flow of fans guide us towards the turnstiles, before breaking away from the crowd and heading for the clubhouse. I could see, up ahead of me, that we might have some trouble.

A hulking Scottish goliath in a donkey jacket and a yellow and black East Fife FC scarf stood between us and the clubhouse.

Evidently a self-appointed doorman, he eyed us with suspicion as we approached 'his' doorway.

'Can I help you gentlemen at all?' he said, standing firmly in front of the entrance.

'Er, yes,' I said. 'I want to meet Dave Gorman please.'

'Do you, now?'

'Yes please. It's very important.'

'I'm sure' he replied, half-turning away. 'Now fuck off.'

'Er . . . no, you see, we've travelled a very long way to meet him . . . all the way from London. . .'

He sighed. 'What's your name?'

'Dave Gorman.'

'Right . . . *fuck* off. . .'

'No, no, it *is*, honestly, look . . .' I pulled out my wallet. 'There's my name there, and that's my face next to it, I really *am* called Dave Gorman. . .'

I had stumped this man beyond belief. I thought for one precious second that the confusion was going to knock him off his feet, before the novelty of the situation and our hazy explanation of the bet got him back on track. He smiled.

'This way gents. . .'

It was a slightly awkward meeting, all told. Imagine it. On the one hand, you're my flatmate Dave, who has travelled hundreds of miles on a drunken whim to meet a man who shares his name, but doesn't really know why, and in the end has nothing he really wants to say or ask him.

On the other hand, you're Dave Gorman the assistant manager, who has just heard that a man with his name has travelled hundreds of miles to meet him on a drunken whim, but has no idea why either, and isn't really being told.

Oh, and for some reason or other, his flatmate's in the corner of the room, too.

He can't have been very impressed. In front of him were two men, shabbily dressed, *clearly* hungover, reeking of booze, and more or less silent. He must've thought we were in awe, when in fact we were just confused and with very little to say. What Dave would really like to have said, of course, was 'I bloody told you so!' and then giggle, but under the very sombre circumstances, this probably wouldn't have been too appropriate.

I felt I had to break the silence.

'Do you like football?' I ventured, but then instantly realised that yes, given his past career and chosen profession, he probably did. Dave had a visible brainwave at that point and jolted into action with a (slightly better) question.

'Um . . . that old football result . . . East Fife 4, Forfar 5 . . . did that ever happen?'

'No, it's never happened, no.'

'Oh.'

'A TV gentleman made that one up, just because it sounds funny.'

'Right. That's a pity.'

Dave blew air through his lips and looked around the room while our assistant manager studied his feet for a moment. He bent down and wiped something off the top of his shoe. Eventually Dave piped up.

'It's just really weird meeting someone with your name.'

'Ah-huh,' confirmed Dave Gorman. For him without a doubt it was, but for an entirely different set of reasons.

Silence. Then. . .

'Er . . . can I . . . can I take your photo?'

I could feel my cheeks now burning with embarrassment. *'Can I take your photo?'* What must this man think of us?

'I've no' got a problem with that. Go ahead.'

Dave reached down into his bag and took out the Polaroid camera he'd bought at the station. He'd already loaded the film, clearly in anticipation of this moment, the pinnacle of his weekend.

Our puzzled interviewee remained seated at his desk for the photo, but this rather odd little moment seemed to break the ice. It was as if Dave had got what he wanted and could now relax.

They started to chat more freely.

'Can I ask you, did the fans at any of the games you played at, ever chant "there's only one Dave Gorman"?'

'Back in the '70s, when we were playing the likes of Rangers or Celtic, I've had games where they chanted my name, ah-huh. It's an enjoyable feeling. But there's not many Gormans about. It's quite a rare name.'

'There's *John* Gorman, of course,' said Dave, doubtless thankful that he'd managed to squeeze a football reference in there, for bonding purposes.

It had quite the opposite effect.

'Oh, yes, there's *John* Gorman, alright. The *Scots*man who decided to help manage the *England* team. . .'

This really didn't seem to be the best subject to talk about, and the atmosphere changed accordingly. There was a chill in the air. Someone, quick, say something. . .

And then Dave asked the question that I would come to wish he'd never asked at all. . .

'Do you know anyone else called Dave Gorman at all?'

'No, I don't,' replied my namesake, as clear as day. 'I mean, there was a Gorman once at my work . . . his first name was Jackie.'

'No good to me, I'm afraid' I said, slightly dejected. 'So you don't know any *Daves* at all?'

'No.'

'And there are none in your family, or anything?'

'Oh. Well. My *father* was named David Gorman. . .'

Wow. From no, I've never met any Dave Gormans, to yes, my dad was a Dave Gorman in less than. . .

'. . . and my *grandfather*, his name was David Gorman. . .'

Crikey! *Two new* Dave Gormans! How exciting was this!

'. . . but apart from that, that's it.'

Didn't matter! As far as I was concerned, any news of a Dave Gorman was fast becoming *good* news. Danny didn't look overly thrilled, but I was over the moon – it was more fuel for my side of the argument, after all. But how – *how?* – had this man managed to forget his own father? And his grandfather! That's *two* generations of Dave Gormans that nearly passed us by!

So you can imagine my delight when, after quite a lengthy pause, another thought suddenly struck this man – the man who'd just told me he didn't know anyone else called Dave Gorman.

'My *son's* called Dave Gorman.'

Wow.

'It's a sort of a family tradition.'

A *sort* of a family tradition? It's the only name that family bloody knows – I was half expecting him to tell me he was *married* to a David Gorman next.

I had to ask. I knew Danny would be annoyed, but I *had* to.

'Is there . . . is there any chance I could meet your son?'

I could sense Dan bristling in the corner of the room.

Dave Gorman looked puzzled for a second and took a moment

to find his words. I'm well aware that by this time the smile on my face had turned to genuine, unconfined excitement.

Finally, he found his voice.

'Er . . . well . . . he's a policeman, he's on duty at the moment, but I can give you his phone number if you want. . .'

Jackpot.

Tosspot.

What was he doing? It's one thing indulging in idle banter in a stranger's office, quite another to demand he hand over his first-born. It took all my willpower not to drag Dave out of that office that instant, something that I'm sure his namesake would have positively *thanked* me for in the long-run. His son! Why did Dave want to meet his son? We had proved that there was another Dave Gorman in the world, and learnt that there was another in existence. As far as I could remember, the bet was that Dave would never meet another Dave Gorman, but it now seemed to have mutated . . . somehow it now seemed I was betting Dave that he couldn't meet *more* Dave Gormans. . .

Now, this was a bet I was still sure I could win, but it wasn't a bet I felt I particularly wanted to enter into – if only for the reason that I would have to suffer the embarrassment of meeting the man I now watched Dave firing off a dozen questions about. 'Where did he live?', 'Would he mind meeting us?', 'Does *he* know of any other Dave Gormans?'. . . it was all becoming rather worrying. Well, rather more worrying than it already was. Which was rather worrying indeed.

Part of me hoped that our new friend was simply making a fictional son up to get rid of us. Perhaps he was frightened of us and simply wanted to palm us off onto a stranger. It would have certainly seemed to back up the fact that, up until a few minutes ago, he didn't know of any other Dave Gormans at all – let alone any Dave Gorman juniors.

Dave took down a phone number and tucked it safely into his jacket pocket. We thanked East Fife's Dave Gorman feverishly and apologised for imposing upon him, before leaving him, and Bayview Stadium, in a rain-splashed taxi bound for Edinburgh.

'No', he said.

'Go on', I said.

'No', he said.
'Go on', I said. *'Please?'*

Dave and I took a seat on a bench off the Royal Mile and I got out the train timetable I'd picked up that morning.

'Dan . . .' said Dave, as I battled to keep the thing straight in the wind, 'I really, really want to stay over and meet Dave Gorman'.

'You've met him. We're going home.'

'No, his son. I *really* want to meet his son.'

I put the timetable down. 'Why, Dave? Why do you *really* want to meet his son?'

'I don't know. I just do. Remember the bet. . .'

'No, *forget* the bet. Okay? Forget it. We were drunk, we were angry. We don't *have* to stick to it.'

'So I'm right.'

'You're *not* right. This doesn't make you any more right than you were last night. You're still wrong, I just don't think we need to prove exactly *how* wrong you are.'

We were drowned out by a passing bus, bound for Leith, and we sat in silence for a few seconds after it had gone. I hoped Dave was taking on board what I had said, and while he was, I picked the timetable up and began to study it again.

'So I *am* right, then' he said.

Gah.

'Look. No. There *aren't* loads of them in the world, and just because you think there are, there's no way at all, just for your information, that we're staying over to meet East Fife Dave Gorman's son.'

'Don't refer to him like that, Dan, it's disrespectful. He has a name.'

'He has a name, yes, but this has the potential to get very confusing, so if you don't mind I'll refer to him as East Fife Dave Gorman's son.'

'Why don't you just call him our Dave Gorman Two?'

'Because he's *not* our Dave Gorman Two! We haven't met him! We can't number him!'

'Yet.'

'No.'

'C'mon, Dan, we've come this far. It's only one night. We're in Edinburgh.'

'Dave, we stink.' And I was completely correct. We did indeed stink.

'I'll get us a hotel, you can have a shower, we'll get a meal, it'll be fun.'

'No. I need fresh socks.'

'I'll buy you some. Any socks you like. Imagine that!'

'*You* need fresh socks as well, you really do.'

'I'll buy some for me, too', he said, and that was the most tempting promise he'd ever made. 'Come on. You think he doesn't exist, don't you? Let's go and meet him, yeah? Please. I'll throw a meal into the bargain. A meal and some socks. And then tomorrow we go home.'

I thought it over. I was exhausted, lacking in willpower, and very hungry. A hotel beats a train journey. A hotel, a meal, and some new socks even more so.

But this is really where the conversation should have ended. This is where the *story* should have ended. This is where we should have gone home. I *had* my chance . . . and I blew it.

'Okay,' I sighed.

'Okay then,' he replied, with some glee. We stood up and began to walk down the hill, at which point Dave muttered something that sounded very much like 'You're *so* going to lose', and looked innocently away.

But he remained true to his word and stumped up for some new socks, and – because I insisted – boxer shorts, too. If I had to stay up here, I was going to bloody well enjoy it, and at that moment in time, the only way I could think of doing that was by having some new pants. Sadly, though, these weren't Marks & Spencer products we were talking about. Considering Dave had already spent £170 on train fares, he was reluctant to buy clothing anywhere other than in the nearest tourist-tat shop, and so I was now the proud wearer of a pair of £1 tartan socks and some boxers with a picture of a big sporran on them. Dave bought himself the same.

This isn't an outfit I'll be showing to many people, and so I would be grateful if you'd keep this to yourself.

We checked into a cheap hotel and made our way to an Italian restaurant on Dundas Street in which the waiters were rude and the food slapped together, but the atmosphere warm and the licence late.

'This is for this weekend only, isn't it, Dave. I want you to know that this is a one-off. I'm not going to spend the rest of the year on this. You were right about the assistant manager of East Fife, and you got lucky finding out about his son. So we know that there are at least two others. I propose that we *both* win. Or we *both* lose. Up to you. But this has to be where it ends.'

'I know. I just enjoyed it, that's all. It was . . . quirky. I liked meeting my namesake, it gave me a warm feeling. I dunno. It's weird. But you have to think, if there are *two* just in *East Fife*, what about everywhere else?'

'No, you see, you *don't* have to think that. Just be happy with what we've done. We have an odd story to tell our mates tomorrow night.'

'It could be odder.'

'Shut up. We'll meet his son tomorrow, yes? The policeman. And then we go home.'

'And then we go home, yes.'

'Yes.'

'Good.'

'Good.'

'Good.'

In the morning I awoke bright, early, and with one thing on my mind; our new Dave Gorman. I'd spent much of the evening before checking my jacket pocket like an obsessive-compulsive, frightened that the small scrap of paper containing his phone number – that day's golden piece of luck – had somehow escaped, never to be found again. Each time I found that it was exactly where I'd left it, breathed a sigh of relief, and could once again concentrate on whatever job was at hand, such as raising a fork to my mouth, or blinking.

I got out of bed, showered and realised that it was only 7am. Was it too early to knock on Danny's door? Probably. So I phoned him instead.

'Danny? Sorry, did I wake you?'

'It's 7 o'clock in the morning, Dave. Yes, you woke me. What do you want? Why are you calling me?'

'Just thought I'd say how much I was looking forward to going and meeting Dave Gorman the policeman today.'

Silence.

'I'm putting the phone down now, Dave.'

'No, hang on, shouldn't we think about getting ready to go?'

'No, we bloody shouldn't! I'm going to go back to sleep now for a very long time. I need my rest. So does Dave Gorman the policeman so don't go phoning him at this hour on a Sunday. Okay?'

'He might be up.'

'Shut up, Dave. I'm going back to sleep. And I'm taking the phone off the hook.'

When I phoned back ten minutes later to ask whether he wanted to go yet, it was true: he'd taken the phone off the hook.

'Danny!' I whispered a little later, as loudly as I could, outside his door. 'It's 8.15!'

Something banged against the wood with some degree of force. It sounded like a shoe. I told him I would come back a bit later.

I paced up and down until 9 o'clock, walked out of the hotel, and made sure to take my mobile with me. I had programmed Dave Gorman's number into my phone in the night in case a fire or burglars or both deprived me of my now well-thumbed scrap of paper. I looked at my phone, pressed the button, and waited with some anticipation.

'Hullo?'

This was as pronounced a 'hullo' as I had ever heard. Not a 'hello' or a 'hallo' . . . a 'hullo'. I decided I should take as early an opportunity to bond with this man as I could.

'Er . . . *Hul*-lo. . .'

A pause.

'Yes? Hullo? Who is this?'

'Er . . . Hullo. Is that . . . Dave Gorman?'

'Yes.'

'Er . . . hel . . . *hul*-lo . . . my name is *also* Dave Gorman . . . I . . . er . . . I spoke to your father yesterday afternoon. . .'

'Ah. Yeah. I *heard*. . .'

There was a tone of dread in his voice. *What* had he heard exactly?

'Um . . . I was just wondering . . . could we come and meet *you*, as well. . .?'

'You'd better explain what this is all about. . .'

'We just want to shake your hand and take your picture, really.'

'"*We*"?'

'You're right, I'd better explain. . .'

We took a train later that morning from Edinburgh out to Kirkcaldy, and from Kirkcaldy, we got a taxi to Methil, the little town that was to hand us our second Dave Gorman.

I trudged behind Dave as he excitedly opened the garden gate belonging to DG Junior, jogged down the path and rang the bell. We were on a small, suburban street, and as is the rule in small, suburban streets on a Sunday, there were children trying to hurt each other with balls, and men trying to hosepipe the grit out of their hubcaps.

After a five-second wait, Dave rang the doorbell again and was just about to poke his nose through the letterbox when a huge shape rushed past the glass. There was a moment of pure anticipation from Dave, like a bloke who's just seen a shark shifting about under the water . . . but then nothing.

'Was that him?' Dave turned to me and said, confused.

'I dunno. If this is his house.'

'Should I ring again?'

'If he's in there, he probably heard it.'

'I'll ring again.'

I have never thought that ringing someone's doorbell three times in fifteen seconds makes a particularly good impression, but I wearily waved my hand at Dave and he took this as 'yes, good idea!'

He rang the bell once more, and we heard the sound of the man on the other side of the glass rattling some keys into the lock and turning them. He'd obviously been running around the house trying to find them while we'd mounted considerable pressure on him with our incessant ringing, but at least he was security conscious – the actions of a policeman if ever I saw one.

The door opened, and a tall, muscular man with spiky brown hair and a black eye raised his eyebrows and looked at us both, quizically.

'Er . . . Dave. . .?' he said.

Dave's arm shot up. 'That's me!'

The two of them shook hands and we were welcomed into his home, as neat and tidy as a policeman's locker.

'So, er, what is it exactly that you two want to know?'

Dave had obviously learnt some social lessons from yesterday's meeting with this man's father, and had prepared brilliantly.

'Do you enjoy your work?'

'Oh yes, I do. Yes. Nine years now, I've been in the force.'

'Are you going to stay there, do you think?'. Nice follow-up, Dave, I thought to myself.

'Yes, I think so. It's a job for life, I think.'

'Great.'

'Yup.'

That, apparently, was the smalltalk over and done with, and Dave cut straight to the chase.

'Um . . . could I take your picture now?'

Dave Gorman, after a nervous pause and some gentle encouragement, agreed, and the Polaroid click-whirred into action. Once again, with the evidence of the meeting safely recorded and tucked away in an inside pocket, we were all able to relax. Or at least Dave and I were. Policeman Dave remained slightly nervous about the whole thing, and I found myself unable to blame him, even though the whole meeting trundled along at an affable and relaxed pace.

At one point, though, he caught sight of my brand new tartan socks and gave me a very strange look. It was only when I watched him notice that Dave was wearing exactly the same sock*s* that a genuine fear flashed across his face. I thanked God he was unlikely to be able to see our matching sporran boxers during the meeting. I just hoped that he didn't suggest we all go swimming by way of a special Dave Gorman bonding exercise.

Thankfully, he didn't. Instead, he put the socks out of his mind and said 'There aren't many Gormans that y'hear of nowadays. I mean, there's *John* Gorman, the *Scots*man who decided to help manage the *England* team. . .'. He looked as if he was about to spit but settled for folding his arms.

'Not a popular decision up here, was it?' I said.

'You could say that, ah-huh. . .'

And then Dave did it again.

'So have you ever met anyone else called Dave Gorman?'

'No.'

'You haven't?'

This seemed strange to me, considering the conversation I'd had with his dad – Dave Gorman – the day before. Certainly worthy of another question.

'What, *never*?'

'No. In fact, I've never even *heard* of any other Dave Gormans. . .'

I looked at him in disbelief. How could this man be so unaware of his own family tree? Surely the fact that his full name was 'Dave Gorman IV' should have been a bit of a clue? I stared into his eyes, willing him to see the error of his ways.

Dave was staring at Dave Gorman in a most disturbing way. It certainly wasn't friendly. Stares rarely are. I started to worry when it lasted longer than a few seconds, and started to panic when it lasted longer still. We were in this man's living room, after all. This man who was a policeman and had a black eye and probably knew unarmed combat and seemed to be about 6'9". Dave didn't blink. Policeman Dave blinked several times. It went on and on and on.

This was painful. It was like watching a man throw away his chance on *Who Wants To Be A Millionaire?*. I knew that Dave had the correct answer available to him. But he couldn't find it. And this was only the £100 question; this was *easy*. 'Have you ever heard of any other Dave Gormans?' He was hovering over 'A: No' while the nation sat on the edge of their armchairs shouting 'B! Your father, your grandfather and your *great* grandfather!'

I stared some more. It was impossible to help him; he either did this for himself or it just didn't count.

I was about to start crying, but then it was almost as if a light-bulb came on above his head and he smiled, 'Nope. I've never heard of any others. You know . . . apart from my own family.'

I wanted to hug him.

I realised I'd been holding my breath for what seemed like twenty tense minutes, and breathed an entirely audible sigh of relief when his answer finally came. The two Daves turned round to look at me, so I coughed, which I think covered it quite well. While I had their attention, though, I thought I'd seize the moment and try and engineer the end of this meeting and the beginning of our return to London and sanity.

I pointed at my watch and raised my eyebrows in a manner that could only suggest 'Hey, haven't we got a train to catch?'

'What are you pointing at your watch for?' I asked Dan. 'And raising your eyebrows?'

'Er . . . haven't we got a train to catch?'

Well that was that, I suppose. He didn't know of any new Dave Gormans. Never mind. Still, it had been a pleasure to meet him and to capture a further Dave Gorman polaroid. To his family he might have been Dave Gorman the Fourth, but to me he would always be Dave Gorman the Second.

I shook his hand and we began to move towards the door.

'Actually, now that I think about it, there *is* another Dave Gorman.'

'Oh yes?'

Oh no.

Oh yes! There *were* more! Danny was *so* wrong. Policeman Dave *did* know of another Dave Gorman – a non-related Dave Gorman, a *fresh* Dave Gorman. This was delightful. I looked at him eagerly, unable to hide my excitement.

'I've never met him, but I've seen his name. He does a show at the Edinburgh Festival most years.'

It was like a punch in the gut. I was deflated.

'Oh. That's me', I said, my disappointment all too obvious. For a moment I'd thought we were onto another one, but the trail had evaporated as quickly as it had formed. It was a dead end. *I* was the Dave Gorman he was telling me about and that was clearly no use. If only I wasn't called Dave Gorman we could have avoided this sort of confusion altogether.

Still, I was happy enough. I had met him. I had the photo to prove it, I'd shaken his hand, and I'd shown Danny he was just that little bit more wrong. Before yesterday and the start of this bet I'd had no idea Dave Gorman 2 even *existed*, and now here he was, a tiny polaroid namesake cupped in my welcoming hands.

Dave was starting to get weird.

But at least he was satisfied. We were done. We were finished. We could get on with our lives.

I started to think about what we would tell our friends when we got home. How we'd show them the photos and laugh at the stupidity and how one day I'd look back on this weekend with warmth and fondness. But not today. Today all I wanted to do was go home.

'That's it, then' I said.

'Yep. That's it, Dan.'

From Dave Gorman Junior's house in Methil, we travelled slowly back into Edinburgh, Dave a delighted man, me a tired one.

At Waverley Station we waited an age in the cold for our train to invite us on board.

'That was a good weekend,' said Dave.

'Let's not make a habit out of it, though, eh?'

Onboard, Dave stared at his two photos and I leant my head against the window as we left Edinburgh. Sleep crept up on me with the evening by its side, and I finally nodded off.

Perhaps when I woke up, I would be in a better place.

I wasn't. I was in Stevenage.

But as the train moved off again, I was nudged back to sleep and finally awoke back in London, where, if only for a little while, everything looked like it was going to be fine.

The adventure was over.

Chapter 3

THE HOME OF TOOTING GORMAN

It felt like the adventure had just begun. I had enjoyed meeting those two Dave Gormans. They were both fine men as far as I could see. Like father, like son . . . especially in the name department. In fact, like great grandfather, like grandfather, like father, like son. They were definitely Gormans that favoured the name Dave; they were men of taste. Not only had I enjoyed it, I think they had enjoyed it and I think that Danny – in spite of not being a Dave Gorman – had enjoyed it also. He didn't say as much. In fact he said quite the opposite. He moaned and moaned about it to my face and I even heard him complaining about it on the phone to his girlfriend Hanne (a Norwegian, whose name you pronounce 'Hannah'). But that's just his way. I know that deep down he had enjoyed it just as much as I had.

I'd enjoyed it so much that I decided it was an experience worth repeating. By which I don't mean returning to Scotland and meeting *those two* Dave Gormans again. That would be crazy! But I did want to meet another. One would do, just one more Dave Gorman would be enough to make me happy and, of course, it would be a lovely surprise for Danny as well.

The phone book seemed like the obvious place to start. This was going to be easy. Unfortunately, I was surprised to find not one 'D. Gorman' in the phone book. Not only that, there appeared to be no Gormans whatsoever. Neither were there any Gorms, or Gorts or Gordetskis, nor any other surnames that you might expect to find nestling near to the Gormans in an alphabetically ordered list. That was peculiar. If this phone book was to be believed, it seemed that no-one in London fell between 'Gordon' and 'Gough'. Then I noticed that a page had been neatly torn from the book. That was even more peculiar. Perhaps Danny would know something about it.

I knocked on his bedroom door. No reply. I edged the door open. He wasn't there. I thought I'd leave him a polite note. There was a pad on Dan's desk but there wasn't a pen to be seen. Now, I don't *like* to snoop, but I thought I'd just take a quick look in the most pen-friendly places. Like the desk drawer, for example. And I was very surprised by what I saw. There were no pens, but there, underneath a roll of sellotape and a packet of mints – almost hidden – was the missing page of the phone book. And it *did* have a few 'D. Gormans' on it. One of them was bound to be a David.

What was Danny doing tearing out pages from our phone book? There was only one answer. *He* must have been planning to find a Dave Gorman too! And furthermore, he must have been trying to keep it a secret from me. He was obviously planning to surprise me with it as a treat. I told you he'd enjoyed meeting the first two.

Well, I'd beat him to it and it would be an even better surprise for him. He deserved it. I soon found a Dave Gorman. He lived in Tooting.

Despite the angriest protestations I could muster, we left the East End at 3 o'clock, crossed the river via the ever-impressive Tower Bridge, and then drove on to SW17. If there were a film version of this story, we'd doubtless also have passed Big Ben, have sixties cloth caps on, and be driving a London taxi painted like a Union Jack, which we'd call the 'Gorman-mobile'. As it was, a *Vauxhall Corsa* with a cracked windscreen and only one wing mirror was all we had to work with.

Dave was whistling a happy tune and tap-tap-tapping the steering wheel, completely oblivious to the fact that what we were doing really wasn't as exciting as he was making it seem.

You, too, should be realising by now the unique pointlessness of all this. I mean, take *my* name. Danny Wallace. I know of a few other Danny Wallaces. There's one in America who writes books about the robots of *Star Wars*. There's another who's just had his first novel turned into a film by Steven Spielberg (sadly, not *this* Danny Wallace, but then I suppose it'd just end up being a film with a bloody 'Gorman-mobile' in it). And there's the absolute bane of my school-days, Danny Wallace, the ex-Southampton and Manchester United player, mentioned immediately by any schoolboy I ever came into contact with for ten tiresome years.

Now, what you should just have noticed is that you're not all that bothered by all this talk of Danny Wallaces. As far as you're concerned, everyone in the entire city of Sheffield could be named Danny Wallace, so long as the country's steel output doesn't suffer as a result. It doesn't affect you; mainly because I'm not forcing you to sit in my tiny car and come and meet them all with me. But relax. You're safe. I wouldn't do that to you. My flatmate, on the other hand, most definitely would.

'This is his road,' said Dave, as we parked up by a Costcutters in suburban Tooting. 'His house should be right over there. Ready?'

'Yes. Is he?'

'Come on. . .'

We rang the doorbell of our new Dave Gorman and he answered it within moments, ushered us into his very tidy semi-detached house and into a wood-panelled kitchen facing the garden. Coffee was immediately made, and a plate of biscuits (three digestives, three ginger nuts) placed on the table in front of us. When it arrived, my coffee was in an *I Love Elvis* mug. So was Dave's.

It turned out that Dave Gorman number three was a bookseller, and, it has to be said, he certainly looked the part. Scruffy in the studenty, didn't-have-time-to-shave-this-morning way (with perhaps 30 years on top), he had a hushed, can-hardly-be-bothered voice, but was a man who wanted us to feel totally at home and offered another mug of coffee almost before we'd had the chance to have a sip of the first.

'What's that on your jumper?' Dave asked.

'It says "The Island of North Ronaldsay,"' replied DG3, pointing at the first and last words vigorously with his fingers. From outside, it would've looked like he was tapping his nipples to see if they were still working. 'It's the most northern of all the Orkney Islands'.

'Have you been there?' I asked.

'Yeah. It's where I got this jumper', he replied, which made sense, because it'd be a strange bloke who'd bring one back from Barnsley.

'I thought I'd better wear it. I thought I'd better make an effort. I was thinking of my dear old mother, God rest her soul, she'd have wanted me to make an effort'. Maybe this was bookseller chic, and Ronaldsay jumpers are what the well-dressed man in *Waterstones* was wearing these days, but to me it really didn't represent too much of an effort. Frankly, by putting on two socks that morning, I'd pretty much equalled this man's effort.

'So your bookshop,' said Dave. 'Whereabouts is it?'

'It's in Crystal Palace,' replied DG3. 'I used to work in a shop in Highgate, but . . .' He took a deep, solemn breath. '. . . it turned into a bit of a nightmare down there'. He raised his eyebrows as if to say, 'I think you know what I'm saying' and Dave and I bowed our heads, in a manner that suggested we could well imagine what a nightmare a bookshop in Highgate could turn into. Perhaps someone was refusing to change the till roll when it ran out, or maybe the bell above the door had stopped working.

'Am I the first Dave Gorman you've ever met?' asked Dave, to which DG3 replied in the affirmative.

'There aren't really that many Gormans about. Hardly any at all.'

'No. I mean, there's obviously *Theresa* Gorman, the M.P. . .' says Dave.

'Oh, yeah, but she married in, didn't she,' said DG3 dismissively. This man was obviously a Gorman purist. If you ain't born one, you ain't getting in without a fight.

'Hey, I wonder if there are any Daves in her family, though,' said Dave, and DG3's eyes lit up.

'That's a good point,' he said, 'I could check!'

And before I knew what was happening, our bookseller legged it out of his own kitchen and disappeared into another room. Moments later, he returned with a huge book; a familiar scene in this house, I'd imagine. As he got closer, I saw it was some kind of *Who's Who* thing.

'Gorman . . . Gorman . . . Gorman . . .' he said, as he leafed through the perfectly-preserved pages, many of which had been marked for special attention with Post-it notes. Surely the mark of a true bookseller.

'Come on,' said Dave, as DG3 flicked through the pages to find the necessary information. 'Please be a David . . . please be a David. . .'

What kind of world did I suddenly find myself in? Standing in a stranger's kitchen in Tooting, while he and my flatmate pray that a politician's husband was christened with the same name as them.

'Aargh. No. He's a Jim,' said DG3, deflated, slamming the book shut.

'Damn,' said Dave. 'Ah well. You can dream, eh?'

This was a man who liked books. He worked with books and judging by a brief glance at the shelves on the way to the kitchen,

he clearly brought his work home with him. I like books too. So
we had something in common. I looked at my mug: 'I Love
Elvis'. Clearly he liked music. I like music too. And coffee. We
had so much in common: reading and listening and coffee. *And*
biscuits. And, of course, our names. This was great, I had a real
sense of bonding. Then I realised that the room was silent. An
independent witness might have seen it as an awkward silence,
but I knew that we were all enjoying the moment. Even so, I
thought it best to speak.

'So . . . you're an Elvis fan then?' I said, feeling this was a safe
bet.

'Not really. The Beatles were more my thing', he said with a
wistful sigh. 'The mugs were a present. No, it's the Beatles for me.
I've got quite a few books about them actually.'

Moments later we were up the stairs and in the back bedroom.
There was a wall full of books. There were books about politics
and art and history and all manner of things. But there in the
middle was a small cluster of Beatles-related books. The third
Dave Gorman I'd met pulled one out.

'This is my Bible', he said, 'It's got every song they did in
there.'

'Really?'

'Oh yes.' He passed me the book as if to prove the point. 'You
can open it up anywhere you like.'

I opened the book at a random page and true to his word there
was some information about a Beatles song. Who had written it,
who had sung the lead vocal, who had performed the hand-claps
– really quite detailed.

'So there is', I said, more than satisfied with his description of
the book in hand.

'Anywhere at all', he said, as if he thought I needed more convincing.

I opened it at another page and sure enough there was another
song. I raised my eyebrows and nodded at him in a who'd-have-
thought-it type of way. He raised his in a go-on-try-again style. I
tried once more and, yes, there was *another* song listed.

I looked at him. I guessed he would have been a young man in
the '60s. It must have been an exciting time. I felt sure he had a
few stories to tell.

'Did you ever see the Beatles live then?'

'No', and then came his deepest sigh yet as he looked to the ceiling and considered what might have been. There was a pause. His face brightened, 'But Ringo winked at me once on Oxford Street.'

There was another big pause. Again I knew we were bonding, as the three of us stood there and contemplated the glory of being winked at by a Beatle.

The silence was unbearable. Both the Dave Gormans were staring into space in some kind of shared Ringo Starr daydream. I had to do something to jolly this along. I had to *say* something.

'So, have *you* ever heard of any other Dave Gormans?' asked Dan.

Dave Gorman seemed suddenly possessed by an idea.

'Ah! You've just reminded me . . .', he said as he left the room with large, urgent strides and continued at pace, downstairs to the front room.

Danny and I, both twentysomething, were left in the starting blocks. Slightly out of breath we arrived in the front room to find lots more books and Tooting Dave searching through them for something . . . something. . .

'Ah!' he said, but it could just as well have been Eureka! '*This* is it!'

He pulled a tatty paperback from the shelf. It had something of a boy's own look about it. Presumably a science fiction, action-adventure kind of thing. Emblazoned across the top of the book in embossed lettering was the name of the author: *Ed* Gorman.

We looked at the book for a moment of shared disappointment.

'I'm sorry,' said Dave, 'I thought it might have been a Dave . . . I couldn't remember.'

'It's an Ed', I said, because at times like these, stating the obvious is often the best way.

'Oh well', said Dave with a shrug of his shoulders.

But I wasn't going to give in that easily. This house might have contained a lot of books. But this man worked in a bookshop. That would almost certainly contain even more books.

'Could you check at work, maybe there's a book out there written by a Dave Gorman? It would be nice to know'.

Dave Gorman was a man who understood.

'I'll check at work,' he said, in reassuring tones. 'In fact – I'll even check the computer'.

We drove home.

Now, perhaps the worst thing about sharing a flat with Dave is that you can be almost certain that he knows where you live.

It's no good disguising yourself with a false nose and hat in the hope of passing yourself off as someone else in the kitchen, either, because he'll recognise you. *Both* times you try it.

I talk of moving flat to you only because, a few days after we returned from Tooting, Dave did something which I found rather disturbing, and not at all in keeping with the no-I-promise-I-won't-let-this-take-over-my-life attitude he had promised me he was going to adopt. It all stemmed from the fact that he was . . . well . . . proud of what we'd been doing.

I was very proud. I'd met three great Dave Gormans. I had three lovely photos as souvenirs. Each one, a photograph of a Dave Gorman taken by me, a Dave Gorman. They were special. Special men. Special photos. Three different faces, three different signatures, but all sharing one name. As I looked back on it – I enjoyed the fact that they were all so helpful as well. The first Dave Gorman had helped me to find a second – largely by having the foresight to christen his son Dave all those years ago. The second had tried to lead me to another Dave Gorman – but that turned out to be me. Still, it's the thought that counts. And now the *third* Dave Gorman had joined the search. He was going to look at work for me – he was even going to check the computer.

I was brought up to believe that you shouldn't ask others to do something if you're not prepared to do it yourself. It's nonsense really; there are many things I don't want to do, that I'm very happy to ask of others. I've asked a fishmonger to gut a fish, I've called the fire brigade and suggested some men run into a burning building, and I've been in the company of sober men on New Year's Eve because we needed someone to drive the car. But looking for my namesakes is not one of those things, and it seemed only right that if in a Crystal Palace bookshop a Dave Gorman was going to look for others, I should do something as well.

Danny was bringing me a cup of tea when he caught me with the phone book in my hand.

'What are you doing?' he asked in mock anger.

'I'm just thinking.'

'You've been through the phone book already. We've met him. That's it now.'

But it was too late; I'd seen something that fascinated me. At the back of the phone book, after all the names and numbers, there are other bits of sundry information that one generally assumes must be tedious. I always had. But today, one sentence in particular had leapt out at me:

'Phone books can be ordered individually, as regional sets or as a complete collection. Paperback phone books £6.50 each and hardback phone books (if available) £7.50 each'

As a rule, you only need one phone book. Anything else you've pretty much already written down on the back of a cereal packet, or can get with a quick ring to Directory Enquiries.

So I found it hard to fathom exactly why, upon returning home from a night at my girlfriend's, I walked into my living room to find that Dave and I were now the proud owners of around one hundred and twenty pristine-condition phone books.

We had a phone book for Plymouth. And for Worcester. And Aberdeen. And Wrecsam a Gogledd Ddwyrain Cymru (or 'Wrexham and North East Wales', if you'd prefer). And yet, as far as I could tell, all we *really* needed was one for London.

Dave was clearly becoming obsessed. This wasn't good news.

I leant down to pick up one of the books. Harrogate. I flicked through. No D. Gormans. Good. I threw it back down. I picked up Bristol. No D. Gormans. Excellent. Back down it went.

Newcastle. No D. Gormans.

Liverpool. No D. Gormans.

Manchester. No D. Gormans.

Well, this was odd. Fantastic, but odd. Not only did it mean that my side of the bet was looking incredibly promising all of a sudden, but it meant that I could put out of my mind the possibility of any surprise trips to Scarborough, Loughborough or Wolverhampton. The relief swept over me like you wouldn't believe.

And then I noticed. A page had been ripped out of the Wolverhampton book. A page in the 'G' section. I checked the others. Many of them were in the same state. They'd had their Gorman page forcefully removed. I thought that was *my* trick.

I knew exactly how this had happened, and as I contemplated the horror, the perpetrator marched into the room.

'You don't need to bother with those,' said Dave, dismissing the mound of directories with a smile. 'We've got this now...'

In his hand was another phone book, this one in no way as neat and ordered as the others. Tatty, ripped pages were stapled unevenly together, and on the front cover Dave had made an unsuccessful attempt to write 'Dave Gormans' in italicised Palatino with Tipp-Ex.

'I've made my own Gorman-specific phone book!'.

Brilliant.

The annoying thing about phone books – even Gorman-specific ones – is that they don't give you anyone's first names. It's just initials. Now, I wasn't interested in simple D. Gormans. Granted, there may have been a time when a chance encounter with a random D. Gorman might have been enjoyable. But in the last few days I'd raised the bar a little. I'd met three full-on namesakes and an initial just wasn't going to cut the mustard after that. I began to make my way through the phone books, ringing the D. Gormans and enquiring after their Davidness. It wasn't proving very fruitful.

I spoke to a Douglas. I spoke to three Darrens. I spoke to a Dorothy who seemed to be offended just because I asked if she was a Dave. I wasn't having much luck. At one point, with so many phone numbers spinning through my head, I was no longer recognising things that should have been second nature. At one point I even rang my own father.

Ring-ring.

'Hello?'

'Hello . . . I'm sorry to disturb you, I got your number from the phone book – I see that you're a D. Gorman, I was hoping you might be a David.'

'No, I'm Derek. You sound familiar. . .'

Click. Brrr. . .

Late that night I recounted the tale to Dan.

'I'm worried Dan. I hung up on my own father. I'm losing it. I'm cracking up. This has got to stop.'

Danny agreed with me. We mixed a cocktail in the kitchen to calm the nerves and I felt a whole lot better about things. And that night, while I was in bed, I came to a decision. If things weren't going to get on top of me, I needed to get a better system. I needed to get organised. I decided that letter-writing would be a more productive way forward.

I got out of bed and began the process. Step one – I found the electoral roll on-line. Step two – I wrote a letter to every Dave Gorman in Britain. All 144 of them.

Dear Dave,
Hello. My name is Dave Gorman. I have recently decided that I would like to meet as many other Dave Gormans as I can. If you'd like to meet me, please give me a ring on *** **** ****.
I look forward to hearing from you,
Sincerely,
Dave Gorman

I would send them in the morning. If I sent them all second-class, I'd have enough time before they arrived to work up the courage to tell Dan what I'd done.

But I got excited and bought the more expensive stamps.

I had hoped that our little chat a couple of nights before had led to Dave hanging up his phone books and retiring from the Gorman hunt. You already know that this was not the case. At the time, I did not.

I woke up one lunchtime when a friend phoned my mobile and barked at me for not answering the phone in the flat. I told him that he must have been mistaken; the phone hadn't rung all morning. I said that if it had, I'd surely have heard it and been up and out of bed in one lean, athletic flash. He laughed at me.

I wandered into the kitchen where I poured some cereal into a glass, drowned it with milk, and took it to the lounge. Dave wasn't around. I was about to turn the radio on when I noticed that the light on the answering machine was flashing, which was odd, because it meant I *must* have slept through the ringing, as accused. I pressed the button, expecting to hear my friend's voice berating me for spending the morning in bed, but hearing, instead, message after message from confused or irritated men.

[in a Yorkshire accent] 'Yes, I got your letter . . . I must say I'm not at all sure what this is all about. I presume it's a wind-up?'

[a West Country voice] 'Ah, hello, it's Dave Gorman here . . . your letter arrived this morning. I'm just phoning to see whether it's a wind-up mate.'

[a posh fella] 'I'm just calling because I received a letter from you. I think it's a wind-up. Can you let me know whether it is or not?'

I listened in quiet disbelief. What letter had they received? When had they been sent? Why hadn't Dave told me what he was doing?

I studied the side of the phone. Dave had turned the ringer off. He was obviously trying to keep his devious operations under his hat.

I knew that Danny would have got a little over-excited at the thought of extending the search for Dave Gormans even further. Well, some people might call it 'angry', but I think 'over-excited' is a far more pleasant way of putting it.

I'd had to come clean, though, when he handed me a sheet of paper with that day's phone messages on it. In all honesty, I was a little upset to discover that so many of my namesakes were so cynical. I re-read the letter I'd sent to see if I could work out exactly what led them to doubt me. It seemed to be perfectly sincere. I even used the word 'sincerely' – if that didn't seal it, I didn't know what would.

But it clearly hadn't worked. So, I proposed to get back on the phone. If I was speaking to someone and they didn't believe that I was truly a Dave Gorman – I could convince them that I was. If they didn't believe that I wanted to come and meet them – I could convince them that I did.

I decided to get organised. I cross-referenced the electoral roll and my Gorman-specific phone book and pretty soon I had a pretty good database of Dave Gormans and their details. I approached my task as if it was a job. On my first day, when Danny was out, I rang 50 Dave Gormans. None of them was at home. Most had answering

machines. So all over Britain, my voice would be heard leaving the same message from one Dave Gorman to another:

'Hello Dave Gorman. It's Dave Gorman here. You've probably had a letter from me. Let me assure you, it is not a wind-up. I really, really would like to meet you. Please, give me a ring on *** **** **** and I look forward to hearing from you. But please, bear in mind, I'm trying to speak to 50 people today – they are all called Dave Gorman, so if you do ring me back and get the answering machine, do give me a bit more information about yourself, and tell me where you're calling from.'

I went out for lunch at the cafe across the road, and then went for a haircut in the barber's next to it. I came back an hour and a half later. There were ten messages waiting for me.

Message 1: 'Hello . . . it's Dave Gorman here. I got your message. I'm going to be out for most of the afternoon. But you could give me a ring around 3.30 if you like.'

Which one was he? What was I supposed to do? I couldn't ring them *all* up at 3.30 on the offchance that that was the one that was available . . . could I?

Message 2: 'Hi, it's Dave Gorman here. I got your message. I'm in now. Bye.'

Message 3: 'Hello, this is Dave Gorman. Just returning your call. Cheers.'

Message 4: 'Hello, this is Dave Gorman's wife . . . you left a message for Dave earlier . . . if there's anything I can do to help, do give us a call back. Obviously, you've got the number.'

Only I *didn't* have the number, did I? Granted, I could narrow it down to one in 50, but that's just not good enough. I was exasperated. In total, there were nine messages from Dave Gormans, not *one* of them giving me any information other than their name. And that was the one thing I was already fairly sure of. What was it about Dave Gormans that made them unable to grasp this simple concept? Was there something in the Gorman genes?

There was one message for Danny. It was his mum. Danny has

known his mum ever since he was a baby. He knows her phone number by heart – it used to be *his* phone number, after all – but even *she* left it just in case. And yet people who were total strangers were for some reason deeming number-leaving an unnecessary and trifling detail.

The phone rang while I contemplated this terrible behaviour in the bath. Just as the answering machine was starting to whirr into action, I got to it, punched it, and picked up the phone.

My heart raced when I heard the person on the other end introduce himself. His name was Dave Gorman. He was charming. He was polite. He said he'd love to meet up.

And what's more, Danny was going to be very excited about this one. There was something very special about where he lived. It seemed like fate. We were going 400 miles, five hours and £170 away.

I walked back into the flat to find a trail of wet footsteps and Dave standing in the living room as naked as the day he was born, the phone in his hand and a broad grin on his face.

'Danny,' he said. 'We're going back to East Fife.'

Chapter 4

THE FIRTH, THE FORTH AND THE FIFTH

At Kirkcaldy we stepped out of our train and into a breezy, sunny day. It turned out that our next Dave Gorman was a greenkeeper, and so our main priority of the afternoon was to get to Ladybank Golf Course, in the town of the same name. Well, the *town's* called Ladybank. The 'Golf Course' bit applies only to the, er, golf course bit.

Neither Dave nor I turned out to be much good at map-reading, but we both have mouths and so finding our way to places by taxis is something that comes quite naturally to us. We found one, and got in.

The driver was an old man in a smart shirt and tie, but who covered both up with a tatty old Pringle sweater. That old men do this has never made sense to me. It's like going to all the effort of wearing your wedding dress and then ruining the whole effect by sticking a knackered beige cardigan over it. I was about to tell him this when he began to speak. His was a breathy voice and his Irish accent made him sound rather weary, so I decided that criticising his dress sense would probably have finished the old fella off. I left it.

'So are you from round here?' he asked.

'No, just up from London for the day.'

'London?' he said, and there was something in his voice that gave me the impression that he didn't quite believe us. It was as if no-one from London had ever been to Kirkcaldy before. Which was ridiculous, because we were there only the week before. Surely news must have spread by now?

'What are you doing up here from London?'

'Er . . . well . . . can I ask you something?' said Dave, shifting forward and leaning his head between the front seats. 'Does the name Dave Gorman mean anything to you?'

The driver considered this for a moment.

'Is it something to do with golf?' he said, which would have been a *great* guess, had he not been a man we'd just asked to take us to the local golf course.

'Sort of . . .' said Dave, and explained the story so far.

The driver was entirely unimpressed. 'It's quite a common name, Gorman,' he said. 'There are one or two in Ireland, an' all'.

We were forced to react with polite mock-surprise, as if the notion of some people in Ireland having an Irish name were an utter revelation to us. It was as if we were saying 'A man called Jean-Claude? In France!? Let us out of the cab, you mad bastard!'.

'Are there *really*?' said Dave, and I realised that the polite mock-surprise was on my part only.

'Oh, yes,' replied the driver, 'I knew one, years ago, before I left Ireland. I think *he* was a David.'

'Are you serious?' said Dave, 'Where in Ireland? Whereabouts?'

'Donegal. A wee place called Raphoe.'

'Raphoe?'

'Ray-fo.'

'Ray-fo?'

'Rah-ay-fow.'

'Rah-ay-fow?'

As far as I could tell, Dave was pronouncing it perfectly well, but then, I couldn't be sure what he was supposed to be pronouncing, as it seemed to change every time the driver said it.

'Raffo, that's right. He used to repair horse's harnesses in Rayphoe. Harnesses for horses, do you know what I mean?'

'Mmm. Horse harnesses.'

'That's right. In Refo. Well, he used to repair them'.

'We're going to have to check that out,' Dave said, shooting me a victorious glance and receiving an annoyed one in return, 'Do you think I could get more details off you?'

At this, the driver seemed unsettled. It had been one thing to keep the two London fellas happy with news of a Dave Gorman, another thing entirely to prove his existence.

'Ah, now, well, y'see, this would have been a long time ago,' he said. 'Over 50 years now. And he was disabled at the time.'

'Well, that's okay. We could still check it out,' said Dave, excited.

'He was a very old man at that time. I don't think he'd be alive now.'

'If we could just get the details. . .'

'In fact I think he might have died before I even left Ireland. Yes, I think he's definitely dead now.'

'Right. Maybe we could still visit the grave', said Dave, down but not entirely out.

'I don't think he was a David, now I think about it. I think he might have been a Phillip.'

'Well, maybe there was a David in his family', I offered, hoping to annoy Dave, but succeeding only in annoying the driver.

'Look, I don't think his last name was Gorman at all, either, thank you. I think he was probably a Phillips. Now here's the golf course, that's £7.40 please.'

We paid up and got out. We hadn't found a new Dave Gorman. But we *had*, apparently, discovered a dead Phillip Phillips from an unpronounceable town.

'Should we still go and find him?' I asked Dave.

'No,' he replied, as petulantly as he ever had. 'Now come on. . .'

I have never understood the appeal of golf. Which is odd because I'm quite partial to a game of *Mini* Golf. The game in miniature makes perfect sense and, ironically, Crazy Golf makes even more sense. In fact, the worse the spelling of 'Crazy', the more inclined I am to like the course. You spell it with a 'K' and I'll be there, and the more 'Z's involved the better. Because when you see a lot of 'Z's you know you're going to find bigger windmills, steeper climbs and obstacles of an altogether more Heath Robinson-style design. All of which makes for a far more enjoyable game. It can be played in under an hour, with only one club, wearing ordinary trousers and the walk isn't too strenuous. There is, in fact, nothing 'crazy' about 'Krazzzy Golf' at all. However, spending a whole afternoon carrying a very heavy bag around for a very long walk while stopping from time to time to hit a ball with a stick . . . well . . . *that's* crazy.

Which is why I was surprised to see many of the Ladybank Golf Club patrons giving Danny and myself a look of suspicion as we walked towards the club house. We weren't wearing dodgy hats, we weren't carrying huge bags, we weren't wearing plus fours, and yet they looked at us as if *we* were odd.

We entered the club shop. The woman behind the counter eyed us carefully.

'Can I help you?', she asked, in a tone of voice that implied the true meaning of her enquiry was probably, 'can I call you a taxi?' or 'are you a plumber?', rather than an actual offer of *help*.

'We're trying to find the greenkeeper. Dave Gorman.'

'You've come to the wrong place – this is the shop'

'Yes,' I looked around at the golfing paraphernalia, the till, the word "shop" that had been above the door. 'I know. But I thought you might know where we'd find the greenkeeper.'

'The greenkeeper will be over at the greenkeeper's hut.'

'And do you know where we'd find the greenkeeper's hut?'

'Yes', she said.

After ten more questions I had got partial directions out of her and we headed off on what I hoped was roughly the right tack. A couple of hundred yards down the lane and we were approaching a large hut-like structure that in no way resembled a shop, so I really was quite hopeful we were going to get it right this time.

There was a low, distant, but noticeable, hum. It got louder. I looked up and saw a lawnmower approaching us. It looked like a regular lawnmower with a tiny man on it, but I've dealt with perspective before so I quickly realised it must be a giant lawnmower with a regular sized man on it.

As it got closer I took it in properly – at least ten feet wide. It was more like a baby combine harvester. On tarmac, with the blades up, it travelled at speed and it looked like rather a fun thing to drive. This impression was reinforced by the smile of the driver. He was a young man with the tan of the outdoor worker and he was sporting the broadest grin I've ever seen. Somehow his smile seemed to be wider than his face. We stood still and let man and machine approach us.

'Hiya . . .', I yelled over the engine noise. 'You wouldn't be Dave Gorman, would you?'

'Aye, that's me', he yelled back.

'Well, so am I', I said, and offered my hand. Dave Gorman 4 looked startled by the very idea that I too was a Dave Gorman. Which is odd because we had arranged to meet, and I would've thought it odder if two other clearly non-golfing Englishmen had been walking around the course that day looking for him. He reached down and shook my hand excitedly.

'Oh, I tell you what, I'll meet you round the corner there on the girls' course.'

The 'girls' course' turned out to be DG4's derisory nickname for a small, roughly triangular, two-hole pitch-and-putt practice area, bounded by woodland on two sides and a railway at the far end. It was where children were allowed to practise their game. I suppose that way the youngsters posed no threat to the tranquil harmony of the course itself – the members no doubt preferring to have them near a railway rather than within earshot.

Danny and I stood contemplating the greenery and quiet, when all of a sudden a bi-plane buzzed overhead, slightly too close for comfort. We looked up. A train whizzed past, and we looked to the side. Then the giant lawnmower raced up behind us. We got out of the way. Given that most of the view was taken up with trees, this seemed like the most unlikely cacophony of engine noise. Dave stopped a few feet from us, turned his engine off, and the beast coughed once, then died. The train passed and a second later the noise passed also. And the plane putt-putt-putted away – as if it was giving advice to a poor golfer. There was silence again; apart from the odd birdsong and a light breeze in the trees.

We chatted to Dave in the sun, and he walked us around the course, telling us about his life, his job, and – mainly – about golf. To be honest – while I recognised most of the words he used, I didn't really understand any of the sentences that resulted. But I nodded a lot and said, 'uh huh' and 'really?' and 'Tiger Woods', and I think I got away with it. I gathered that Dave was quite a player himself – he'd been a promising junior who now needed to practise a bit more, but he loved golf and he loved his job. Slowly I tried to work the conversation away from his passion and towards mine.

'So . . . golf, eh? Tsk. So . . . tell me, have you ever heard of any other Dave Gormans?'

Subtlety is very much my trademark.

'Oh, aye', he said brightly. My heart raced. He'd said it with such nonchalance that it seemed the most natural thing in the world that he should know of another Dave Gorman – we were onto one for sure!

'There's the ex-goalkeeper. You know, the assistant manager at East Fife.'

Damn. Of course there was. I should have expected that – a young man, he was no doubt a fan of The Fifers.

'So, you follow the football then?'

'No, not really. My dad works with him.'

I wasn't expecting *that*.

'I beg your pardon?'

'My dad works with him at the football club.'

This was odd, and my brain struggled to make sense of all the facts.

When we'd met the first Dave Gorman, in his office at the stadium, he hadn't known of any other Dave Gormans. He'd even forgotten to mention three generations of his own family. But then I remembered; he *had* said that he'd worked with a *Jackie* Gorman.

Our greenkeeper was still smiling. I wasn't.

'Um . . . your Dad isn't Jackie Gorman, is he?'

DG4 looked a little startled, clearly surprised by my seemingly psychic ability to pull his father's name out of thin air.

'Er . . . aye, that's him, yeah.'

I was nonplussed. I kept replaying the conversation with the first Dave back through in my mind. How could this have happened?

I mean, if *I* was to work alongside a Jackie Gorman, I think it wouldn't be too long before our shared surname became the subject of a conversation. I think one of us would at least have *mentioned* it. And if we were *having* that conversation, I think it'd be pretty remarkable if Jackie didn't then mention the curious fact that, while we shared a surname, he had a *son* who shared my *whole* name. That's the kind of fact I would find hard to forget.

Then, when a young man and his flatmate travelled *all the way* up from London to Glenrothes because of my name and asked if I knew of any *other* Dave Gormans, I would have remembered that fact and I'd have said, 'yes, there *is* actually, he's the son of a colleague of mine', meaning that those nice young men would have got to meet the *other* Dave Gorman, and the one who'd had to pay for it all wouldn't have had to fork out another £170 travelling back up from London *a week later* in order to stand on a golf course, ten miles away from the office in which we'd had our conversation, meeting the Dave Gorman that slipped my mind along with pretty much all the menfolk in my family!

I was furious. The way I saw it, East Fife Football Club Dave Gorman's little memory lapse had cost me £170! But I controlled my anger because it wasn't the fault of DG4. He was a completely innocent Dave Gorman. It was all that other one's fault.

I changed the subject.

'Can I have a go on your big lawnmower?'

Before today I had witnessed my flatmate meeting three of his name-sakes. So I thought I knew what to expect from this encounter. Dave Gorman would shake Dave Gorman's hand. Dave Gorman would take a polaroid of Dave Gorman. Dave Gorman would ask Dave Gorman to sign the photograph. Dave Gorman would ask Dave Gorman if he knew of any other Dave Gormans. And then we would leave. All very straightforward.

What I wasn't expecting was for Dave Gorman to ask Dave Gorman if he could have a go on his big lawnmower.

Dave clambered on and his namesake rattled a few things and started the thing up. And then Dave was off, riding the jolting, clunk-ing monster with glee. He started to speed up, and shouted with pride, and waved one of his arms around his head. It was difficult to hear over the growling engine, with its roars and splutters, but at one point I swear I heard him yelling, 'Look at me! I am a cowboy!'.

'Are you sure he's allowed to do that?' I asked DG4.

'Oh aye. He's not going to be doing any damage. The blades are up.'

We looked back at Dave. He'd somehow managed to make the blades go down. Butchered grass started to shoot up behind him as he whooped and hollered and drove really quite fast in a figure of eight. I looked back at DG4. He had gone quite white.

It is difficult to describe what happened to me while driving that mower. I am not a religious man, but I definitely felt as if I was in touch with some kind of higher power. Maybe this was symbolic of man's ability to control the forces of nature as I, driving a man-made, diesel-drinking beast, tamed that unruly grass and shaped it to my own satisfaction. I felt utterly reborn. And a Dave Gorman had made it so. Any anger I'd felt before this subsided. It was an epiphany. I knew now why DG4 sported such a broad grin. *This* was *his* job. The greenkeeper was a grinkeeper was a Dave Gorman, halleluja.

Our greenkeeper looked at what Dave had left in his wake. It was green, but it didn't look very kept. If grass could ever be described as wonky, it was now. He surveyed the scene, sucked some air through his teeth, and looked back at us.

'I'll just tidy this up and I'll be right with you'.

He did so masterfully, and met us back at his greenkeeper's hut, where Dave was trying to explain to me the sense of sublime exhilaration he'd felt on the lawnmower, and I was trying to tick him off for knackering the nice man's grass.

DG4 walked around the corner, wiping some oil from his fingers onto his dungarees.

'What are you two up to now?' he asked

'We've got to get going, really,' I said. 'We've got a train to catch.'

This wasn't strictly speaking true, but then it wasn't – strictly speaking – a lie, either. We'd made no firm plans for the day, but I wasn't going to get caught in another overnight fiasco with my flatmate, so a train really was the only idea I could muster.

'I'll give you a lift into Kirkcaldy Station if you want?'

For one glorious moment I'd thought that we were going to drive to Kirkcaldy on the lawnmower. But Dave insisted we go by car. It was faster, he said, and indeed it was. Faster than anything I've ever been in in my life. He was a bit of a boy racer, as it turned out, and clearly the novelty of driving that lawnmower had made way for the novelty of scaring the hell out of family and friends by driving like a nutter in a souped-up *Fiesta*. He assured us we were perfectly safe, mind you; a suggestion more than contradicted by the fact that it was impossible to open most of the doors because of 'a small knock' he'd been involved in. We didn't ask.

At Kirkcaldy train station I clambered across from the passenger side to the driver's seat and then out of the only working exit, while skilfully avoiding an embarrassing incident with a gear stick.

We shook hands again and then, with a screech and a roar, that particular Dave Gorman disappeared – the only clue that he'd been there being the three metres of tyre rubber that he left on the road as he squealed off into the distance.

I'll tell you a secret. I'd had quite a nice day. It had been sunny, we'd been out in the fresh air and we'd made a happy, grinning friend. I'd enjoyed myself.

As the train trundled over the Forth Bridge towards Edinburgh, Dave started fumbling in his bag and eventually produced a deck of cards.

'I thought this would help to pass the time,' he said. 'You deal.'

I started idly shuffling the cards, looking around the carriage as I did so. There must have been people on that train who travelled this route on a daily basis and yet I couldn't see one person who didn't stop for a moment to take in the surrounding beautiful scenery.

Except Dave, of course, who was back with his head in his bag, rifling through its contents.

'Hold this a minute', he said, handing me the polaroid he'd taken of his latest namesake. Then, from within his bag, he produced a small black photo album.

'What's that?', I asked, although the word 'photos' splashed across the front had pretty much already given it away.

'It's the Dave Gorman-Specific Photo Album.'

Oh, God.

'The. . .?'

'I thought it would be nice to have somewhere special for the photos.'

He handed me the album. Sure enough, there they all were. Four polaroids of Dave Gormans, all neatly placed in the album, their faces displaying various degrees of confusion, bemusement and, in one case, possible fear.

'Think about it, Dan. You can't just leave photos like this lying around. And you can't put them in another album. With *other* photos of *other* people with *other* names.'

He looked disgusted at the thought.

'That would be . . . *wrong*. It would sully the memories. The importance. No, *this* is the best way'.

'I wasn't arguing, Dave. Do what you like with them'. See? I *was* in a good mood.

'I wish we'd asked them what their middle names were.'

'Why?'

'Then I could arrange the photos in alphabetical order.'

'Mmm' I said, handing the album back to him before my mood was destroyed. I started to deal the cards. 'Now let's have no more about these Dave Gormans, okay? We've had a nice day out, let's not spoil it. Put your album away and let's play cards.'

Dave ignored me and opened the album up again to stare at his namesakes.

'Just think, Dan,' he said, flicking through the dozens and dozens of empty pages.

'Just think what?', I said.

'Just think how much nicer it'll be when we've filled the whole thing up.'

Danny stared at me. He stopped dealing the cards and simply stared.

'We are *not* filling that whole photo album up.'

'I'm sure we could do it.'

'No, Dave, you don't understand. We're not doing it.'

'Why not?'

'Because *we* are not idiots. *You* can do what you like, but if you think I'm coming with you. . .'

'You've *got* to come with me, Dan, otherwise it's weird.'

'What do you mean, *"otherwise"*? This is already very, *very* weird, Dave.'

'You said I couldn't meet "loads" of Dave Gormans.'

'I know, and that's what this whole bet has been about. But there's no way we're going to be able to actually prove it. Neither of us is ever going to win, neither of us is ever going to lose . . . because how many *is* "loads", anyway?'

'Well, I'll tell you what *isn't* "loads" . . . four. *Four* isn't loads. That's all we've met and it *isn't* loads. There weren't "loads" of Beatles, there aren't "loads" of horsemen of the bloody apocalypse, but there *are* "loads" of Dave Gormans and we can't give up until we've *proved* it. I mean . . . there's space for "loads" of Dave Gormans in this album, for example. . .'

'We are *not* going to fill that album, shut up about the bloody album. . .'

'Then we have to define what "loads" is. Pick a number. And that'll be the bet. If we meet that many, then that means that there *are* loads of Dave Gormans in the world and I win. If we don't meet that many, *you* win. Go on. Pick a number. But it has to be loads.'

Dan and I were locked in eye contact. This was a battle of wills. We were both determined men, but now, I suddenly realised, everything rested on him. What would he say? Would he say 'five', and put an end to all my fun a little too early for my liking? Or would he come up with a ludicrous, six-figure number and cast me into a world of torment?·

His eyes unlocked themselves from mine. He looked to the table. Collecting up all the cards, he slowly, calmly ordered them, and held them out flat in the palm of his hand.

'*That* many', he said.

I looked at the cards. I reached out and cut the deck at random. I got a seven.

'Well, I don't think that's "loads"', I said with a sigh, an ache in my heart from knowing that the power was his, and the adventure was nearly over.

'No, Dave', he said, and I looked back up at him. He put the two halves of the deck back together again. '*That* many'.

I looked at the full deck. Is that what he meant? A Dave Gorman for every card in the deck? There was spirit in Danny if you got him riled!

'What . . . 52?' I said.

'And the jokers', he said.

Fifty-four Dave Gormans! The challenge was set. We'd just been playing, up until this point.

Now it was time to get serious.

Why, you may well ask, when I was now starting to regret ever having met even the Dave Gorman sitting opposite me, did I now decide that, yes, 54 would be a good number of others to meet?

It's not as if people walk around thinking, 'well, my neighbour's name is Ian Fletcher, but . . . oooh . . . wouldn't it be so much better if I could only meet another 50 like him? That'd *really* round it off nicely.'

What was I thinking? I didn't want to meet *any* more Dave Gormans, and yet, here I was, making things harder for myself by setting him a high hurdle and then making it even higher for no reason other than I was enjoying the power.

I mean, what about the extra card that no one reads explaining the rules of bridge? Why didn't I just throw that into the challenge as well? Why not 55?

It felt like signing my own death warrant. If Dave was as determined to prove himself right as I was to prove him wrong, this could go on for quite a while. Even just the rest of today was going to be hellish.

But I had a plan. In London, I'd make a bid for freedom. I'd spend the next few nights at Hanne's. She'd take care of me. She'd make me soup, stroke my forehead and call Dave a bad man for what he was making me do. I would lay low. It would all calm down and go away.

Our train would arrive in Edinburgh soon, then before we knew it we'd be on another one to London. It couldn't come soon enough.

And then I noticed that Dave had his Gorman-specific phone book out on the table in front of him, and was quietly leafing through the badly stapled pages, searching for one page in particular.

'Edinburgh . . . Edinburgh . . . Edinburgh. . .'

Four down, 50 more to go. We may as well bag the others as quickly as possible, as far as I was concerned.

I got my mobile phone out and dialled the first D. Gorman I found, in the nearest place possible.

Our train deposited us neatly at the centre of Edinburgh, at Waverley Train Station on the eastern side of Princes Street, just down the hill from Edinburgh Castle. Local legend has it that upon arriving in the city, some visiting Americans once noted with glee how clever it was of the Scottish to have built the castle so conveniently close to the train station.

We walked up the steps of the adjacent shopping centre, and stood at the foot of the towering, Edwardian Balmoral Hotel. It's a hotel I am sad to say I've never slept in – my stays in Edinburgh have always been at least a month long and usually in a grubby flat nine hours' drive from anywhere I needed to be in a hurry – but I persuaded Dave that we really didn't need to go straight to the place where he'd just annoyingly agreed to meet the fifth Dave Gorman. A cup of tea was what we needed. Actually, a whiskey would have been better.

So we ventured into The Balmoral, which, as I write this I now decide, seeing as I am suddenly technically an author, is precisely the sort of place in which I should be staying from now on, even though when the Maître-d' first spotted us he had an expression on his face that'd make you think Dave and I had *invented* the clothes we were wearing.

We stood, for a moment, just staring at the reception area with its marble and red velvet, its tall, plush armchairs and its men in waistcoats drinking port. The restaurant downstairs, I noted, had been awarded a Michelin Star for its rich and exquisite food, a fact which becomes all the more impressive when you consider the head chef's name was Jeff Bland. A more perfectly *English* chef's name I don't think you'l ever find.

'Would I be able to help you gentlemen?' asked the *Maître d'*, a youngish man proudly wearing the kind of uniform that meant he really had a bit of a cheek raising his eyebrows at the likes of *us*. We might have been a bit rough around the edges, but at least we weren't *tassled*.

'We're just after a cup of tea,' said Dave,

'Or whiskey' I muttered.

'Is there a cafe in here?'

'There is a Burger King just across the street there', said the *Maître d'*, perfectly politely. We looked behind us, and yes, there was, but could he not see in us the look of the gentry? How dare he suggest we drink tea there rather than in the cultured and historical surroundings of The Balmoral? We might have been eccentric Scottish Lords dressed up as scruffy London twentysomethings, for all he knew.

What would we say to put this Edinburgh snob in his place?

Well, nothing, obviously. Dave brought me my *Whopper* meal and we discussed exactly what the afternoon was to hold for us.

'So,' I said, heavily. 'What do we know about this one?'

'His name's Dave Gorman,' replied Dave, 'and he lives in Edinburgh'.

'Is that it?'

'Isn't that enough?'

Apparently, it was. Dave also knew where we were meeting him and when, of course, so it seemed that we had more than enough facts to be getting on with. We finished our meals (Dave had the Chicken Royale) and, in a thin rain, ran across the road to North Bridge, walked up to the High Street and over to Hunter Square. Despite being born and bred in Scotland, I'd never really seen Edinburgh in any month other than August – the frenetic festival month – and so I was surprised that a journey that would normally take me up to an hour was over in ten minutes. Usually, I'd be fighting off dozens of leafletters, trying not be stopped by groups of students who want to tell you all about their all-nude production of Hamlet, which takes place in 1983, is translated into Spanish and set to the songs of ABBA ('it's not really very good, but it's only £5'), and bumping into everyone I'd ever met in London, all of them 'just up for the weekend'.

The Edinburgh we were making our way through today was an altogether different one. It was much . . . greyer. It seemed somehow more . . . damp. There was no-one swallowing swords, for one thing, and we all know that every good city needs a good sword swallower. There were no garish posters plastered across the walls, no chatty groups of people wearing backpacks and smiles. And everyone you saw looked like they belonged in Edinburgh. Residents. Actual Edinburgh residents. This may sound odd, but the *last* thing I expect to find in Edinburgh is people who live there.

We arrived at the City Cafe a little before four o'clock, and took a seat on one of the tables nearest the door. This was so we could play a game. If any strangers walked in we could see them and assess whether or not their name might be Dave. We did this for a while before realising that it was really quite a limited game, and anyway, the coffee-drinking bloke in the suit who kept looking over at us was most likely our man.

Edinburgh's David William Gorman, unshaven and bespectacled, works at the Royal Bank of Scotland, is 32 years old, and had until today never met another Dave Gorman. 'Well, I've heard of John Gorman, the Scottish ex-*England* assistant manager', he said, and oddly, we sort of guessed he would have. We bought him a Guinness and asked him about his life.

'Well, at work, I'm the account manager for technology within technology,' he said, taking care to leave a pause big enough for a wry smile. 'Which is a bit bizarre!'. We gave up trying to work out what his job actually was and just cut straight to the agreeing about its probable bizarreness.

'But I was born in Glasgow, I lived in Alloa, I studied Business Studies in Dundee, I joined the Royal Bank in 1991 as a graduate. I've owned my own flat since 1993 . . . and that's largely it.'

There was another pause, this one nearly big enough to be awkward. Dave had obviously taken in some of his namesake's information and was processing it into some golden question.

'Dundee United . . . Alloa . . . East Fife. . .'

'Yes. . .', said DG5.

'All those football clubs. . .'

'Y . . . yes. . .?'

'They all begin and end with the same letter.'

DG5 considered this.

'Quite true!' he said. 'Yes. Quite true.' He swilled the last of his coffee around the cup and then finished it.

'That's rare. You can tell people that!' said Dave, like he was doing his new friend a favour.

DG5 nodded but didn't say anything. I didn't actually think he *would* be telling anyone that. Not unless it was in a story about how he met these two freaks in a cafe and that's all one of them said.

'Would anyone like a drink?' I asked, and escaped to the bar. I was determined to be the normal one who bought people drinks in that particular story.

I was enjoying meeting this Dave Gorman. So much so that I became uncertain as to whether 54 would be enough Dave Gormans to meet. I mean, to a civilian, like you or Danny, 54 might *sound* like loads. But Dave Gormans are different. I was fast becoming an expert on them, and I knew we were an ambitious people: 54 would certainly not sound like "loads" to the likes of *us*.

'So what's the point of all this, if you don't mind me asking?' said DG5.

'To prove *him* wrong,' I said, indicating Danny, now fumbling with change at the bar. 'He said that I couldn't meet loads of us.'

'Us?'

'Dave Gormans.'

'Oh, right, yeah.'

'I mean, there *are* loads of us, aren't there? You've heard of more, right?'

'No.'

'Oh.'

'And where have you been to find them?'

'Well . . . pretty much just up here, really. This has been a bit of a hotspot, all told. Edinburgh, Glenrothes, Kirkcaldy, Ladybank . . . oh, and Tooting.'

'And how many are you going to meet?'

'Well, it *was* going to be "loads", but now it's just going to be 54.'

'Well, that sounds like "loads" to me!'

'Hmm. Have you got any ID on you, by the way?'

The City Cafe is one of those 1950s-styled cafe/bars which serve all-day breakfasts and, unless you argue, try to put your drinks in pitchers. The two pool tables have red baize – a mark of the self-consciously cool – and there are booths with leather seats and those little American squeezy tomato ketchup dispensers for anyone who's ever wished they were in an episode of *Happy Days*. I paid the barman, apologised that I didn't have time to change my pounds into dollars before walking through the door, and took the drinks back to the table. The polaroid album was out, and DG5 was studying each of his four namesakes with some care.

'Wow. This is weird. I mean, I used to resent the name when I was younger,' he said. Dave looked startled. 'It seemed odd to me. I wanted to be something normal, like MacGregor, or something. It's crazy, isn't it, because it's just two syllables at the end of the day. . .'

Dave visibly flinched at this point.

'. . . but aside from my family, I didn't really know any other Gormans at all. But I like the name now. It's got something about it. I mean . . . it's unique.'

This from a man sitting opposite a Dave Gorman and looking at pictures of four other Dave Gormans . . . most of whom lived within spitting distance of his house. Not exactly unique in the true sense of the word, if you ask me, but I kept schtumm.

We took the man's picture, added it to the album, and started to bid him farewell.

'So this search of yours . . . are you confining it to the UK, then?"

'Absolutely', I said, and looked at Dave, who looked back at me, and then nodded.

'Only from what you were saying earlier, Dave, it sounds like this could go all over the place. . .'

'Er, no. And anyway, I'm sure it'll be over quite quickly,' said Dave, and I took this to mean that he was finally realising that this was a bet he couldn't really practically win.

'Are you sure? Because from what you were saying earlier. . .'

'Yep, I'm sure,' Dave said, and before I could ask exactly when all this talking took place, he was shaking DG5's hand and telling him what a pleasure it was to meet him and that we really had to go now. I joined in, and we left him sitting at the table, awaiting the arrival of a few friends, who would doubtless listen in amazement as he told them of the London nutjob and his polaroid nightmare. And all about his kind-hearted, hard-done-by flatmate, of course.

We returned from Scotland with five pictures in the album and a thoroughly satisfying day behind us. Danny, too, seemed to be satisfied. So satisfied that he couldn't even manage a word to me in the flat when we got back and just went straight to bed. Clearly the mark of a *deeply* satisfied man.

This was a healthy start to my challenge. Life was good. But

sometimes life tricks you. It can seem *so* good that you think it can't get any better. And then it gets better.

This was about to happen to me.

When we'd arrived home, there'd been a parcel waiting for me. I'd taken it under my arm and popped it on the kitchen table while I made tea and toast.

But I'm like a little boy with parcels, and soon enough all thoughts of tea were abandoned as I ripped away at the packaging.

Now, I can only assume that this was a parcel sent to me by Dave Gorman in Tooting – the bookseller. Because without a note, or card, or letter, I'd been sent a book.

Not just any old book, but a very special book. A book written by a Dave Gorman.

The title alone sent a shiver down my spine. It seemed the perfect description of my own personal task. It was called '*Looking At Ourselves* – by David Gorman'.

I sat down on the sofa and started to read. Dave Gorman the author appeared to be some kind of expert on the Alexander Technique . . . it was interesting; I very much wanted to meet him.

But then you probably guessed that.

Most interesting of all was an introduction to the book from Dave Gorman himself. It contained this sentence:

'You'll recognise me in the South of France – I'm the one with the Canadian accent and a computer under his arm.'

Wow. The South of France! And a Canadian! Or, at the very least, someone who can do a Canadian accent. So many treats, all at once.

Danny was going to love this. I couldn't wait for tomorrow to come so that I could tell him. So I didn't. I ran to his room and banged excitedly on the door.

It was the second time in one week that Danny had thrown a shoe.

Chapter 5

JEUX SANS FRONTIERS

Danny seemed much happier about this trip than the last. When we had been sitting on a train bound for Scotland I got the distinct impression that he was a tad grumpy. But now, as we sat on a plane bound for the South of France, he was a far more cheerful travelling companion.

'So, when we get to Marseille, how far do we have to travel?' he asked, smiling.

'I don't know.'

'Roughly?'

'I've no idea. I don't really know where he lives.'

'What?' His smile hadn't lasted long.

'I know the name of the village . . . I just don't know where it is.'

'You've got his address, though, right?'

'Dan, he lives in a small village. In the South of France. He's Canadian. How hard can it be to find him?'

'Answer my question. You don't have his address, do you?'

'Well . . . no'. There was a huge pause. It was definitely Danny's turn to speak next but he didn't seem too keen, so eventually I continued.

'We know it's in the South of France. And so is Marseille. So we're going to get close, whatever happens.'

'You don't know his address! You don't know where this village is! I don't think being in the same country counts as "close", Dave', said Dan, who I noticed had been getting a degree pinker with each incremental increase in volume.

'We're not just going to the same country Dan; we're going to the *South* of France. That's *half* a country. We're not going to the *North* of France are we? No – we've eliminated that from our enquiries. We're already narrowing it down. We'll find the village, then we'll ask.'

'Ask *who?* For God's sake!' Dan half-yelled, throwing his arms in the air. He was about to carry on when he realised the stewardess was leaning in making her presence felt. I was glad to see her, because tea has always had a calming effect on Dan. But her expression was not the cheerful smile that precedes the 'tea or coffee?' question. She leant in close to Danny.

'I'm going to have to ask you to calm down, sir. The airline takes air rage very seriously these days. It is a criminal offence.'

She stood up straight and gave me a stony look, too, before turning on her heels and walking off.

We spent the rest of the flight in silence.

As soon as we touched down in Marseille, I insisted we try and find a phonebox. Well, we got off the plane first, and rushed through customs, and *then* I insisted we try and find a phonebox. I'd managed to somehow persuade Dave that it really would make sense if we got in touch with France's Dave Gorman *now*, rather than turn up at his house too unexpectedly.

We found a telephone near the exit of the arrivals lounge and Dave clambered into the booth. The number for directory enquiries is one of many pinned on the wall inside. We dialled it up and waited.

Neither of us, it suddenly occurred to me, speaks French.

Someone answered.

'Hello?' started Dave, uncertainly.

'No,' I whispered, 'Say "Allo?"'

'Er. . . "Allo?"' he repeated, and it seemed to work. The person on the other end said "Allo" back.

'Avez vouz the number for Dave Gorman in St Alexandre merci?'

There followed a stream of French to which Dave listened with wide eyes all the way through, before quietly replacing the handset.

'I'm not really sure what was going on there.'

'Well, we should really get in touch as soon as we can.'

'Yeah. But let's try again later. Let's get on our way and stop at the next phonebox we see.'

We walked out of the arrivals lounge and into the baking sun where we instantly realised that we should have worn shorts. There was a Rentacar place up ahead and we asked them for whatever they had. We were presented with a small green *Renault* which Dave eyed up like a matador eyeing up a bull. Which would have been a *great* simile, had we been in Spain rather than France.

'I think I can handle this one', he said, and we took it.

Dave decided that he would be the driver because he'd had the most speeding tickets and so we'd get there faster, and we set off. Within ten minutes, however, I was beginning to regret not having decided to walk to St Alexandre instead.

A quick glance at the atlas revealed that St Alexandre is approximately 150km north of Marseille. It appeared that, all being well, we should be able to get straight onto the motorway without getting caught up in town centre traffic – a nightmare that I was keen to avoid.

Getting out of the airport was easy enough, and I was relieved to see a sign almost straight away for the N7. This was going to be a doddle. But then, as we happily tootled along, I found myself approaching a decision. There were two routes, both marked N7, but the signs were not helpful to my idiot English eyes. They didn't say north or south (or even *nord* or *sud*), preferring instead to give French towns as a clue. But my knowledge of French geography is worse even than my knowledge of the French language, so that was of no use to me. I followed, instead, the laws of physics and took the line of least resistance. I took the route that involved the least manoeuvring and moments later discovered that we were now heading into the very heart of rush-hour Marseille.

Now, when I drive in England I instinctively know how wide the car is. I'm on the right hand side of the car, I can see the centre of the road and I know how much of my vehicle is to my left. But for some reason my brain is incapable of reversing this scene when I'm on foreign soil. Even though it's no longer necessary, my head still wants to drive while leaving a car's width to the left of me. Consequently, I find myself driving far too far to the right. I could tell that I was too far to the right because Danny was wincing and involuntarily moving towards the centre of the car. It looked as if he had developed an allergy to the car door.

Driving around the town centre of Marseille while desperately looking for a way out was a very quick way of getting into the French way of driving. Why use your indicators when you can honk your horn? Especially when you're stuck behind an Englishman who won't let you pass because he's driving across two lanes, too slowly, for fear of passing the turn-off that'll get him and his terrified flatmate out of this nightmare.

I try never to be a backseat driver, or to warn grown men that they really are driving quite close to the pavement and on the wrong side of the road, or that they've just caused a minor explosion, but this is something I now find myself kicking myself for. While Dave becomes accustomed to the new car and the whole new style of driving that our French cousins seem to have adopted – if you've ever been rally carting, imagine that, only with death a real possibility and a lot more screaming – I'm trying not to shout out in terror, and to stop my legs from shooting up to my chest every time we nearly rear-end the car in front. It's only when we've been round a round-about the wrong way and end up down a narrow street, clipping the wing mirrors of three thankfully empty cars as we do so, that Dave decides that maybe we'd best slow down and take a quick gander at the road map, as well as find that phonebox we've come to realise we really should try and use.

Eventually, more by luck than judgement, we found our way onto the *autoroute* and we were heading in the right direction. I relaxed into the driving and attempted to cheer Danny up with some interesting conversation.

'Did you know they drive on the left-hand side in Australia?'

'Really', said Dan, hiding his interest well.

'Yeah. Only you'd think they wouldn't. You know, because their water goes the wrong way down the plughole, and all that. So their roundabouts go the *right* way, and their water goes the *wrong* way . . . whereas here in *France*, of course, the water is *fine*, but the roads are back to front!' I left a pause long enough for him to contemplate this wisdom.

'That said, in England the water *and* the roads are *both* okay, so we're lucky, really.'

Enduring what Dave deems stimulating conversation can be a rather tough gig, and by the time we were nearing Orange, I was beginning to fantasise about how I would eventually hide his body. The weather, however, made any thoughts of strenuous excercise, particularly in this car, really rather unappealing. It was a very hot day, and we'd somehow rented an inordinately hot car with an air conditioning system that blew warm, sickly air no matter what you asked it to do. We stopped at a service station just outside Marseille which Dave decided would be a good place to practise his gear changes, and then we'd hunt for something cold to get inside us.

'Could we buy some ice-cream?' Dave asked the man behind the counter.

'No, ice-cream, no.' he said.

'Oh. They don't sell ice-cream, Dan.'

'On a day like this? What about lollies?'

'Do you have lollies?' asked Dave.

'Lollies?', the Frenchman looked puzzled at the word, but his mind was made up anyway. 'No.'

'Just some ice?' I asked, 'Avec . . . l'eau?'. Then, to Dave, 'I'm just asking for some ice in some water, Dave', and Dave, in turn, reminded me that he too had a 12-year-old's grasp of French.

'Ice, no, l'eau, no. End. End'.

'Well, what *do* you have?' asked Dave.

And so it was that we ended up sitting in a very hot car, in the very hot sun, eating very hot chips for no other reason than we were too embarrassed not to buy the only thing the man could sell us, and too embarrassed to be seen eating them. To drink, we'd managed to buy some milk from the man, whose fridge had obviously packed in, accounting for the rather depleted nature of his stock. But lukewarm milk, chips and a car like a speeding, bumpy oven don't make for particularly happy bedfellows, and we both agreed that perhaps finding somewhere en route for a rest before our morning assault on St Alexandre would be a good thing for two now quite poorly lads to do.

Looking at the map I'd decided that Avignon would be the best place for us to stop off for the evening, mainly because I've heard of it through the medium of song. About six years before I'd spent a perfectly good night on Ilkley Moor (without a hat) on the same basis and that had worked out fine. It's not a fail-safe system, but it's as good as any. Mind you, I once spent an evening with a girl who insisted her name was Ruby Tuesday, and that was a disaster, so there are no guarantees.

Sur le pont d'Avignon, l'on y danse, l'on y danse. **On the bridge**

of Avignon, everyone dances, everyone dances. Presumably this is why James Brown wants you to take him to the bridge. Although I'm not sure he'd be that impressed with it. The bridge was originally built in the thirteenth century but it was constantly damaged by the violent swelling of the Rhône and finally abandoned in the seventeenth century. Today only four arches remain. If I were in charge, I'd call it a pier and have done with it. But then I suppose that would spoil the song.

We parked up and headed for the centre of town, our first priority being to find somewhere to stay. The first place we happened upon is the *Hotel du Mons*, a thirteenth-century chapel converted into rooms that looked more like something out of a Habitat catalogue than they should have done for the very reasonable price Dave had to pay for them. I had a skylight in my room. Dave had a big round window in his. Forget tiny trays with packets of coffee and tubs of milk; novelty windows is all it takes to make us two happy. Pleased with our find, we ambled down to the courtyard and walked the short distance into the town centre.

According to a leaflet thrust into my hand by a girl in a baseball cap, a man called Petrarch once called Avignon 'a sewer where all the filth of the universe has gathered'. But in fairness, that was 700 years ago, when the Black Death, pestilence, overcrowding and famine would turn even the most fairminded man grumpy. I know it would annoy me. I'm glad to say that Avignon is an altogether more friendly place than it was in Petrarch's day, with wide squares and narrow streets, chapels, convents and churches wherever you look, and many dozens of restaurants spilling their customers out onto the pavements.

Our evening in Avignon was a pleasant one, largely spent swapping stories and ordering imaginative cheeses from the lady who ran the outdoor cafe we'd chosen from the many on offer. It was one of those evenings that seems to stay perfectly warm until well after midnight, and for a moment – just for a moment – I had a feeling of real warmth towards Dave and what we were doing. It was a feeling that would soon pass, but nevertheless, I was enjoying myself. Yes, it was stupid, and no, I still couldn't see the point, but I'm afraid that as far as I'm concerned, a bet is a bet, and Dave had to be proved wrong. But if he'd asked me that evening – which he didn't – whether I regretted being there and wanted to call the whole thing off, I'd have said no. Of course, that might just be the fact that dining in Avignon is, in many people's eyes, a nicer way to spend a Spring evening than traipsing around misty, damp Kirkcaldy. But, like I say, I wasn't asked, and the next morning as we again met in the gravelled, white court-yard, I'm pleased to say that my weary cynicism had returned to me in the night, and I was once again regretting every single moment we were spending on what was starting to become a very tiresome quest.

Dave had managed to get one of the hotel staff to track down the number of Dave Gorman in St Alexandre, and had tried ringing from his room. There'd been no answer, but that was okay, said Dave, because he was probably on his siesta, or something.

We clambered into our car and made our way over the river *Rhône* and out of *Avignon*.

We made good progress that day. The car was still too hot, but the serene atmosphere of Avignon had affected us for the better. We travelled through Orange and some glorious Provence coun-tryside before pulling off the motorway and finding our way quite easily to the village of St Alexandre.

It's a tiny, toy-like village that sits atop a hill, surrounded by wide open vineyards and acres of green. I drove slowly up to the entrance to the village; it looked unreal, like a film set had been built to resemble a village in Provence. It is undeniably, a stun-ningly beautiful place.

I parked the car next to a beaten-up old blue and grey 1950s *Renault* that the film unit art director had presumably placed there to create a lived-in, rural feel to his set, and we continued on foot.

Five minutes after leaving the car and beginning to walk around the village, we were yet to bump into a single resident. Although we saw two cats and a dog on our stroll, the rest of the village appeared entirely deserted. There were houses with full washing lines outside them, and we'd been forced to negotiate our way around a kid's upturned skateboard in the middle of the street as we first drove in, but there was not one actual person to be seen, anywhere. I mean, our *flat* in London wasn't all that big, either, but with a population of two, it could certainly take St Alexandre in a fight.

A minute later and we realised we'd come full circle and were now back where we'd started.

'We're back at the car' I said to Dave. 'What now?'

'Sssh,' said Dave, finger-to-mouth. 'Do you hear that?'.

In the distance, there was music. Barely audible, but definitely there.

'Perhaps all the villagers are at a traditional French dance', said Dave.

Somehow this made sense. Until, after standing in total silence for a few moments more, we realised that if they *were* at a traditional French dance, they were dancing to 'God Shuffled His Feet' by The Crash Test Dummies.

We followed the music and made our way through a narrow street and up a covered, stone stairway until we reached what looked what must have been the town hall; a tall and imposing building that we realised we'd seen from the bottom of the hill on our drive in. But the music wasn't coming from there . . . it was coming from round the back. We cautiously made our way down a pathway and into a gravelled courtyard until we were almost upon it. We wanted to be careful not to surprise anybody too much – judging by our experience today, they might not have seen another human in quite some time.

And then, there he was: a mechanic in a blue t-shirt, hosing his van down. Finally, we were getting somewhere.

Just as the village itself looked like a film set, so this mechanic looked like an actor who had been perfectly cast as 'French mechanic'. He had a face weathered by the sun, he was smoking, but more importantly, everything about him had an air of Gallic nonchalance. His cigarette drooped 60 degrees below the horizontal because he couldn't be bothered to apply any pressure with his lips, the ash on the end of his cigarette was almost an inch long because he couldn't be bothered to flick it away, and the water from the hose was, well, it was going in the general direction of his van most of the time so that was all right. He saw us approach and as if to complete the picture, he shrugged.

'Bonjour', I said. This was going well.

'Bonjour', came the reply.

He was quick. What could I come up with next? I trawled my memory, back to my schooldays. There must be something? Then it came to me:

'Parlais vous Anglais?'

'Non.'

Damn. Well that was the end of my conversational French. We should have thought about this. Maybe I should have bought a phrase book. Then it occurred to me – I had the only book I really needed right there with me. I delved into my bag and produced, *'Looking At Ourselves'* by David Gorman. His smiling, moustachioed face was beaming back at me on the cover.

I smiled at the mechanic. I showed him the book, and I pointed at the cover.

'Où est l'homme ici?' He stared back at me in silence. 'Er . . . Monsieur Gorman? Dav-eed Goour-mon? Où est?'

He continued to stare. Then he turned and walked back into the garage. He returned a few moments later with a friend who somehow managed to look even *more* French. His cigarette drooped lower, there was more ash magically suspended from its tip, and he too shrugged. As he shrugged, I saw on his face the familiar expression that accompanies the gesture: the corners of his mouth were turned down, his eyebrows were arched up. But then his shoulders relaxed and his face remained the same. It seemed that irrespective of his shoulders, this man's face was permanently shrugging. Maybe years of shrugging had taken their toll. Maybe his face had been shrugged into that position. He spoke without moving his lips. I don't know what he said, because it was in French. The two men stared at me.

'Où est Monsieur David Gorman?' I tried again.

There followed another burst of conversation between the two. I was worried. If they failed to understand me, would they then retreat and return with another even *more* French man? Would we repeat this scenario over and over until I was speaking to 100 increasingly Gallic men smoking cigarettes suspended vertically from their lower lips and with three feet of ash delicately poised?

In the gabble of words I could make out only one: 'Gorman'. They said it several times. With a question mark on the end of it, then without, then with an exclamation mark on the end of it, with the emphasis on the first syllable, and then on the last, before finally the first mechanic addressed me.

'Gorman?'

I showed him the front of the book and the author's name.

'*Oui*. Gorman.'

The mechanic turned to his friend, '*Oui* – Gorman', he said, as if it was necessary to translate my two words.

There followed another quick dialogue between the two and then the first walked past me, in the direction from which we had approached him. He spoke, but I have no idea what he said. I looked to Danny for help but he just shrugged. It was obviously catching. I don't know what the mechanic had said, but I think it was 'follow me', because that's what I did, and he didn't seem to mind. He led us back to the town hall, and though Danny decided to wait outside in the sun, I walked straight in after him.

Inside, there was immediately the library-like silence that exists around authority. There was wood-panelling and a marble floor, which made every footstep sound giant as we approached a large door. He wiped his hands on his shirt and then knocked tentatively, like a naughty schoolboy summoned by the head-master. We waited. Eventually he knocked again. The door opened and a smiling, middle-aged woman's face appeared.

I spent about 25 minutes in that office but I can't report accurately on what happened because I didn't understand a thing that was said. There were about eight members of staff in the room. The mechanic explained my question to them, then made his excuses and left. They all stared at me, they had a look at the book, there was a lot of shrugging, and the repeated use of the word 'Gorman'. Then one of them walked to a filing cabinet and produced a map of the village. They photocopied the map and then three of them hunched over it drawing directions. I guessed we were getting somewhere. There seemed to be much delibera-tion, but finally they handed me the photocopy of the map and pointed out the arrows they'd drawn showing me the way to Dave Gorman's house.

'Merci', I said, to the room. And I meant it.

The woman who had opened the door waved my thanks away with a gesture that implied it had been no trouble at all. I repeated my thanks. Maybe the weight I gave my gratitude pricked their curiosity, but it sparked a small conversation and then, for the first time, somebody spoke English.

'Tell me, why do you want to find this man?'

'Je m'appelle Dave Gorman', I said proudly.

The office stopped. There was silence. Then there was a flurry of '*Non*'s and '*incredible*!'s then there was laughter. They didn't believe me. I showed them my passport. There was more laugh-ter, a few handshakes, a 'bon chance' and they waved me on my way.

I went back out to meet Danny, confident that I had been proved right. Dave Gorman the author lived in a small village. In the South of France. He was Canadian. And how hard had it been to find him? Not very hard at all.

Dave, bubbling over with pride, showed me the map as I played in the sun with a cat I'd decided to name Geoff. I'm not sure why I decided on the name Geoff, but as far as I was concerned as long as I wasn't giving the world another thing called Dave, I was happy enough.

'So if we just follow these arrows, we'll be right on track' he said. 'Let's go'.

'Are we going to take the car, Dave?'

'This place is tiny, Dan, and he only lives around the corner.'

I bade Geoff a fond farewell and warned him quite sternly never to get sucked into a journey like this, just because his mate Pete reckons there must be 'loads' of cats named Pete in the world.

Dave was already striding purposefully down the road, and I jogged after him to catch up.

'Just down this road here, then. . .'

Now, I'm not sure what the people Dave had met in that office do for day jobs, but I can only assume it has something to do with creating badly-drawn and inaccurate maps. Because although the little village of St Alexandre appeared to be entirely in proportion, the surrounding countryside must have become warped in the photocopying process. A journey that looked like it'd take five minutes at the most became a long, tiring and mainly uphill walk to the house they'd marked with an 'X'. It was mid-afternoon in Provence, and the sun was making our eyes water and our necks burn as we negotiated our way over fences in fields, down hedge-lined little roads and, at one point, across a mud-bottomed stream. After nearly 45 minutes, though, we made what the map promised us would be our last turn, and began to battle against the hill up to Dave Gorman's house.

Each of the large family homes we were passing was surrounded by lush, healthy gardens, and ancient trees which stooped to embrace the entrances, providing household pets with shade and cool. I think Geoff would have liked it here.

'So, it's one of these, then. . .'

'It's that one there . . . and look. Cars.'

This was a good sign. It meant he was home. There was nowhere nearby that you'd go without your car – and you certainly wouldn't bother walking into the village once you'd worked out from your dodgy map how far away it was.

'I'm going to go and ring the bell,' said Dave, and he started to walk towards the driveway.

'No, hang on a second. Just wait. What are you going to say to him? You can't just turn up like this and say "Hello, can I take your picture?"'

'We have no choice, Dan, he wasn't in when we called earlier. I'll just walk up and introduce myself.'

'You can't do that, he'll think you're weird. You might scare him. He might have a gun. People who live in the sticks always have a gun.'

'I really don't think he'd harm one of his own, Dan.'

'So how are you going to introduce yourself?'

'Like I've been doing my whole life. "Hello, my name's Dave Gorman, what's yours?"'

'You're going to get your head kicked in.'

'By *this* bloke?'

Dave pulled the book out once again and pointed at the author's huge smiling face on the cover. 'I don't think this bloke is going to do any kicking. He's zen. He's a guru. He knows about . . . stuff.'

'Oh, well, if he knows about "stuff", that's great. Go on, then. I'm staying up here until I'm sure he's not got a gun.'

Dave left his bag by my feet and, book in one hand, camera in the other, walked down the gravelled driveway to the house of Dave Gorman number six.

The house, thank God, the house. There had been some nervous moments earlier on in this trip when I'd really thought we'd never make it to Dave Gorman's house . . . and yet here I now was, ambling down his very French driveway, enjoying his very French garden with its very French pool, all the time taking in the very French weather. I couldn't believe my luck. Not only was he an author, but he lived in foreign climes! I was heartily impressed by him already.

So impressed that I didn't mind when he took his time answering the doorbell. Hey, he was probably relaxing, practising his Alexander Technique, whatever. I didn't mind. I was in France!

I knocked on the door again. Bit harder this time. And waited.

I could feel Danny's eyes burning into the back of my neck, so I turned round, smiled confidently at him, turned back towards the door and hit it again. I could feel a sweat beginning to break. Why wasn't he answering his door? I simply couldn't come up with a logical reason.

I rang the doorbell again, and could hear Danny using some really rather foul language faintly in the background. There was still no answer. I hadn't been expecting this.

I looked back over my shoulder to see Danny still standing at the top of the driveway, arms folded. I tried to adjust my posture so that I now resembled someone who really wasn't panicking in the slightest. I tried to hold my shoulders in a way that would suggest to Danny that there was absolutely nothing wrong with the world. That I, his trusty flatmate, had a plan.

But I *didn't* have a plan. All I could do was open the book to check my facts. And yes – I was right! There it was in black and white: 'You'll recognise me in the South of France – I'm the one with the Canadian accent and a computer under his arm.'

It didn't say, 'You won't find me in the South of France because I won't be in', did it? No, there was positively no mention that this might be the case.

I took a deep breath and walked what seemed like ten miles back to Danny.

'He's not in, Dan'. I tried to say it as casually as I could.

Danny remained perfectly silent. But if he *had* spoken, I think it would have been quite loudly, because he went very pink.

I decided that the best plan of action was *in*action. We would hang around and wait. He couldn't be far away. It didn't seem possible.

Twenty minutes later and I was getting a bit anxious. I was trying to hide it, but Danny was refusing to play another game of I Spy with me, and without having some form of distraction, the full horror of the situation began to spin frantically through my mind.

I wasn't happy. I was in the South of France, I'd made my flatmate come with me – what the hell was I doing?

I'd come all this way to meet a Dave Gorman. And I still fully intended to get my man.

I had an idea. I decided to ask his next door neighbours. Surely they'd know where he was. He might even be round at their house. It was a brilliant idea.

I walked down the slope of the hill towards a neighbouring home. I was halfway up its driveway when the lady of the house came out to see what I wanted. Unfortunately, in the last hour or so, my French really hadn't improved all that much, and so our conversation was fractured and confused. But then I remembered that I had a visual clue in my hand . . . I showed her the book and she immediately recognised her neighbour's face on the cover.

'*Où est?*' I asked.

She pointed at his house.

'*Non. Il n'est pas dans le maison.*'

Blimey – where did that come from? Well who cared, she seemed to understand me, because she said 'Aaah, okay. Il n'est pas dans le maison.'

'Er . . . so . . . *où est?*' I asked again, my voice becoming slightly more frantic. She shrugged. I returned her shrug. We both shrugged together.

'*Où est?*' I tried once more. I was sweating, and I could feel my eyes bulging with the sheer frustration of the situation, and I think she must have felt it too, because she suddenly walked very quickly back to her house and locked the door.

I trudged out of her garden not a little disheartened. But I still had the other neighbour to go.

'That one was very helpful,' I said with a forced smile as I passed a silent Dan. 'We're definitely making progress.'

On the other side of Dave's house, neighbour number two was less helpful still. She was apparently unaware that she had a neighbour at all, and seemed unwilling to believe that the face on the front of the book belonged to him. So that was perfect. One didn't know *where* he was, the other didn't know *who* he was.

I dreaded to think what colour Danny would be when I told him.

So I didn't.

'Great. Come on Dan', I said, picking up my bag. 'We've got to go back to the village.'

This wasn't a lie, as such. We did indeed have to go back to the village. It was where our car was, after all, and we couldn't just leave it there, could we? And hey – if Danny was under the impression that I'd discovered from Dave's neighbours that he was to be found in the village somewhere, well, that was no fault of mine.

I just hoped to God he *was*.

'I *told* you to phone him, Dave,' I said as we hopped over the stream for the second time that day. 'I said we should, but oh no, that was too easy for you.'

'Look, I *did* phone him. I phoned him this morning, and he wasn't in. He still isn't.'

'So what did his neighbours say?'

'Er, well, they weren't entirely sure about a few of the facts I asked them to clear up for me.'

'Which facts in particular?'

'Where he is. When he'll be back. That kind of thing. But we're heading back into the village, and we can ask around some more. Someone's *bound* to know where he is. He's probably just gone out walking, or become caught up in a particularly interesting game of *boules*, or he's eating some grapes in a vineyard. You saw, his cars were there, he's around here somewhere.'

'What if that's his holiday home? What if those aren't his cars? What if. . .'

'Shut up. He's around. He's just . . . hiding. We'll find him. It's all part of the game. No one said this was going to be easy.'

'*You* said this was going to be easy.'

'Well, yes, but no one said I was right, did they?'

'*You* said you were right.'

'Yes, well. I thought I was.'

We were heading back into the village in an altogether more frantic manner than we'd left it. My sweat-soaked trousers were beginning to chafe on my inside leg, and I'd never worn such very hot socks before. The mid-afternoon sun had become a late-after-noon sun and St Alexandre, still perched wonkily on its little hill, took on a golden glow as we approached it at pace.

'He'll be back soon, I'm sure of it,' said Dave, and I tipped Geoff a wink as we passed him, still sprawled in front of the old town hall. I was glad to see that Pete hadn't got to him yet. I took a second to stoop down and stroke him.

Suddenly, the door of the town hall flung open, and there stood a frantic-eyed middle-aged woman in a floral dress, who waved her arms at Dave and beckoned him over.

'Monsieur! Monsieur!', she said.

There was a smile playing around her lips, and she beckoned some more.

'I'll be back in a minute, Dan.'

'Be careful, Dave,' I said. 'She might be a mugger.'

The woman led me by the hand back down the marble-floored corridor and into the very same wood-panelled office I'd stood in earlier that afternoon. There was a hushed sense of anticipation as my new friends, the office workers, watched me walk through the door. There were smiles all around. It appeared that while Dan and I had been loitering with intent outside Dave Gorman's house, the good people of St Alexandre had been doing some detective work on my behalf.

Clearly thinking that it would make me a very happy man indeed, they revealed to me a very, very alarming fact about Dave Gorman the author.

I sat down in disbelief.

He was in London.

Chapter 6

A REFUSAL AT THE NINTH

Dave Gorman number six had been surprised enough to hear that we were coming round to meet him at his mate's house in Greenwich just because of his name.

He was even more suprised, however, when we showed him a polaroid of Dave standing outside his house in France the day before.

I saw fear in that man's eyes.

The same kind of fear I'd seen in my flatmate's eyes as he'd walked nervously out of the town hall in St Alexandre to deliver to me the news that the man we'd travelled hundreds of miles to meet was, at the precise time we were on our way to France, on his way to England.

To be more precise, he was on his way to Greenwich. He would be five miles from our front door while we were one yard from his.

I. Was. Furious.

I was furious as we drove from St Alexandre, through Orange, past Avignon and into Marseille. I was furious as we flew out of France and back into Britain. I was furious in the car from Heathrow to Greenwich and from the meeting with DG6 to our flat. And I was furious as we sat in silence in our living room trying to pretend we were watching the news on Channel 5.

In the end, I had to get out of the flat for a while and so my girl-friend and I arranged to meet at a restaurant with the slightly odd name of Wagamama. Text messaging aficionados might like to note that this is one of the most satisfying words you can possibly type.

I didn't really understand much of the numbered menu and so I instinctively went for number 54. It seemed rather fitting.

'I expect you're wondering why I asked you here,' I said.

'Er, no. *I* asked *you* to meet *me* here', replied Hanne.

'Oh, yes, that's right. I'm sorry. My mind's elsewhere.'

'I know. So what's been going on with you and Dave lately?'

Thank God. I could finally pour my heart out. I reached across the table and squeezed her hand a little too tightly.

'I'm trapped in some kind of terrifying nightmare.'

'What do you mean?' Her face had a look of genuine concern. 'What's he making you do this time?'

'You know about the whole namesake thing?'

'Yes. Well, I know you went up to Scotland that weekend. It sounded quite fun.'

'Fun? It sounded quite "fun", did it? I haven't told you about the rest. I've been too ashamed. . .'

I paused. I had to build up to this.

'I've done something I really shouldn't have done with Dave.'

The words hung in the air. Hanne looked shocked. I realised she could have taken my words in any number of unpleasant ways and so I quickly continued.

'You know when you make a bet you have to stick to it otherwise you look stupid?'

'No, I don't.'

No. Hanne was far too sensible for that. Norwegians generally are. Clearly I had some expaining to do. 'Well, when you make a bet you have to stick to it. Otherwise you, um . . . look stupid.'

'Why?'

I didn't know.

'That's the way it's always been.'

'A British thing?'

'Maybe. No. Yes. A bloke thing, certainly.'

'I don't understand.'

I started to repeat what I'd just said but she cut me off.

'No, I understand the basic words . . . I just don't see why you don't just stop. So what, you look stupid to your flatmate for five minutes. It makes no sense to me.'

'I'm in too deep, Hanne. I made a bet with him. That's almost like an oath. And I had my chance to get out of it, but I messed up. Instead of ending it, I made my life much harder.'

'It can't be that serious.'

'We were in France yesterday.'

Hanne put her chopsticks down. I always know things are serious when Hanne puts down cutlery. It means that there's pointing to be done.

'I warned you about him!' she said, her finger in the air.

'I know. . .'

'Look at what he's got you doing! I mean, running all over the world trying to meet people with your name I can vaguely understand. What I *can't* understand is why anyone would run all over the world trying to meet people with their *flatmate's* name.'

I made a sulky face.

'It's for a bet.'

'What does that even mean? So what if it's for a bet? Drop it. Move on.'

'It's not as simple as that.'

'Just don't go back to the flat for a while. How hard is that? Listen, let's go away for a couple of days. Let's go away this weekend.'

'I can't.'

'Why?'

'I'm . . . busy.'

'Busy with what? I thought we were spending this weekend together?'

'Yes. Of course we are. But not the Saturday.'

'That's *half* the weekend! You'd better keep Sunday clear, okay? Because I want to have a nice day on Sunday. I said we'd meet the others at the pub on the park. Sit outside, have lunch, that kind of thing.'

It sounded normal enough. Which made it sound great.

'Sounds good. It sounds really, really good.'

'So why not Saturday? I thought we'd agreed.'

I wanted to lie. But I remained silent instead, while she put two and two together and came up with a seventh Dave Gorman.

'You're an idiot', she said. And she was right.

My number 54 arrived. We ate our food and went our separate ways.

When Danny arrived back at the flat, I was sitting in the kitchen making my way through chapter two of 'Looking At Ourselves – by David Gorman'. I was very proud of this book. Dave Gorman really knew his stuff when it came to the Alexander Technique.

I'd asked him to sign it for me – because it'd be rude not to, wouldn't it? – and he'd done so quite happily.

'To David Gorman, from David Gorman'.

Now, obviously, if you saw that in a second-hand bookshop, you'd be forgiven for thinking that the world's loneliest man had given himself a birthday present. But to me, it represented the fruits of some rather hard work and a bad situation made good. I turned each page eagerly, not really understanding much of it, but determined to read it anyway.

'Tea?' said Danny.

'Naturally', I said.

He clicked on the kettle and joined me at the table.

'Nice meal?' I asked.

'Kind of. What've you been doing?'

'I arranged that trip to Wolverhampton I was telling you about.'

'Oh. Still for Saturday?'

'Oh yes.'

'Right.' Danny sighed. 'It's very important that I get back at a reasonable time, though, okay? I realise that this bet is taking place and that I'm half of it, and I accept my responsibility. But I'm not going to risk falling out with Hanne over this.'

'Sure. It's just a quick trip to Wolverhampton. We'll be there and back in no time. Well, three hours there, three hours back. With maybe a stop in Bromsgrove for another one, but don't worry. I can even drop you off at her house on the way back.'

'That won't be necessary'.

It's odd, but Danny has been seeing Hanne for a couple of years, and yet I'd never found out exactly where she lived. It was as if Danny was keeping it quiet from me. Maybe she was homeless.

'Listen, Dan, there's something I think we should do. . .'

'What?'

When we'd been in Greenwich meeting our author, the three of us had shared a bottle of wine in an ample, airy dining room, and Dave Gorman had taken his shoes and socks off, which I can only imagine is a level of relaxation around strangers that only a continental expert on relaxation techniques like him could truly manage. Or maybe he'd had another bottle of wine before we'd arrived. Whatever it was, it had led to him having rather a good idea. As we'd discussed swapping e-mail addresses, his face had brightened and he'd said, 'Of course, there's another thing you can do, right there. . .'

'What's that?' I said.

'You could send out some random e-mails to addresses you think might work. Send a message to every 'davegorman@whatever.com' you can think of. You could send them to Hotmail . . . to AOL . . . to Freeserve . . . to anything, really. If they come back undelivered, you know that there's no Dave Gorman on the other end. But if they don't come back immediately, that means there might be . . . So write to them. Explain what you're doing. You never know. . .'

This was a brilliant idea. And one that I now had to convince Danny to help me do.

'Dan, it won't take five minutes. . .'

'Then do it yourself. . .'

If I was going to do this, I wanted to do it properly. And it was going to be a two-man job. I bribed Danny with tea and sat him down at the computer. He could start. After all, the more we found, the sooner all this would be over for him.

First of all, we scoured the internet for as many domain names as we could find, and as many Internet Service Providers as we could summon up. We found ISPs in Britain, in America, in Taiwan, in Finland, in Africa, in Iceland, in Japan, in Italy and just about anywhere else you can think of.

Then we sat down and began the process of thinking up what addresses a Dave Gorman might choose for himself.

We mailed messages off to davegorman, to dave.gorman, to dave_gorman, to gormandave . . . to davidgorman, to david. gorman, to david_gorman, to gormandavid . . . to daveygorman, to davey.gorman, to davey_gorman, to gormandavey . . . all these variations – and plenty more – we sent to every service provider we could possibly find.

I'd promised Danny it would take five minutes. It didn't. It took all night, and the day that followed it. All in all, we sent out around 4,000 e-mails, each one of them explaining the quest, and each one a tiny electronic message in a bottle that we hoped would wash up on someone's laptop. . .

And then we sat back and watched the computer almost explode. Messages were bouncing back in their dozens . . . 'Undelivered mail – return to sender' became burned onto our retinas as we scoured the inbox for just one, single, solitary response from a human. Surely this plan must lead us to at least one Dave Gorman? Surely they couldn't all be luddites, fearful of the world of electronic mail? Danny had long since walked out on the scheme, citing a severe headache and temporary blindness as an excuse, but I kept checking . . . just in case . . . just in case . . . but to no avail.

We'd just have to keep doing it the hard way.

It is likely that you, the reader, live somewhere other than Wolverhampton. Imagine your horror, then, when you realise that you actually have to go there. Imagine further that you'll be going there unpaid, leaving momentarily, and travelling for several hours in your flatmate's small blue *Vauxhall Corsa*.

This was fast becoming the repetitive nightmare that I felt was sure to haunt my life, but at least I'd learned how valuable a bit of preparation could be. Before the car had left our street, I reminded Dave of that lesson.

'You've remembered to phone these men to tell them we're coming, haven't you?'

'I thought I'd do it on the way.'

'No, you'll do it now, or I won't be responsible for my actions.'

Dave sighed and we pulled up outside the petrol station on the Mile End Road. He got his mobile out and scowled at me while he dialled. I was spoiling his fun. He was spoiling my life. I needed to be back in London by the evening. Hanne had not been impressed with my behaviour thus far, and I needed to make it up to her with at least half a nice weekend. The only thought that would get me through today was that tomorrow I would be free of it. For a little while.

'Hello . . . is that Dave Gorman? Hi . . . it's Dave Gorman here. . .'
And we were off.

And so to Wolverhampton, a town that's just been awarded city status for no other reason, apparently, than 'cities are more likely to attract tourists'. Which may be true, but it seems like a cruel trick to play on them. Getting them to traipse all that way in the hope that they'd buy a few postcards during their attempt to get to know the city – a mammoth task that would take all of an hour. If the tourist board was that desperate to change the place's image, why not call it Wolverhampton-on-the-Wolds and pretend it's a pretty little village in Yorkshire? Or call it *Wolverhampton World*, and tell people it's a theme park modelled entirely on Wolverhampton. At least give them their money's worth, eh?

This wasn't on our minds as we trundled into Wolverhampton, though, because it was still a town at that stage and the world was a more sensible place. Well, as sensible as it could have been, under the circumstances.

We were trying to find a pub called the Holly Bush, which was off a main road populated by many other pubs. We'd stopped along the way and bought some pick 'n' mix and I discovered for the first time that Dave doesn't like fudge.

'Don't you, Dave?'

'No. I never have, really.'

'That's weird. I thought you'd like fudge.'

'Did you?'

'Yeah.'

'Nah. I've never liked fudge, really.'

It's at times like this that you as a reader have to be grateful that people writing books can edit themselves. That fudge thing really can't have been all that interesting to you, but to me it was just one of many dull things that a long car journey forces you to pretend is interesting. I'd been spending more time in enclosed, moving spaces with Dave than I was used to, and was picking up dozens of little nuggets of information that made each journey that little bit more bearable. Or so I told myself. Did you know, for example, that Dave used to compete against Badly Drawn Boy in a Manchester pub quiz? Or that one of his nipples is pierced? I didn't think you did. It would be odd if you did. Did you know that he once trampled a nun at a rollerdisco? The most interesting thing to note about that is, if you ask him about it, he'll completely deny it. Many people who find themselves travelling all over the place will often like to tell you that, on their very personal odyssey, they learnt a lot about themselves. I didn't see this happening on ours. I was pretty sure we'd just learn a lot about *each other*, most of it entirely useless.

Inside The Holly Bush, Dave Gorman was sitting in a green bomber jacket at a table by the window, a pint of bitter already on the go.

He was keen to talk about the Gorman name. I was keen to talk about the name Dave Gorman.

'Now, I think the name is from County Leith, County Monahan in Ireland, that's the first thing. . .'

That's good to know. But it was really whether he knew of any other Dave Gor. . .

'. . . and the original surname was Gor, which means 'Man of Blue' . . .'

Again, I'd rather know that than not, but. . .

'. . . and it then became O'Gorman, which means 'Son of Gor' . . .'

Great, but. . .

'. . . and here, look at this . . . when you switch my phone on, look what it says. . .'

He switched his phone on. I looked at what it said on the display.

'. . . it says 'Tosach Cath A Deire Air', which is Gaellic, and means 'first and last in battle', which is the Gorman motto. . .'

This was news to me. I think my personal motto would probably just be 'last in battle'. I resigned myself to letting him get all this out of his system before popping the vital question.

'. . . it's a pity, 'cos I'd have brought the coat of arms and the Irish tartan if I'd have thought. . .'

'Not a problem,' I said, and took a deep breath. 'So, do you know anyone else named Dave Gorman?'

'No.'

Damn. But I thought back to the first two Dave Gormans we'd met and, by way of a safety measure, added 'So there are no other Daves in your family?'

'Nah. There's a John, a Tony, a Ron and an Ian. But that's not what you're after, is it?'

'I'm afraid not.'

Wolverhampton's Dave Gorman – whose accent makes it very apparent where he's from – was going to be 35 the following Thursday. A father of three, he spent fifteen years in the RAF as an aircraft engineer, before being made redundant. 'It was when the Conservatives were on their last throw of the dice . . . they thought "let's just cut out the middle of the Air Force . . .". And that was me.'

He was now dividing his time between family, working in The Holly Bush, and training under-10s to play football. 'It's just one way of putting back into the sport what I've taken out'. That was admirable.

But he had one slightly worrying hobby.

'I like to drive around in Ford Capris. I'm a Capri nut.'

'What . . . have you got more than one Capri?' I asked.

'I've got three.'

This man had *three* Ford Capris.

'I've got a 3-litre, a 2-litre, and a 2.8-litre in bits.'

This man had *three* Ford Capris.

'It's interesting, because the production span was from '69 – '87, and I picked up a B reg 2-litre 'S', for £300. Only done 66,000 miles, pretty good condition throughout, you know. So it is possible to do.'

This man had *three* Ford Capris.

We took his picture, still shaking our heads in disbelief, added it to the album, and bade him farewell. But not before he'd run around the back of the pub, promising to bring us back a present each. When he returned, he had two t-shirts with him.

'Here's an Irish Harp t-shirt each,' he said, tossing them onto the table in that shy way men do when trying to play down a touching gesture. In giving us these two, free brewery t-shirts, he confirmed for me a wonderful truth. That we, Dave Gormans, are a kind and giving people. I couldn't wait to meet the next one. We jumped back in the car and drove down the road to Bromsgrove. I'd thought it wise to arrange to meet two in one day. Both had got in touch as a result of either a phone call or letter, and if I was going all the way to Wolverhampton, it seemed silly not to swing by Bromsgrove on the way home.

I'd arranged to pop by at 4 o'clock. At 2.15 we were already parked outside his house.

We sat in the car in the rain, waiting for it to be four o'clock. The fudge had all gone, and so as you can imagine, it was a depressing scene. We tried to start up a game of I Spy but the rain made it hard to see outside and there are only so many things you can spot on the inside of a Corsa. But we had a tiny darts board with inch-long darts that we bought for £3 from a Help The Aged shop we passed a while back, and eventually we succumbed, took it out of the glovebox, set it up on the dashboard, moved the seats back, and began a game of 301. Bizarrely, the miniature darts kit turned out to be some way under professional standard, and so we had to resort to listening to an odd compilation tape Dave appeared to have put together while deaf.

Forty minutes and what felt like four years later, we were still slightly early but decided it was an acceptable arrival time and so made a dash in the rain for Dave Gorman's house. It's large and detached, in front of a cow field on a cul-de-sac, and the man himself greeted us as we arrived at his door.

'Hello,' he said, cheerily. He's a grey-haired chap with a soft voice and a strong West Midlands accent, and as soon as we were in his hallway the kettle was on and the tea on its way.

'So what's all this about?' he said, bringing the tea from the kitchen, through the dining room, to his lounge.

'We just wanted to meet you,' said Dave, 'because of your name.'

'It's great to meet someone else with my name. I've often wondered if there were any others out there. I'd like to think there's some common link between us. You two must have been thinking about this for quite some time.'

'About a fortnight', I said, and sipped at my tea.

Bromsgrove's Dave Gorman is a social worker and teacher, in a school where the kids need both. We arrived in his house on his son's sixteenth birthday, and there was a strong sense of good, wholesome family life in the air.

Born in Birmingham, he opted for the excitement of The Villa over the drudgery of The Blues as soon as he was able to make basic decisions. He's also handy around the house. 'I did all the wiring myself', he told us, and Dave and I found ourselves rather impressed, both of us finding the prospect of even untangling wires so great a task we'd rather get a man in to do it. Dave Gorman also plays badminton 'two to three times a week'.

I'm pleased to say that by this stage in the operation, Dave and I were becoming quite slick in the meet 'n' greet department. Quite different from the way we started in East Fife. We were now able to drink tea and ask questions, very nearly at the same time. I think that we both started to realise that if this quest was ever to be concluded and our minds laid to rest, we'd have to get a move on. Therefore we realised that with one polaroid taken, and two choice pieces of trivia collected (the self-wiring, and the fondness for badminton), we had achieved our immediate goal and the afternoon could progress. Preferably with a speedy trip home to avoid the wrath of Hanne.

'That was a good day,' said Dave, as we moved into the medium lane of the M40. 'I enjoyed that. Two very nice Dave Gormans, bringing us up to eight in total. Not long now, Dan.'

'Well, quite long, Dave. So long, in fact, that it might be worth your while just giving up now. Petrol ain't cheap.'

'No, it isn't. And you still owe me 50p for that fudge.'

'I'd call that reasonable expenses. I gave you the receipt, anyway.'

'Two in one day makes it financially much more worthwhile, though. Three would be better.'

'Yeah, three would obviously be better than two. But there aren't any more. That we know about, anyway. Which makes my side of the bet look a lot more promising, I'd say. . .'

Danny was right about petrol not being cheap. The same could also be said of plane tickets, train tickets, taxis, hotels and, yes, fudge. I don't even like fudge. I'd been putting off thinking about the money side of things, preferring instead to focus my attentions on the actual bagging of Dave Gormans. And I certainly wouldn't want to bore or embarrass you with vulgar, grubby talk of how much this bet was beginning to cost me. But costing me it was. Or, at least, it was costing my credit card company. But that's okay, because then it's sort of free, isn't it? No actual cash is changing hands, is it? And as long as I didn't open their letters for a bit . . . well . . . maybe they'd just forget about me.

I listened to Danny talking about his side of the bet and realised that the best way to win it would also be the cheapest. We had to start meeting as many Dave Gormans as we could in each trip we made. It made good financial sense. And it meant that I'd get to meet more of my namesakes quicker than I would have done.

I knew Danny needed to get home to avoid his girlfriend leaving him, but I made an instant decision.

'So if I were you – which I'm pleased to say I'm not – I'd make this our last trip and have done with it. What are you doing? Why are you pulling in?'

Dave had moved the car from the middle to the slow lane while we'd been talking about fudge, and was now slowing down to get us into the Royal Leamington Spa Welcome Break service station.

'What's going on? What . . . are you hungry?'

'No, it's just . . . I'd like to make a call.'

'Who to? Why do you need to call them now?'

'I need to call them before it's too late.'

'Too late for what? It's . . . 10 past 5, now.'

'No, I mean if we drove past this service station it would've been too late. You said it yourself, three would be better than two.'

'Eh?'

'If we could meet three Dave Gormans today, that would obviously be better than two. You said it yourself.'

'Better for you, yeah, but I need to get home! What's happening here? Have you arranged to meet another one? Here?'

'Not exactly. Listen, this sounds weird, but I couldn't drive past Royal Leamington Spa knowing that there's one there.'

'There's one in Royal Leamington Spa? Please say you're kidding.'

'I bet he's a really good one! And he's probably just sitting about. Probably just watching telly or something. Or scratching. I can't go home yet, I need to meet him. D'you know what I mean?'

'No.'

'Aw, c'mon. He's had a letter. He knows I want to meet him. And yet he hasn't bothered to call. What drives a person to torture another like this?'

'Maybe he's on the witness protection programme. Maybe he changed his name to Dave Gorman to escape the clutches of the mafia.'

'I thought he might just have been busy.'

'That's also a possibility.'

Dave reached down beneath his seat and pulled out a street map of Royal Leamington Spa. This was clearly not a spur-of-the-moment stop. He unfolded it, very nearly taking my eye out.

'Look, I know where he lives. I looked it up. We're here . . . he's there . . . we're about fifteen minutes away from his house. I just want to call him up and say hello.'

'And then, presumably, tell him we're parked outside his local Little Chef and we're on our way round?'

'Hopefully.'

'No.'

'Please?'

'Fine.'

I stared out of my window while Dave rang him up.

'Hello, can I speak to Dave Gorman, please?' A pause. 'Yeah, um, my name is also Dave Gorman. . .'

Here we go.

'No, yeah, honestly . . . yeah, well, all I was wondering was whether it'd be alright for me and a friend . . . no . . .'

This wasn't going too well. I could sense the desperation in Dave's voice.

'No, honestly . . . look, did you get my letter? No . . . just ten minutes . . . no, all it'd be is. . .'

This wasn't going well at *all*. I shook my head in a mixture of relief and annoyance. Which is a handy shake to know.

'Okay. Thanks, then. Bye.'

Dave hung up. 'I don't believe it,' he said. 'He wouldn't meet us!'

I was numb. How could a Dave Gorman do this to another Dave

Gorman? It seemed inhuman, almost. Whatever I said to him, no matter how much I'd pleaded, he simply replied with a flat 'nope', a 'don't want to', a 'not playing', or just a 'no'. It was absolutely unbelievable. I was deeply wounded.

But maybe I could still convince Danny to let him count.

'I spoke to him, though, Dan. One on one. *Gormano y Gormano.*'

'Yeah, you *spoke* to him.'

'I spoke to another Dave Gorman, that's another one. . .'

'Ah, you didn't meet him, though. . .'

'No, but I spoke to him. . .'

'I heard you speaking to someone, but we haven't met another Dave Gorman. That's cheating, Dave, and you can't cheat. . .'.

I was secretly impressed by Dan's decision. This moral streak of his, this deep-seated sense of right and wrong, was only likely to make his own life harder, and yet he was sticking to it. So fine, Royal Leamington Spa Dave Gorman didn't count, because I hadn't actually shaken his hand. A renewed enthusiasm for the bet swept over me, and I stepped on the gas. The quicker we got home, the less time we'd spend in the car, and the less time we were in the car, the less petrol we'd use. See? I was using my sensible, financial head straight away.

When we got to London, I dropped Danny off at what he promised was a convenient tube station, and off he went to Hanne's house. He'd promised her a nice Sunday, and I respected that. I watched him buy a half-price *Terry's Chocolate Orange* from the man in the sweet shop next to the station. Presumably, this was a peace offering. If it was, it was a bit of a rubbish one.

I drove home. I watched a little TV, yawned a lot, and decided that bed might be an option. As I brushed my teeth, I switched the computer on, figuring I'd just check my e-mails before crashing out.

I almost swallowed my toothbrush.

There was one e-mail that virtually lit up my in-box. It was from 'The Gormans'. My mind raced . . . I didn't want to get too excited in case I was heading for a fall. Were any of my family on e-mail? No. So it wasn't 'The Gormans' I'd grown up with. This was another lot entirely. One of the thousands of e-mails must have actually got through!

I clicked the e-mail open.

'Dave. This is David Gorman. Your quest sounds very interesting but I am afraid I cannot meet you as I am leaving the country on

Monday and have to prepare the family. Otherwise it would have been fun. Thanks. David Gorman.'

I'd found one! But he couldn't meet me! I was suddenly wide awake. I looked at my watch – it was only just after ten. I fired off a quick reply.

I told him that we'd travel to wherever he is before he left the country. I said that we'd spend such a short time with him that he wouldn't even notice we'd been there. I begged, and made more promises, and begged some more.

And then I waited.

I waited, and checked my e-mail, and then waited again. There was nothing doing. Well, there was one e-mail from a company in America promising a revolutionary new way of resolving debts in just ten easy monthly payments, which I printed out and pinned on my wall, but apart from that, nothing.

And then at midnight it arrived.

David,
My flight is now scheduled for Tuesday morning, so I will have a couple of hours (1200–1400) on Monday 22 May, we could get together if you can work it out. I am staying in a hotel on a US military installation in Vicenza, Italy, my number is **** **** ****. Feel free to call and we will work out the details.
Thanks
David

Oh my God. We were going to Italy. And we had to leave as soon as possible.

Chapter 7

THE ITALIAN JOB

Try and put yourself in my shoes for one moment of your life.

Imagine that it's a Saturday and you have travelled to Wolverhampton and to Bromsgrove where you have met two fine namesakes. You're happy. But then you've suffered the trauma of rejection in Royal Leamington Spa from a namesake who, frankly, seems to have a right royal attitude to the whole thing. You're unhappy. But then, on returning home you find an e-mail from a namesake saying that he'll gladly meet you. You're happy again.

I hope you are successfully imagining yourself in this situation, dear reader, because only that way will you understand the emotional roller coaster ride that I was on. The ups and the downs, the highs and the lows; the good, the bad and the Royal Leamington Spa. There was no way I was going to let myself fail with this new Dave Gorman.

So as we've established, I opened his e-mail at midnight on Saturday. He could meet me at noon on Monday. In Italy. Suffice to say that Sunday morning was a bit of a panic. I knew that if we were to meet this man, we had to fly out to Italy that day. And we *were* going to meet this man.

I got on the phone and booked two tickets from Luton to Venice. We were flying on an airline that is commonly referred to as 'cheap and cheerful' but we all know that phrase is a polite way of saying 'cheap'. I knew this wasn't going to make Danny cheerful. But first I had to find him.

I knew he was at Hanne's house. I just didn't know where Hanne lived. I didn't even know the phone number. Every time I asked, Danny had always 'forgotten' or Hanne had 'just moved'.

It didn't make much sense to me, but Hanne definitely looked too clean to be homeless.

But I'd bought the tickets and we had to go. Which meant I had to find Danny. Which meant I had to find Hanne. I headed off to Columbia Road flower market.

A Sunday morning on Columbia Road is a wonderful thing. Six days a week it's a nondescript little road in the East End, running off Hackney Road from the Shoreditch end. The surrounding streets are full of neat, cared-for terraces with freshly painted front doors and elegant, clean brickwork. It is one of the curiosities of London that somewhere so homely is only a couple of miles from Liverpool Street Station and the edge of the highrise office blocks that form the centre of commerce that is the City of London.

On Sunday mornings, Columbia Road becomes a centre for a different kind of commerce. Both sides of the street overflow with a mass of colour as every kind of flower is sold by every kind of cockney. The crowds fill the width of the road and it's impossible to do anything but meander slowly through it all taking in the sights, sounds and scents.

To take advantage of the crowds, several shops open up on Sundays. You can buy trendy foodstuffs in foccacia bread or more traditional cockles and muscles. There are antiques shops selling everything from eighteenth-century furniture through to 1950's Americana and there are several small shops run by individual craftsmen who do interesting things with leather and tin.

It's in one of the antique shops that I knew I would find Guro. Guro is a friend of Hanne. I had met Guro a couple of times before – on our first meeting I had caused great offence by assuming that she was yet another Norwegian. 'Never assume', she had told me, 'you make an "ass" out of "u" and "me"'. It turned out that she was in fact, Swedish. How very foolish of me. When I entered the shop Guro was in the middle of a sale, persuading a wealthy-looking couple that they really needed an antique bookshelf. Somehow this seemed like an act of anti-patriotism. Surely, any good Swede would be taking the couple aside and whispering a paean to *Ikea*.

I coughed. Guro looked up. She glared in my general direction and continued her sales pitch. I coughed louder. The couple looked up.

'I'm sorry,' I said, 'I need a word with Guro.'

I grasped her elbow and steered her round the corner.

'I'm working', she said in an urgent whisper.

'Yes. . .'

'And I'm Swedish.'

'Yes, we established that. . .'

'And I don't want to talk with you.'

'I need your help. I need Hanne's phone number.'

But Guro had returned to her couple. I picked up a vase and wandered nonchalantly in to her view. I held the vase up to the light. I'd seen this in films where the nasty gangland boss tries to intimidate someone with a tacit threat to their worldly goods.

'You are an idiot', snapped Guro. The couple looked alarmed, I could see them looking at the vase and thinking, 'it's not that bad'. Guro continued, 'I don't own the vase, and if *you* break it, *you'll* have to pay for it!'

'I need Hanne's phone number.'

'I can't give it to you. I promised Hanne. Danny made me sign a contract.'

I put the vase down. I looked into her eyes. Her Swedish, over-seas-student, working-on-a-Sunday, eyes.

'I can give you £30.00.'

She smiled.

'Have you got a pen?'

There is no solidarity amongst the Scandinavians.

So it was Sunday morning and I was waking up late and happy at Hanne's house after an evening out with her and her Norwegian flat-mates. I'd arrived late in the fun, but I'd caught up quickly, and my head was now paying the price. The plan, as I saw it, was to stay in bed, drink tea, and then head to the park for a kickabout and a pub lunch.

And then the phone rang and for some reason my entire body tensed up.

'What's the matter?' asked Hanne

'Sssh. Listen.'

Hanne's flatmate, Janne, had answered the phone. She was speaking in English, which struck fear into me. Dave speaks English. Almost exclusively.

'Maybe it's Dave', I said.

'Dave, Dave, Dave,' said Hanne. 'Always about Dave. It can't be, anyway. He doesn't have this number.'

This is true. Hanne's house had become something of a safe haven for me since I moved in with Dave. I don't tell him when I'm going to be there, or even where 'there' is. It's always meant that there's somewhere to avoid the intensity of Dave's obsessions; more specifically, somewhere I can hide when I suspect any more trips to Wolverhampton might be on the cards.

I listened in terror as Janne said, 'Just one moment please' and walked towards Hanne's room. She knocked twice and poked her head round the door.

'Morning,' she said. 'Hanne, call Nuala when you have a moment.'

Phew.

'Oh, and Danny, Dave's on the phone for you.'

Gah. This wasn't right.

'I promise you I didn't give him this number', I told Hanne, with the most earnest face I could muster.

'You better not have.'

'I didn't! Why would I? He must have found it in my room somewhere, or got it from someone else.'

'I don't want him calling up here all the time.'

'He won't. It must be important. I'll make sure he destroys the number.'

I jumped halfheartedly out of bed and stumbled in my shorts to the hallway. I picked up the receiver.

'Dave?'

'Hi Dan. Listen, bit of an emergency. How quickly can you get home?'

'Well, I'm kind of staying here today.'

'Where's here?'.

Thank God. He didn't know where the house was.

'Oh, you know, London.'

'Give me the address, I can come and pick you up.'

'No! No, that's okay, I'll come back to the flat.'

'Er, actually, can you meet me in Luton?'

'Luton? So there's a Dave Gorman in Luton, I presume?'

I calculated the distance. I could be in Luton and back by two o'clock, and still meet Hanne and the others in the pub. I'd even have time to pick up the football for the boys.

'No. Though we should check – good one! No, I need you to meet me at the airport. Where's your passport? I've checked all your drawers, it's not there.'

'There's a secret drawer under my bed.'

'I checked there.'

Sigh.

'Under the papers on my desk, then.'

'Cool. Get there, I'll meet you at the check-in for Venice at one.'

'Venice?'

'Oh yeah, we're going to Venice. Well, Vicenza, but Venice is on the way. See you at one?'

'Do we have to? I'm going to get into trouble.'

'It's now or never.'

'I could choose quite easily.'

The bet, Dan. The bet.'

'But. . .'

'I've already bought the tickets, okay?'

Tsk.

'See you at 1 o'clock.'

'Bye.'

'Bastard.'

'What?'

'Bye.'

I walked with my head low back to Hanne's room, and picked my watch up from the floor. I'd thought it was about 10 o'clock, but it was now quarter to 12.

'I have to go. Right now.'

'I knew it. Danny, this has to stop,' said Hanne, sitting up. 'Where are you going? Where is it this time? Will you be back today?'

'I'm going to Venice.'

'*Venice? Danny!*'

'Sorry.'

'Why are you doing this to me?'

'What do you mean "to you"? I'm not doing anything to you! I'm not enjoying this, you know. I don't want to go to bloody Italy with bloody Dave.'

'Shut up. Just go, then.'

'Hanne, come on. . .'

'And don't come back, either,' and with that, she pulled the covers over her head and made as close a sound to a harumph as I'd ever heard her make.

You might think that this was a bit of an over-reaction. But this was Venice we were talking about. The one place I'd spent months promising to take Hanne to, but never got round to. And now I was going not with her, but my idiot flatmate. You must understand – I was in big trouble.

'I'll try and call you later on', I said, and left her room, cursing Dave Gormans everywhere under my breath as I did so.

When we met in Luton Airport, Danny was in another one of his moods. I'm not sure why; he'd always wanted to go to Venice. He'd been talking about going for a long time. Admittedly he'd been talking to Hanne about it, and not me – it is, after all, one of the world's most romantic cities. This is something that was brought home to me when we were checking in. There was a neatly-groomed young man behind the desk. He was going through the various formalities, but there were calculations going on behind his eyes. He was examining our paperwork, and he was examining us. With just one small rucksack between us, it was obvious we were not businessmen. We were two young, vaguely scruffy men taking a two-day trip to a famously romantic location. He took in my smile, and then Danny's scowl, and he raised his eyebrows and whispered conspiratorially, 'Lover's tiff, is it?'

Without thinking I looked at Danny's sorrowful eyes. I knew he'd had a row with Hanne, so yes, he'd judged Danny's situation about right. I turned back to the check-in man, 'Yeah', I said, with a nod in Dan's direction. 'Lover's tiff.'

Danny kicked me.

But Venice's reputation is widespread, and the man at the check-in wasn't the only person to make that assumption. On the plane, the stewardess brought me my pudding.

'Would you like two spoons with that?' she asked, smiling.

Venice is a quite spectacularly wet place. We might complain about the weather in Britain, but at least we don't have to travel about by boat.

Marco Polo airport is about eight miles from the centre of town, and we took a bus from there to Piazzale Roma, and checked the train times from the nearby Stazione Santa Lucia to Vicenza. With a couple of hours to kill, Dave cheerily suggested a wander around town, and so we set about making the best of things and went for a walk.

We were heading for Piazza San Marco, the place Napoleon called the 'drawing room of Europe'. My mind, however, remained guilt-locked in the 'bedroom of Hanne'. We passed an internet cafe, and the urge to make amends with her overtook me.

'Dave, I have to go in here for a second, okay?' Dave nodded and said he'd meet me outside in ten minutes.

I handed over a few lire and took a seat with a coffee and a complimentary biscuit, and headed for Hotmail.com. I started to set up an e-mail account with which to smooth over the cracks in my relationship that this bet was starting to cause. I chose the address '*danny_is_sorry_for_being_in_venice@hotmail.com*', but bizarrely, after the computer had had a think about it, I was told that my chosen name has already gone. Clearly, this wasn't a new situation for a Danny to be in. However, the name '*danny_is_sorry_for_being_in_venice_2@hotmail.com*' appeared still to be up for grabs, and although this new address rather ruined the sincerity I'd set out to convey, time was short and I grabbed it before any other Dannies in the city beat me to it.

'Hanne,' I typed. 'Hello. Danny here. Sorry for being in Venice.' There. What woman could resist forgiveness with an opener like that? But I decided some white-lying might also be in order, to stop her from thinking that any fun was involved in our trip. 'The weather is rubbish. I have hurt my ankles. The cars are really loud. There's a scary man outside.' That should do it, I thought. 'Back tomorrow, love, Dan.'

I signed out, took a bite from my biscuit and wandered back into the sunny street. Dave was waiting in a new pair of sunglasses and a hat.

'Hiya. Not a bad way to spend a Sunday afternoon, eh?'

'Mmm.' I said. 'So what now?'

'Dunno. I'd really like to call Dave Gorman to make sure it's okay we visit him.'

'Sorry?'

'I said I'd like to call Dave. Just to make sure it's okay to go and see him.'

'Yes, I heard that. Are you telling me that you haven't actually spoken to Dave Gorman in Vicenza yet? I thought I'd asked you and you said it was sorted.'

'Well, it *is* sorted. Kind of. But no, it's not been possible to actually speak to him, Dan.' He said it as if I had suggested the most insane and impossible course of action in the world. 'We've e-mailed each other, though.'

'Okay. Yes?'

'Well, he said he could meet us tomorrow for an hour or so.'

'Where?'

'Vicenza.'

'*Where* in Vicenza? And when?'

'I don't know.'

'Bloody hell . . . do you remember *France* at all? Eh? Remember what happened there?'

'That's why it's quite important that we speak to him before we go all the way there.'

'We're already in *Italy*, for Christ's sakes!'. I felt like crying with desperation. Here I was, in trouble at home, and in even deeper trouble in Venice. We *had* to meet this Dave Gorman, now. There was no way on God's green earth that I was returning to London and Hanne without there having been a point to the trip. I was willing to take *any* point at this stage. Even a pointless one like this.

'I think we should definitely find a phone, then', I said, trying to keep calm.

'That's what I was thinking too', said Dave, and off we went to find one.

At the crowded Piazza San Marco, Dave dashed off to stand in the queue for the phonebox, while I trudged towards the Basilica di San Marco. It's a building that points almost universally upwards like no other, forcing your eyes up to the sky at which point, if you're not religious, you just stand there going, 'yeah? It's the sky. What are you pointing at?'.

An old man in a dirty grey hat – a Spaniard, I think – stood near me with his wife, both observing with some awe the arches and artwork of the Basilica. He began to talk to me in what sounded like broken Italian, but I gave him a Frenchman's shrug, which as we already know involves a good deal of bottom-lip work, to show I'd no idea what he was saying.

'Inglese?' he said, and that sounded enough like 'English' to convince me he was on the right tracks.

'Yes', I said.

'My wife . . . was wondering . . . why this building is so bubbly.'

'Bubbly?' I say. What could he mean? Luvverly?

'All these bubble, she wonders why the building have so many bubble.'

'Bubble?' I said, like a simpleton, repeating any word I heard. 'Are there bubbles?' Where would these old Spaniards have picked up such a word?

'We never seen such a bubbly house.'

'I see. Well. Yes. If you like.'

'Do you know?' asked his wife, her eyes filled with hope.

'Um . . . no. It was puzzling me, too', I said. 'Ah well. I hope you find out', and I took a few steps backward, still staring intently at the crucifixes and ornate windows, before turning round and pegging it.

I saw Dave up ahead and he was looking pleased with himself. So pleased he had two ice-creams in his hand. He held one out to me as I arrived.

'Good news, then?' I said.

'He wasn't in.'

'But you spoke to someone?'

'No one was answering.'

'But he knows we're coming?'

'Not really.'

'So why were you looking so pleased with yourself?'

'Ice-cream. What were you doing?'

'Those two over there kept asking me about all the 'bubbles' on the Basilica.'

'What . . . the domes?'

Of course. The domes. They were on about the domes on top of the Basilica.

'Er, yes, that's right. The domes. That's what I told them.'

'What did you tell them?'

'That they were domes.'

'They asked you about the domes, and you told them that they were domes.'

'Er . . . yes. Thanks for the ice-cream.'

'I think you need it.'

Vicenza is situated midway between Verona and Padova about 60 miles west of Venice. The train journey there takes about an hour, and once you're there it's very easy to become overawed by the sights. It's a city famous for its Venetian Gothic, Renaissance and Neo-classical architecture and, most notably, it was home to the sixteenth-century architect Andrea Palladio. Many of his finest buildings, such as *La Basilica Palladina*, remain within the heart-shaped city walls. But the most striking image of our brief stop in Vicenza was not a building. On leaving the train I was struck by an amazing vision. On the platform I saw my first uncool Italian; I saw an Italian train-spotter. He appeared very much like the English breed, only in the hot weather there was no anorak. To him, that wasn't a garment, merely a state of mind.

We went for a walk to try and find a suitably cheap hotel for the night.

The second most striking thing about Vicenza was the number of nuns on bicycles.

The hotel we made our way to is to be found down a street as narrow as anything the Middle Ages could have thrown up, lit up by a crude red and blue neon sign proudly bearing its name. We walked into the lobby to find a short man in a shirt two sizes too small for him, scribbling, hunched, into an accounts book. Dave coughed politely to grab his attention. He slammed the book shut.

'Gutentag', he said, looking up and smiling at us both knowingly. The cough must clearly have had a German lilt to it, and we weren't sure how to tell him that wasn't what we were.

'Er . . . gutentag', I said, probably not helping matters very much.

'Do you have any rooms?', asked Dave. The man looked slightly startled that we suddenly weren't German, but played it off perfectly.

'Of course, you wanna room, yes?'

'Yes.'

'Yes, we have room tonight.'

The man gave us forms to fill in, but he only had the one pen, so I had to wait while Dave filled in his details. While I did, I noticed that the man was trying to catch my eye. When he did, he just smiled at me, then looked at busy Dave and smiled, then back at me. I smiled back, confused.

'There you go, Dan,' Dave said, and handed me the pen. I leaned on the desk to complete my form but glanced upwards to see that the man was now smiling at Dave, and then at me, and then at Dave. I looked up at Dave. He smiled at me, confused. I smiled back, looked at the bloke (who was now smiling at me again), smiled, and finished my form. This man was certainly very happy that we were here.

'Excellent, my friends, so . . . you are in room 112.'

Hang about.

'Just the one room?'

'Yes, come, come, you can take the stairs.'

'Er, well . . . is it a double?' asked Dave.

'Yes, nice bed, good window.'

'No, a double *room* . . . with *two* beds?'

'No, one bed. Good one.'

'I'm sure it's lovely, but, er . . . we were actually hoping to get a room *each*, you see.'

'Room *each*?' he said. His face was flitting from Dave's to mine, like a man watching a game of bewilderingly fast tennis. 'Room for each?'

'Yes', I said.

He made a face which implied he thought that any second we were going to shout, 'Only joking!' at the tops of our voices, but we weren't budging on this one. We're very good friends, but given the choice, we'd always rather sleep apart.

'Okay,' said the man, sighing, and opening up his accounts book again. 'A room for each of the Englishmen.'

Maybe he'd thought we'd had an argument, or were as repressed as the British have a reputation for being, but both Dave and I were relieved, five minutes later, to find ourselves walking down a musty corridor to our adjacent, but very separate, rooms.

I was also interested to note that, on the way up the stairs, we'd passed two men, gabbling German and walking really rather close to one another. Clearly this place had found itself a real tourist niche. Phew. For an awkward moment back there, I'd thought that Dave and I were going to be the only two German homosexuals in the whole hotel.

We decided to pop out for a quick meal before phoning Dave Gorman the soldier on his military installation and breaking the news that we were suddenly in his town. We were halfway down the narrow street outside the hotel when Dave had a thought.

'Just in case there are any problems with getting in touch with Dave Gorman, Dan. . .'

'Don't even start. . .'

'. . . we need to find out where the military base is. That way at least we know where we can go to track him down if worse comes to worst.'

'What, you want us to infiltrate the American base, do you? You want us to break in under cover of darkness?'

'No, of course not. But if we *had* to, we'd have a good reason.'

'It's not much of a cover story, Dave. We'd sound like spies.'

'Who's ever heard of a British spy, Dan? I just want to find out where it is so we can plan our trip in the morning. I'll ask someone. Hang on, I'll ask the fella at the hotel.'

We turned round and walked back into the lobby, where our friend was still behind his counter, still scribbling into his book.

'Excuse me,' said Dave. 'I need to know where all the American soldiers are.'

'You wanna meet a soldier?' he said, his suspicions about us now suddenly confirmed.

'Yes. An American one. Where do I go to meet American soldiers?'

The man looked at me with sad eyes. He must have thought I was very forgiving.

I rang the military installation with my heart in my mouth. I had sent an e-mail saying that we were on our way but I had had no reply. I had spent the rest of the time trying to find Danny or in transit. Now, I was here, in Vicenza and the phone was ringing and ringing and ringing. It rang for nearly twenty minutes before a recorded message told me in both English and Italian that I was ringing the US Military Base in Vicenza but that all the lines were currently busy. I tried again.

Eventually, someone picked up. It was a female voice. An intensely nasal, American, female voice. I held the phone away from my face but I could still hear her as she told me that I had successfully got through to the US Military Base in Vicenza and asked how she could be of assistance.

'Hello, I'm trying to get in touch with David Gorman.'

'Just putting you through.'

The phone buzzed a few more times. Then a male voice: 'Yo.'

'Errr . . . hello,' I said, 'is that Dave?'

'Speaking.'

'Oh good. Hi – I'm the other Dave. I don't know if you've checked your e-mail, I tried to let you know we were coming.'

'What?'

'We've come to Vicenza. We're really hoping you can still meet us tomorrow.'

'Are you shitting me?'

'What?'

'What are you talking about? Who are you?'

'You e-mailed me. I e-mailed you. My name is also Dave Gorman . . . me and my flatmate Danny have come from London in order to meet you.'

Silence. Then laughter. Then, 'Dude, you got the wrong room. My name is David Goldman.' Then laughter. Then click. The phone was down.

I rang back. I was at the back of the queue again. I got the recorded voice again. I rang back. I got the nasal voice again.

'Hello, I'm trying to speak to David Gorman. That's David G-O-R-M-A-N.'

'Just putting you through'

Brrrrrrrr. Pause. Brrrrrrrr. A soft southern female drawl, 'Hello?'

Who had the nasal lady put me through to this time – Jane Grossman? Gail Morgan? Elaine Baldwin?

'Hello. I'm trying to get in touch with David Gorman.'

'I'm afraid he's out right now, can I help you?'

Finally we were getting somewhere. I chatted to my name-sake's wife for ten minutes. They had received my e-mail. They'd been hoping we would make it. We arranged to meet the whole Gorman family at a restaurant, *Il Fauno*, near the base, at twelve the next day.

Il Fauno's sign proudly boasts of its excellent *aria condizionata*. It had other signs, too, probably bearing equally proud boasts. One in particular caught my eye. It read *'Qui si fa creditor sola ai novantenni se accompagnati dai genitori'* . . . which, although it was clearly in Italian, seemed to ring some kind of visual bell with me. Then I remembered the cafe opposite our flat and its fondness for these kind of signs, and worked out that it was probably the one that went 'We only grant credit to 90-year-old people accompanied by their parents.'

And they say humour doesn't travel. I started reading every other sign hoping to recognise the Italian translation of 'You don't have to be mad to work here, but it helps.'

'I think that's them,' said Dave, excitedly, pointing at a man in a green shirt, his wife, and four kids. They were sitting at a table in the sun and next to the garden, and chatting happily. One of the kids pointed at us, and her dad stood up to greet us.

'My name is Dave Gorman,' said Dave Gorman.

'Dave,' said Dave, shaking his hand. 'Gorman. Too.'

I think Dave was a bit stunned to be meeting an American name-sake. Americans are . . . y'know . . . glamorous. This man was likely to be the most glamorous Dave Gorman we were going to meet, and Dave appeared to be momentarily starstruck.

'Take a seat, guys. It's a pleasure to meet you. . .'

Our new Dave Gorman was a 40-year-old, shaven-headed warrant officer from Alabama. 'Well, being a military family,' he says, in a Southern accent so drawly it almost sends us to sleep, 'we're kinda from all over the place. Me and my wife are Alabama born. Those guys . . .' he pointed at his two daughters, '. . . they're from Louisiana. He's from Georgia,' he said, pointing at his oldest son. 'And this little guy . . .' he wiped the drool from his baby's face. 'He's from Langstuhl, Germany.'

I looked over at his wife, who was gazing adoringly at her husband. She had the look of a country and western singer about her, but one who probably only ever sang happy songs. About having nice kids, and a plump dog called Barney, and about travelling the world in an army van with the husband she'd been with since she was sixteen.

She took one of the green glass bottles of cold water they'd ordered and collected a couple of cups together for Dave and me. I looked around us. We really were the only people in the restaurant not dressed up in military uniform, and so therefore the only people in the room not wearing our names on our chests. I scanned the place for Gormans, more for peace of mind than anything, and thankfully found none. But I did spot one man, sat between a 'Lester' and a 'Vincent', with a name so phonetically rude that I now find myself unable to bring it your attention.

'So let's get some food . . .' Dave Gorman number 9 said, as a waiter arrived at our table. 'Two hotdogs, please, Spaghetti a Ragu, Penne Pasta, Pizza a prosciutto with funghi . . . and you guys?'

'Um . . . I'll have a hotdog, too, please,' said Dave. I wasn't sure whether he was asking for this in order to bond with the Americans, but the way he said it made him sound incredibly English. It didn't sound like it was coming from someone who was ordering a sausage. It sounded like someone who actually wanted a dog to be brought to our table, and hot.

'Same please', I said.

We sat around the table having a pleasant meal. It felt easy and relaxed and the conversation flowed. With our earlier Dave Gormans there had been a certain sense of awkwardness. The Dave Gormans had been wary of us – unsure as to why we were there. And we didn't really know why either. But then the bet had lent us a sense of purpose and I think we'd grown to be quite comfortable with the whole thing. However, our later Dave

Gorman encounters had been against the clock, so there was a sort of slickness about it.

But now we were in Vicenza. We were never going to find a second Dave Gorman here and while we did have to return to London later that day, there was no need to rush. For the first time we were able to completely relax and take our time in the company of a DG. It was also the first time the Dave Gorman hadn't been alone. I realised that the look I had seen in so many of their eyes so far was the look of a man who felt cornered. This Dave didn't feel cornered; he was holding court. He was the patriarch and he and his family made us welcome in their environment. I didn't just feel like I was sitting with his family. I felt as though I was a member of his family.

'Hey, you know what?' asked Dave. 'We could be related!'

I guess the feeling was mutual.

We spoke about many things that day but Dave had two startling facts to reveal. There was one piece of good news and one piece of bad news. The bad news concerned the youngest of his kids. In his mother's arms, blissfully unaware of the situation, was their eighteen-month-old son. A tiny, angelic-looking man with a mop of curly blonde hair, who went by the name of. . .

Justin.

David.

Gorman.

I mean – can you imagine?

Not David Justin Gorman. No. That would have been too convenient. Instead, for no sensible reason that I could come to terms with, his parents had decided to call their son Justin David Gorman. I mean . . . *Justin*, for goodness sake! It was like a punch to the gut. This little devil child – and no, I don't think I'm being too harsh, actually – just sat there, gurgling and smiling, taunting me, virtually making fun of me, blissfully unaware of his near Dave Gorman-ness. So near and yet so far.

Justin was just out.

I couldn't believe it.

'Are you okay?' said Mrs Dave Gorman. 'You seem kinda . . . quiet all of a sudden.'

I wanted to tell her it was because I was a ball of supressed rage. Instead, all I could manage was to say, weakly, 'Just a bit of wind.'

I looked at Danny, the only person who'd know what had

affected me so. He avoided my gaze, embarrassed, and tried to start up a new conversation.

'How about your other kids? What are you lot called?'

'Well,' said Mrs Gorman, 'I was just about to tell you . . . this guy here, he's our eldest son. And his name *is* David Gorman. . .'

Saved! They may have taunted me with their eighteen-month-old Justin David Gorman, but they'd been waiting to present me with ten-year-old David Jacob Gorman all along! I loved these people. I even forgave little Justin. He wasn't all bad.

But what great value Italy held – here we were in Vicenza, and we were scoring two-for-one. This was the first time I'd ever been part of a Dave Gorman triangle. But now the three of us sat in quiet contemplation – a ten-year-old, a-29-year old and a 40-year-old Dave Gorman. If only that eighteen-month-old baby had *also* been called Dave, eh? All of a sudden Justin David started to cry. I think he understood.

After a while, when there were clean plates and smiling faces all round the table, I began our formalities. I produced the polaroid camera and snapped our ninth and tenth DGs. They signed their photos eagerly, and I looked on and smiled, like a proud father.

'So where exactly are you going this afternoon?' I asked Dave Gorman junior, by way of making conversation.

'Fort Louis, Washington, sir.'

'Are you looking forward to it?'

'Yes, sir.'

This was great. The more questions I asked, the more times I was called 'sir'. You don't get this in Britain nowadays. You're lucky if you get a 'mister.'

'Do you want to go into the military?'.

'Yes, sir.'

'Do you want to be a warrant officer, like your dad?'

'Yes, sir.'

Maybe he thought I was a teacher.

'Do you go to a military school?'

'No, sir, I'm home schooled.'

'But did you go to school before you moved out here?'

'No, sir, I've *always* been home schooled.'

'That's cool.'

I looked down at his polaroid. He'd signed his name 'Davib Gormam'. I wondered whether perhaps home schooling was quite as cool as I'd just said it was.

They were a lovely bunch of Gormans and it was a real shame that this meeting had to end. But it did. After all, we only had to get back to London but Dave had to get him and his family en route back to America. We walked back out to the front and we waved them goodbye as they clambered into a people mover and drove off.

I was a very happy man. I'd stuck my neck out and come to Italy hoping to meet my ninth namesake and against all the odds I'd found my tenth as well. We watched them drive off round the corner before making our way back to the train station. We travelled home by planes, trains, automobiles, gondolas and a speedboat, but not in that order.

On the flight home Danny was as relaxed as I'd seen him since all this began.

'I'm really glad I met him,' I said, while Danny just kind of nodded. 'I mean, bet or no bet, I'm really glad I met him.'

'Listen, Dave. Don't tell Hanne this . . . but. . .'

I knew what was coming.

'. . . nothing.'

He'd enjoyed himself.

Chapter 8

GORMAN WISDOM

On our return from Venice, there were several letters waiting for me. The ones that looked like they were from an ever-more-anxious bank manager somehow ended up stuffed in a kitchen drawer. There was also one message, left that morning by a concerned-sounding lady from my credit card company, who'd been studying my spending and urged me to check my bill as it was possible that my numbers had been stolen by some internet gangsters. I deleted the message, and opened the final letter.

It was from a gentleman in Warminster.

I think you can probably guess what his name was.

He'd been away on holiday and so hadn't been able to get back to me, but was now back, rested and tanned, and up for a meeting.

I took my road atlas down from the shelf and studied the page with Warminster on it. He wanted us to meet him at work, in a little village called Bishopstrow, at the fish factory where he worked as someone in a shirt and tie. I flicked through the adjacent pages of the atlas . . . there had to be somewhere nearby that contained a Dave Gorman? If I could score two Dave Gormans on a trip to Italy, I was sure I would be able to bag a brace between London and Warminster.

I phoned Dave Gorman in Warminster to tell him we were on our way round, and dragged Danny outside and sat him in the car.

We drove to the South West, found the village, found Lyons Seafoods, and bagged ourselves another Dave Gorman. This one, it turned out, had once played golf on Ladybank Golf Course and was shocked to learn that he had strolled along the grass cut by a fellow Dave Gorman. 'I remember thinking it was very well tended,' he said. 'Now I know why!'.

He'd never met anyone else called Dave Gorman, but did reveal to us how he'd go about finding more.

'Car stickers! They're very underrated as a form of advertising. I'd probably go about it that way. You know. . . "I'm in the Dave Gorman Club . . . Are You?". Something like that. . .'

I promised to carry his idea out. We took his picture, shook his hand, and left. We were becoming very professional at this lark.

From Warminster, we drove to Swindon to meet Dave Gorman number twelve. Now here was a man who knew about the Gorman name. Forget Wolverhampton; Swindon rapidly became the centre of all knowledge on the Gorman clan and their history.

Dave Gorman number twelve, a lorry driver, had the look of the new man about him. Some kind of Native American necklace hung around his neck, and he lavished cup after cup of tea upon us, as well as – a little later on – a piping hot home-made apple pie. He had a pair of huge, clear blue eyes that he kept hidden behind glasses, and his enthusiasm for showing us what ample evidence of his Gormanhood he'd amassed never wavered. We sat in his back garden, the three of us, carefully studying photo album after photo album, following his family back through the years, back to Ireland and the tiny cottage they'd owned back there. He showed us his cousins, his parents, pictures of himself when he was two, photos of the Gormans on holiday in the New Forest, and maps, documents and postcards tracing the movements of the Gorman family for hundreds and hundreds of years.

He truly had more proof of his Gormanness than anyone I'd ever met before. He liked canoeing and camping, and proudly showed off the old blue van he uses to drive him and his son Jonathan from adventure to adventure. He enjoys his life, and it was a heart-warming thing to see. We spent several happy hours sitting, laughing, exchanging stories and drinking more and more tea. As it got later and darker, though, I realised that we had to make a move. We had one more Dave Gorman to meet. And this one, Danny would be pleased to note, was back in London.

'I wish you wouldn't go,' said Dave Gorman, the emotion of the situation making his voice crack the words as they came out, and I could see that Danny felt the same way. We'd made a friend, here.

'Maybe we can come back sometime,' said Dan.

This was a real breakthrough. Danny had really, truly enjoyed himself.

We got into the car and drove out of Swindon.

'That was my favourite Dave Gorman ever,' said Dan, as we stopped for petrol. 'Present company . . . er . . . you know. . . .'

'You enjoyed yourself.'

'No, I wouldn't say that.'

'Yes, you did. I can tell.'

'No, you can't.'

'Yes, I can. You enjoyed yourself.'

'No, I didn't.'

Yes he did.

'Not at all, in fact.'

Yes he did.

'Stop thinking in your head that I enjoyed myself.'

He did, y'know.

I smiled a quiet smile and drove us back to London.

If there's one word you could use to describe Highbury in London, it's 'leafy'. We parked the car on a huge mound of them and tried our best to battle our way through some more before we got to the high street. From there, it was a case of asking directions, forgetting almost instantly what we'd been told, and guessing our way there. Dave and I can usually find our way anywhere, just by using the following technique.

'Dave, I think we should go left.'

'Right. Well, I think we should go right.'

'Hmm. Well, how about we go left for a bit, and if that doesn't work, we can then come back here and then go right for a bit?'

'Okay, that should be fine.'

We then buy a streetmap.

Luckily, on this occasion, we were covered by the *London A–Z* and Dave offered to navigate on the basis of whatever it gave us.

Incidentally, there are approximately 55,000 streets listed in the *London A–Z*. Only sixteen of them begin with Z, and I have never walked down any of them. I think it's about time they brought out a cheaper A–Y for people like me.

It turns out the doctor's surgery is roughly five minute's walk, and, in our usual way (but mainly because of the bloody leaves), it took us half an hour to get there.

'Okay, this is where we're meeting him' said Dave. 'I'll go in and ask for him, okay?'

Now, you could say that this is asking for trouble. Why not tell the receptionist that Danny Wallace was in reception for Dave Gorman? Why send a Dave Gorman in to ask for a Dave Gorman? Well, this was our first chance to confuse a receptionist, something that we were sure would be fun.

'Hello,' said Dave, 'would you mind telling Dave Gorman that Dave Gorman is here to see him?'

'Certainly' said the woman, without a flinch. Clearly this was a reception desk where miracles regularly occur and time was scant for mere coincidences. Disappointed, Dave and I took a seat.

'Sorry,' she suddenly called over, 'Did you say your name was Dave Gorman as well?'

'Yes,' Dave replied, shooting me a wink as he did so.

'Right. Just a minute then.'

This was a very disappointing reaction.

Still, at least the patients were giving us odd looks, and if Dave's little performance was taking that woman in the corner's mind off whatever it was that was causing her to itch quite so much, then as far as I'm concerned it was more than worth it.

Finally, a tall and wiry man walked into the reception area and had a word with the receptionist. I craned my neck and managed to make out that on his chest is a badge declaring his name and position: David Gorman, Practice Manager.

I wondered to myself whether this could be our man.

'Dave? Danny?'

It was, yes.

And with those words, spoken loudly and clearly in a Highbury doctor's surgery and in a North Eastern accent, your two friends met their third Dave Gorman of the day; their thirteenth Dave Gorman so far.

I wonder if you spent your day doing something similar.

I knew I'd sleep soundly in my bed that night. It had been a very, very good day, and we'd met a whopping three Dave Gormans. The photo album was by my bed, and I couldn't help but flick through it every now and then, just to stare at my ever-increasing

collection. In the morning, I made a trip into town and ordered 500 car stickers bearing the words 'I'm in the Dave Gorman Club . . . Are You?', exactly as Warminster Dave had specified. I added our phone number to the end of the sticker, so that anyone who found their curiosity pricked by the words could always phone up and have a chat about it with either Danny or me. Though it would probably be better if it was with me, to be honest. I picked them up later that afternoon and attached the first one to the side of my trusty car. Now all I had to do was find another 499 places to stick them and everything would be fine. I stuck one on the other side of my car. I stuck one on Danny's bag, as well as on the back of his leather jacket, but he couldn't see the practical side of this and tore them off without even wearing them once. He's weird sometimes.

As it turned out, the car sticker was having very little effect, even after two or three days of it being there. I'd driven to *Tesco*, all around East London, and even to the petrol station on the Mile End Road, and yet not one Dave Gorman had got in touch off the back of it. Unbelievable.

However, life was about to become a little bit strange. Oh, all right: life was about to become a little bit stranger. I received my first anonymous tip-off. I couldn't really explain how this occurred. As far as I knew, no-one else was really aware of my search. Unless they were called Dave Gorman. Or they printed car stickers. Or they were Danny.

But Dave Gormans must have been telling their friends, and their friends must have been telling other friends, because I was beginning to get all sorts of e-mails about the bet. A couple at first, and then a few more. And then, one day towards the end of the week, I got rather an exciting one.

It arrived from a clearly made-up Hotmail address, and the sender hadn't bothered to write anything by way of an explanation. Instead, they'd attached a document. It was a list of names and phone numbers from a business directory.

In New York.

'Danny! Come quick! Please!' Dave must have got his big toe stuck in the hot water tap again.

'What is it?' I shouted.

'Come and see this!'

I wandered into his bedroom. He was printing something out.

'Someone's sent me something brilliant,' he said, reaching down to pick the piece of paper up. 'Look at this'.

I started to read it. 'Gorman, Cheryl. . . Gorman, Jack. . . *Gorman & Silverman* . . . *Gorman, Gorman & Thompson* . . . I think I can guess, but what exactly am I looking for here, Dave?'

'There, in the middle!'

And there, in the middle, it was.

'Gorman, B, David (Dr.) . . . 911 Park Avenue, New York, New York. . .'

'He's a doctor!' said Dave. 'We haven't got one of those yet! Number Thirteen worked in a Doctor's surgery, but this one is a bona fide doctor in his own right!'

'You're not serious.'

'What? What do you mean?'

'You're not seriously about to suggest that we fly to New York to meet this man?'

'Well . . . why not . . . I mean . . . he's a doctor. . .'

'Yes, but . . . he's a *New York* doctor.'

Danny was right, of course. It was stupid to go all that way to meet just one Dave Gorman. Particularly given the fact that I was now finding myself stuffing letters from bank managers in drawers. I mean, the unofficial rules of the game were supposed to be that if I find out about one, I go and meet him. But this . . . this was different.

'You're right, Dan. I guess it's just too far away'

Danny smiled at me. 'You're slipping,' he said, with an annoying smile. 'I guess the bet doesn't mean that much to you any more. . .'

I managed to buy two fairly reasonable flights to New York, and found a half-decent hotel to go with them. I'd teach Danny for being cheeky. I'd teach him a lesson he'd never forget. I'd take him to New York.

That'd wipe the smile off his face.

Chapter 9

START SPREADING THE NEWS. . .

Now, I don't know if you've heard about New York, or seen it on the telly, but it's rather a big place, all told. Far bigger than the old one, at any rate, and with far more Americans in it (which, if you've ever stood in York town centre in the middle of July, you might actually have trouble imagining).

There's a lot to see, and I planned to see as much of it as soon as I could. I ambled out of my hotel room at elevenish, first planning on a casual stroll and a bite to eat at the restaurant next door, which I'd been pleased to note served breakfast all day and all night, all week.

We were booked into the Roosevelt Hotel in Manhattan, on the corner of the excitingly-named Madison Avenue, and it was as plush and grand as you could hope. Well, its lobby was. Its rooms were actually rather hot, stuffy and noisy, with air conditioning units that could double as machines for making people deaf (should such an industry ever arise). I also found a broken Panasonic toaster under my bed, though I later checked our bill and they'd forgotten to charge me for it.

Marble floors and men with cigars are wall-to-wall, as are, rather bizarrely for this time of the morning, Albanians. Everywhere I looked, in fact, there were Albanians. Some were carrying instruments, most were in waistcoats, and all of them were . . . well . . . Albanian. An Albanian flag hung between two of the 30-foot marble columns, and the receptionist's desk was lined with small, paper Albanian flags on sticks. A sign said 'Welcome Albanians', which, to be honest, was what first tipped me off that they were Albanian.

By the time my jetlagged, foggy head had worked out that there must be some kind of international conference going on, the Albanians that had been everywhere a minute before were now completely gone. The receptionist was taking the flags off her desk, and the welcome sign had been removed. There was a ping from behind and Dave stepped out of the lift. I looked at him in confusion . . . where were all my Albanians? How could I explain what I had just seen? The way cockroaches scatter and hide the moment you turn the light on, the Albanians seemed to have pegged it the moment they sensed Dave getting out of a lift. Out doors, through windows, under desks . . . the lengths they must have gone to disappear in unison and make me look like a fool is astounding.

'Breakfast?' asked Dave, 'And then we should go and find Dave Gorman.'

'Dave, about fifteen seconds ago I was totally surrounded by Albanians.'

'Cool. Hey, the place next door does breakfast all day. I fancy pancakes.'

'I was totally surrounded by Albanians.'

'Cool. There are taxis outside, the fella in the hat will get one for us. We should get going as soon as we've eaten.'

'A little under 30 seconds ago, I, Danny, your flatmate, was totally surrounded by Albanians.'

'Were you?'

'Yes.'

'Cool.' He stared at me. 'Pancakes?'.

I sigh, I nod, and we walk down the stairs and past two men and a ladder, presumably about to remove the huge flag, and the last of my evidence.

Dave ordered the pancakes, I had coffee and a croissant, and we planned the day ahead. It took about 30 seconds. We had only one thing to do, and it involved a single taxi journey and the doorstepping of a Dave Gorman. Hardly a day you'd need a diary for.

'I've done some research. He's an opthalmologist' said Dave. 'It says here that he works until five or so, and sometimes he's at a different office altogether, but I think he's here today.' He unfolded a tatty Post-It note on which he'd written 'DG 14 – Eye bloke. 911 Park Avenue.'

'And he has no idea we're coming to meet him?'

'Well, no. There hasn't really been time. The time difference always seemed to get in the way. And think about it: he'd think we were crazy if he thought we were coming all the way here to meet him. If we surprise him, he'll think it's just a happy coincidence. We'll catch him off guard. It'll be brilliant. And I mean, we had a plane to catch, and a hotel to sleep in, and I guess I *would've* phoned eventually, but I got sidetracked by those Albanians.'

'What do you mean you got sidetracked by those Albanians?'

'I got up early and popped my head round the door of some sort of conference, and it looked like fun, so I stayed awhile. I met some very nice Albanians.'

'Dave, why didn't you tell me? I was trying to tell you all about the Albanians and you ignored me. And you conferenced with them. How could that not be the first thing you told me when you got out of the lift?'

'It didn't seem all that relevant.'

'Not relevant? To a conversation in which all I talked about was the fact that I was standing among dozens of Albanians?'

'We've got work to do, Dan. Let's not forget our focus, here.' And with that, he wiped the syrup off his fingers and stood up.

'Let's go get 'im.'

As I got into the taxi I felt excited for a myriad of reasons. I'd never been to New York before and yet the place felt incredibly familiar. I recognised the buildings, the streets, and I felt like I recognised the people. Basically, New York is the world's largest film set, and for an Englishman – striding out of the Roosevelt Hotel, leaping into one of the famous yellow cabs and barking at the driver, '911 Park Avenue' – it felt like taking centre stage in a proper American movie.

At the same time I also had a rush of adrenaline caused by the sheer recklessness of what we were doing. Plainly speaking, I couldn't afford to take me and my flatmate to New York. But I'd done just that. It was a sensation I'd last felt while jumping out of a plane.

I made a parachute jump a few years ago and it was one of the most frightening things I've ever done. Until I was actually doing it, that is, when all of a sudden it became one of the most exciting. But at every moment prior to actually falling through the sky with only ropes and canvas to protect me, it was . . . well . . . scary. When I was being talked through the procedure on the ground, when I was sitting in the plane on the way up, when they opened the door of the plane at 10,000 feet: at all these times I was petrified. I was scared because I knew that I was still in control; that I could still opt out. I didn't *have* to get in the plane, they didn't *have* to open the door and I didn't *have* to jump out. But when I *did* jump, there were no more choices. I was strapped to an instructor who was strapped to a parachute, and that was pretty much that. I had no choice but to enjoy myself. Well, now that self-same sensation was coursing through my veins as we sat in a cab and it jerked its way through New York traffic. I'd done something foolish, there was no turning back, there was no choice but to enjoy myself.

And most exciting of all, of course, we were en route for Dave Gorman number fourteen. We were trying to find one for every card in the deck (including the jokers) and number fourteen meant we were starting a new suit.

We'd found all the spades. Bring on the diamonds, baby!

We pulled up a few doors down from number 911 and I took a deep breath. I paid the driver and we clambered out of the back seat. This was it. The glamour and excitement of our first New York Dave Gorman.

I strode up to the door with Danny lagging a few paces behind me. I was about to ring the bell when I looked up and saw a terrible thing. There, on the wall, was a brass plaque. And on the brass plaque, was Dave Gorman's name.

'ARSE!' I shouted.

'What?' said Danny. 'What is it now?'

'His . . . name. I . . . it's . . . David Gorman's name. . .'

'Well . . . what about it?'

Danny caught up with me, and studied the plaque.

'Oh', he said.

David Gorman's name wasn't David Gorman. It was *B.* David Gorman. Not David B. Gorman, you understand. No, that would have been fine. This was B. David Gorman.

Can you imagine the fury? The pain? The frustration?

Well, can you?

If I was trying to meet 54 Scott Fitzgeralds, I wouldn't make do with an F. Scott Fitzgerald. If I was trying to meet 54 Edgar Hoovers, I'd tell J. Edgar Hoover where he could stick his extra consonant. And just as Justin David Gorman had been a disappointment back in Vicenza, so this B. David Gorman was an utter, crushing, disappointment now.

I didn't know if he was a Bernard or a Bruce or a Brian but I didn't care because at the end of the day he wasn't a David and that was all I knew.

I felt frustrated and I felt panicked; all of a sudden it was as if my parachute had failed to open. What was I doing in New York? What were *we* doing in New York? How could I make sense of this situation?

I turned and started walking away. I didn't know where I was going but I knew I didn't want to be here, in the shadow of Dr. B. David Gorman.

'Oi,' called Dan, who remained still as I stormed past him. 'Where are you going?'

'He's not a Dave Gorman is he? I'm going home.'

'What?'

'I'm going home.'

'*Hotel* home or *home* home?'

I didn't know the answer . . . 'Look, I'm getting a taxi, Dan, and if you want to be in it, you'll need to start walking.'

Dan could see I was upset. He turned back towards the sign a final time, as if to make sure it said what it said. He stood where he was for another moment, desperately trying to come up with some way of making it all better. He was trying to find a way to persuade me that this impostor counted.

Now, I know he only wanted me to feel better, but there was no way through it. If we accepted this man as a namesake there were no rules any more. The world would be chaos. What was the point? If we counted this man, I might as well admit defeat. And that was worse.

Eventually Danny scurried after me. We hailed a taxi and headed back to the hotel in silence. It didn't feel like we were in a film any more. It felt like we were in hell.

On the way back I turned my head away from Dan, pretending to be fascinated by the sights outside my window. In reality I was hiding my eyes, which were betraying me, welling up with emotion, and threatening to spill a tear with every jerk and jolt the New York cabbie could bring from his machine.

I hated New York.

I'd never actually found myself disappointed that someone didn't have the Christian name I'd thought they did before. It's not something that worries me, usually. I don't find myself at parties desperately hoping that the girl I'm about to be introduced to is a Jennifer and then throwing my beer over her when I find out she's a

Tammy. Although I imagine that if any girl deserves to have beer thrown over her, she's probably a Tammy. But this time, when I had witnessed my flatmate's ride from anticipation to fury to sheer, heart-breaking, broken-heartedness . . . well . . . it got *me*, too.

Dave was sitting by my side as the taxi roared through New York, saying nothing. I could tell from his body language – face turned against the window, arm up to protect himself against the world, legs crossed away from me – that he was more than just angry. There was high emotion in the air. It seemed physically impossible to speak, as if words had no place in this life any more, and just one thoughtless utterance could have fearful, yet unwritten, repercussions.

I stared out of my side of the cab, trying to work out when the journey had turned from fun half-obsession and boyish whimsy to what was now, seemingly, something far bigger. What had New York done to this? How was Dave treating it now? Self-discovery? A search for identity? To feel he wasn't alone in the world? That there were others out there with something fundamental in common with him?

Bollocks.

He was doing it to prove me wrong. I felt less sorry for him instantly. Perhaps the let-down at the hands of B. David Gorman was for the best. Maybe this would prove to Dave how ridiculous things had become – stuck on the other side of the world with nothing to show for it apart from jetlag and a huge credit card bill. I had no doubts that we'd be catching an earlier flight than we'd anticipated. We wouldn't be out celebrating tonight. We'd be in our rooms, pack-ing. Probably with the tellies off. It was that kind of mood.

Dave didn't seem like he was up for a spot of sightseeing, some-how. He told me in no uncertain terms that he wanted to be alone for a while. So I left him in his room and found myself a taxi driver who'd take me wherever people usually go when they visit New York for the first time.

And so it was I began to get to know the place on my own. I stood on the Brooklyn Bridge, and had a stranger take a photo of me in front of lower Manhattan, and New York harbour. I got on a boat and took a ride to the Statue of Liberty, reading its inscription 'Give me your tired, your poor, your huddled masses yearning to breathe free' and hearing someone quip that if it's breathing you want to do, you really ought to do it somewhere other than New York.

I bought a bagel from a man in the street, a t-shirt from a lady in a shop, and a blackcurrant drink called Welch's, which was so sugary I very nearly passed out.

I walked past a queue of tubby people waiting to be allowed to take their place in the audience of that afternoon's *Rosie O'Donnell Show*. I saw Tim Robbins and Susan Sarandon go into a big building. Tim was wearing shorts. Susan was quite smart. I bought a hotdog and then threw it in a bin.

And I was doing all this without my mate. I felt a pang of guilt and instantly told myself not to be stupid. It was his bloody fault, all this. If he learnt nothing from our trip to France, he was an overexcitable fool who should really learn to check the minor details in life, such as whether someone is actually called Dave Gorman or not. Yes, he might be sitting alone in his hotel room watching repeats of *The Golden Girls*, eating his free biscuits, wearing his complimentary shower cap and feeling very sorry for himself, but whose fault was that? Not mine. Not bloody mine. He could stay there and consider exactly how he was wasting both our lives with these insane shenanigans, as far as I was concerned. He wasn't going to make me feel bad about it. I had New York to discover. And plenty more of it to discover this afternoon.

I looked at my watch. I'd been gone five hours. The pang returned at twice the strength. I jogged to the nearest junction, hailed a cab, and asked the driver to take me back to the hotel as fast as he could. As we drove down Fifth Avenue, past the zoo, past the Museum of Modern Art, past an old woman who looked a bit like Kirk Douglas, I realised that I really should have been there for him, no matter how much I disagreed with his methods.

I arrived back at the hotel to find Dave waiting in the lobby.

'Where the hell have you been?' he asked, and instantly, all guilt and regret vanished from my mind.

'Out. Looking at stuff.'

'I've been waiting ages for you. I've found another one.'

'What?'

'I've found another Dave Gorman. He's going to be turning up here in about half an hour.'

'Why have you found another one, Dave? Why couldn't we have just packed our bags and left?'

'We're in New York, Dan!'

'Yeah, so let's see some of New York!'

'I think you're missing the point. We're in New York, so let's find some New York Dave Gormans! It's fresh hunting ground. . .'

'Oh, so *that's* why people come to New York. I'd thought it was for the museums, or the architecture, or the clubs, or the shops, or the sights, or for the bloody baseball. Not for finding namesakes at every available opportunity.'

Dave considered this for a moment. He wrinkled his nose and shook his head.

'So he's arriving in about half an hour.'

'Great. How did you find this one?'

Back at the hotel I'd gone to my room to be alone and sulk. I'd packed my bag. Made a coffee. And then I'd done what I always do when I'm in a hotel and I've packed my bag – I opened every drawer and every cupboard to check that I hadn't forgotten anything. I hadn't. But I did find something else. Something that got me rather excited again. I found a copy of the New York Phone Directory.

Suddenly a strange mix of hope and tension flooded over me. I'd lost the battle, but what if there was still a chance that I could win the war? I opened the phone book and flicked to the Gs. Then the Gormans. Then the D Gormans.

There were loads of the bastards.

This was exactly what I needed! Something to get my teeth into. . .

It was like starting all over again. With renewed enthusiasm I began leaving messages on answering machines, speaking to Dominics, Dylans, and even one Dagwood Gorman. But in amongst them I found and spoke to one, wonderful, real-life New York David Gorman.

I convinced him I was genuine. I explained the story so far. He placed his trust in me.

'Look, you're a stranger in town, so why don't I come down to your hotel?', he said. Nothing, but nothing, could have made me happier. Such was my excitement that I arrived in the lobby 30 minutes early. Which is where I was when I saw Danny returning to the hotel, looking every bit the tourist in his shorts and sunglasses. What did he think this was? Some kind of holiday?

We sat in the cafe opposite the lobby, I bought Danny a coffee, and we waited for Dave Gorman to arrive. I was fairly confident that I'd recognise him. I'd met thirteen so far, and I was getting a feel for it. And then it happened: a man walked in. I'd say he was about 30 years of age, he was wearing cool sneakers, a pair of very baggy jeans, and one of those fashionable retro American workshirts with a company logo on the back and the name of whoever once wore it sewn above the pocket. This looked like a Dave Gorman to me.

I made my approach, 'Excuse me . . . Dave?'

He looked at me with complete disdain.

'Do I look like a Dave?'

'Er . . . well. . .'

'What does that say?' He pointed at his shirt. There, neatly embroidered, was the name 'Frank'.

'It says "Frank".'

'Right, so I guess my name is "Frank", huh?'. He strode off muttering something under his breath about shooting tourists, and I sat down, with a bit of a blush on the go.

'That wasn't him', I explained to Dan, just in case he was in any doubt.

'I guessed. That fella over there, though . . . do you think *that's* him?' He was indicating a large, bespectacled man, in bermuda shorts and a bright blue shirt with a striking floral print. That wasn't the look of a cool New York resident. That was a tourist if ever I'd seen one.

'That's not him,' I said. 'Trust me.'

'Excuse me' said the man, suddenly standing by our table. 'One of you guys called Dave?'

Our newest Dave Gorman took us for a walk through the city, ending up at the Bowling Green. This isn't actually a bowling green; it's a small triangular park in front of the Museum of the American Indian at the southern end of Broadway. It has shady trees, and plenty of benches, and was crowded with workers from the financial district, relaxing and talking in the evening sun. We got a small table on the fringe of things and sat chatting. This was one of the most relaxed men I'd ever met. Here was a man who seemed to be comfortable in his skin, he liked who he was, and where he was in life. He was great. I showed him the polaroids of all the Dave Gormans I'd met so far and he asked a lot of questions. And he laughed. And he made me laugh. And he made Danny laugh. For a while this seemed like the most normal thing in the world to be doing.

I learnt that this Dave Gorman had an Irish background: his father had been an Irish-American who wrote about sports for a Jewish newspaper. Dave had moved to New York after college in order to pursue an acting career but early on, while following the usual career path and waiting tables, he'd realised that his 40-year-old colleagues in the restaurant still harboured the same ambition but remained men waiting tables, so he jumped ship and made moves towards publishing. He enjoyed his job, but he fancied a change, and so he'd begun studying interior design.

Prior to this, I'd met two American DGs – the father and son team in Vicenza. Was it too much to hope that this man might also be a father to yet another?

Well, yes, it was.

'I'm gay,' he said.

'Are you?' I said.

'Yes.'

'Brilliant!'

And it *was* brilliant. It was brilliant because here, in front of us, sat our first gay Dave Gorman. Things just got better and better.

By now, I think at the back of my head there was an idea that Dan and I would somehow manage to find Dave Gormans who would come to represent all humanity. Now, I'll be honest – I don't think this was ever likely to happen. The Irish origins of the surname meant that I was condemned to meet more than my share of men who, like me, had aspirin white skin and ginger beards.

However, all and any cultural diversity amongst the DGs was to be celebrated. So all of a sudden, this Dave Gorman sitting in front of me, became extra important to me. Unique. Special.

Things could only have been better if he'd told me he was a part-time nightclub bouncer. Surely there's no one with a fondness for the English language who'd not want me to have met a man we could come to call 'Dave Gorman the Gay Doorman'?

Alas, that was not to be. But I wanted him to know how much this meeting had meant to me. As with every meeting, I was taking away a souvenir in the form of a signed polaroid, but what about him? Was there anything *I* could give *him* as a souvenir?

I delved into my bag, hoping I'd find something, anything. It couldn't have been more perfect. There, at the bottom of my rucksack, was a t-shirt. But not just any t-shirt. This was the Irish Harp t-shirt given to me by Dave Gorman in Wolverhampton.

'I've got you a present', I said, shyly, 'it's not actually from me, it's from Wolverhampton Dave Gorman. He gave it to me, but I think he'd want me to pass it on to another Dave Gorman. He's that kind of bloke. This is a present from one Dave Gorman to another, from Wolverhampton to New York.'

I passed him the shirt. People often say that Britain and America share a special relationship, but could there be a more potent symbol for it than this? I, Dave Gorman was an envoy delivering a gift from Wolverhampton Dave Gorman to New York Dave Gorman; this was a hands across the water moment.

Dave looked at the shirt. He looked at me, and he looked at Danny, and then, to no one in particular, he said, 'Thank you, Wolverhampton, wherever you are.'

Dave and I stood at the edge of the park and waved Dave Gorman the New Yorker off. He walked for a good distance before turning round to see us waving, then waved back a little, looking slightly embarrassed. As he reached the tall park gates, he seemed to have forgotten about us, and stopped to readjust his tiny black backpack, look at his watch for a few moments, and then kneel down to tuck an errant shoelace into his sneakers. As he did so, he absent-mindedly glanced back to where we'd been standing earlier waving, only to see that, yes, there we still were, and yes, there we were still waving. We looked like simple-minded fools fresh from the institution waving at their new best friend, but then that's how I suppose we really must have appeared to him all evening. Well, Dave probably had. I'd simply met a man who managed to represent and sum up his country based solely on the shirt and shorts he was wearing.

'He was fantastic,' said Dave. 'He's so happy in his life. That's so warming. So nice to meet someone who's gay in the old-fashioned sense of the word as well as the modern.'

'Yeah. Though I'm not sure what he's going to do with the t-shirt you gave him. How's he going to explain that to his mates?'

'It represents his Irish roots.'

'It represents an Irish lager he's never heard of, that's about it.'

'I just thought it'd be nice, y'know. I think, in an odd sort of way, Wolverhampton Dave Gorman would have wanted me to give New Yorker Dave Gorman the t-shirt. I could feel Wolverhampton Dave willing me on. "Give him the t-shirt," he seemed to be saying. "He needs it more than you. . ."'

'Let's not forget Wolverhampton Dave Gorman has three Ford Capris, Dave. That doesn't paint him as a particularly wise man. . .'

'Shoosh your lips up. Keep waving. He might turn round again.'

'I can't see him. Where is he?'

We stopped. We'd been waving at various stunned strangers in the vague middle-distance, none of whom had bothered to wave back at us, or even acknowledge our existence. I guess Crocodile Dundee had been right about New Yorkers all along.

''*Shoosh your lips up'?*' I said.

'Sorry.'

All in all, the day could have been a disaster. As it was, Dave deemed it an unmitigated success. 'It almost went so wrong,' he said, as we walked through the park, 'but we rescued it . . . we found another one. That's fourteen, now, Dan. Only another 40 to go!'

The evening sun still warmed our bare necks and ankles, and there was a happy breeze in the air. I decided on reflection not to pick him up on the fact that, all told, another 40 Dave Gormans would be a gargantuan task, and one single Dave Gorman here, there, or on the Bowling Green, really wouldn't make much of a difference. But I remembered his face that morning, when dejection and despair had unexpectedly kicked in, and I shooshed my lips right up.

We dined in fine style, at a restaurant facing the park. Dave ordered the fish, I opted for the chicken.

'So what now?' I asked, hoping that the answer would involve words along the lines of 'sightseeing', 'shops' or 'home'.

'I dunno. Dessert?'

'No, I mean what do we do now that we've found our New York Dave Gorman?'

Dave went quiet. He prodded his fish.

'Dave? Don't go quiet. Don't prod your fish.'

'I'll prod it if I want to.'

'Look, what's the matter? You should be happy. We came all this way, we flew 10,000 miles, and we found a Dave Gorman. We almost didn't. Think of it as winning a little battle in this ever-more-tiresome bet you're fuelling. You got one!'

'Yeah, I got one. I got one Dave Gorman. That's not many, Dan, considering where we are.'

'But it's better than none, yeah? You'll feel better later on. We'll go out, have a couple of pints, stare at some women, not talk to them, and spend the last of our time in New York having fun.'

'I'd like to find some more.'

'I'm sure you would, but I'd like to see some of New York.'

'You will. We can get one of those horse and carts around Central Park. But we have to meet more Dave Gormans, now we're here.'

'No,' I said. 'I can't face going to find some more. We can't do this.

We can't turn this trip to New York into just another pointless excercise in tracking down random namesakes.'

'A *what?* A pointless excercise? This is more than that, Danny
Wallace,' he said. 'This is a bet!'

Part of me – a foolish part, I was now coming to realise – had
hoped that this trip would at least be a little about two friends going
away for the weekend. Friends do that from time to time, I've heard.
Granted, there are usually more than two of them, and they usually
go to Amsterdam to tie some bloke called Steve to a lamppost and
paint his privates blue the night before his wedding, but even so.

The Dave Gorman-hunting was, I had thought, a neat excuse to
justify a short trip to the States. A good cover story for a much-
needed holiday. Something to tell our mates we did. But that's not
how Dave saw it at all. Of course it wasn't.

'Where's your focus, Dan? If we're ever going to get to 54, we can't
be satisfied as soon as we hit fourteen. That's not how it works at all.'

'Can we talk about this tomorrow, please, I'm getting quite tired.'

We took a silent cab ride to the hotel and walked through the lobby.
I'm pleased to report that the Albanian flag had been successfully de-
rigged, and the hotel staff were now preparing for the next day's
mid-morning arrival of a group of executives from Panasonic. Maybe
I'd fetch that toaster from under my bed and give it back to them.

We took the lift up to our rooms, and I ran myself a long, hot,
well-needed bath.

When my head hit the pillow that night I fully expected sleep to
take me straight away. I had a very satisfying day behind me, and
I was exhausted, both physically and emotionally. And I had
drunk two bottles of wine.

But something kept me awake. In the darkness, I was sure I
could see a small orange light. Just every now and then, but definitely there. I shut my eyes and turned my back on it, but it was
no good. What if it was a tiny mouse with a flashlight? I sat up in
bed, straining my eyes in the darkness and waiting for the next
time it flashed.

There it was again. On the table opposite my bed.

I turned the bedside lamp on to help me negotiate the unfa-
miliar landscape of the hotel room. The orange light was on my
phone.

This meant I had a message. I jumped out of bed. Nobody

knew I was here apart from the various New York D. Gormans who would have got home and discovered a strange message from a strange Englishman who hoped that they, too, were Dave Gorman.

There were two messages.

'Hi there. This is Dave Gorman. I got your message earlier today. I'm gonna be in all night – so call me back if you get this.'

Gah! Not here in New York as well? He hadn't left a number! Which one was he? It seemed that the American Gormans shared some of the less-favourable traits of the British Gormans.

But there was another message. Oh, joy of joys. And it was from another Dave Gorman. And he understood what had become my mission in life. He left the address of his workplace and cordially invited us to meet him there during our stay.

I was so happy. And I knew Danny would love this, too. I had to share this with him immediately. I rushed out the door and turned towards Danny's room before realising that I was in a hotel corridor wearing only my boxer shorts. Panic gripped me. I skidded to a halt and looked back towards my door. Everything seemed to be running in slow motion except my bedroom door which was swinging back into position where its lock would click into place. I threw myself back towards the room and managed to get the fingers of my right hand between the door and the frame as it swung shut. I screamed out in pain.

'Aaaaaaggggghhhhh. Arse!'

Three rooms down the dimly-lit corridor, a door opened and a young woman wearing a dressing gown and with her hair wrapped up in a towel-turban stared down at me. She was looking at an almost naked man, lying on the floor screaming in pain.

'Sorry', I said. And then, in my best accent, 'I am from Albania.'

She shut her door as if I'd just given her a perfectly good explanation, and I scurried back into my room.

What had I been thinking anyway? Dan would be sound asleep by now. Even if I was dressed, I'd end up knocking on his door and he'd only throw a shoe at me. I'd learnt that much by now.

I did it anyway.

The next morning I met Dave at the lifts. I was humming a half-happy tune when a young couple joined us. They smiled at me, and then looked to Dave. Dave smiled at them, and they looked to the floor, trying to stifle some approaching giggles. Dave looked confused. So, I imagine, did I. Eventually, the young woman looked up at Dave.

'Send my greetings to Albania', she said.

Something dawned on Dave's face.

'Come on Dan,' he said, in a funny accent. 'Let us take ze stairs. . .'

We made our way to Fifth Avenue by foot and stood, staring and aghast, outside the office block which promised us a fifteenth Dave Gorman.

'Big, isn't it?' I said.

Danny looked impressed. And slightly nervous.

'What have you told him?' he asked. 'I don't think this will be a man we can mess around.'

He had a point. We were just down the road from Trump Towers, with its look-at-me, golden facade, and most of the skyscrapers around us had well-groomed, gloved doormen waiting to carry sir's shopping or welcome madam into her offices. This was a street of success. A street that probably didn't suffer fools gladly.

Dave Gorman had told me on the phone that he was a stockbroker. From the look of the imposing building in which he housed his operations, he was good at his job.

We entered the building, took a lift up to a floor somewhere in the twenties, and stepped cautiously out. We were met with outright suspicion.

'Okay, before we go any further, gentlemen,' he said, two of his buddies standing behind him for protection. 'Let me see some ID, please?'

DG15 was about 50 years of age. I'd expected to find a collar and tie, but his shirt was open, and the short sleeves revealed tanned, muscular arms. His friends, I noticed, also had tanned, muscular arms. The kind of arms that could quite easily crush two jokers from England who turn up with nothing apart from a ridiculous story about having the same name as one of them.

I nervously handed my passport over to them. Danny didn't have his with him, but showed them an old gas bill he found at the bottom of his rucksack, and they seemed to think that was fine and handed it back. But this was weird for me. Usually, *I'd* check that the people we met were real, genuine-article Dave Gormans. That was *my* job. I wasn't used to them checking *me* out. He studied my passport for a while, and then studied me, and then my passport once more. All in all, I'd say he scrutinised it more than any customs officer ever has. I was nervous. For some reason I began to worry that I was going to be found out – that any moment now he was going to realise that I wasn't really a Dave Gorman and I'd be kicked out of the building.

But he smiled. A broad, relaxed smile. The sternness that had been there a moment ago just melted away.

'So how can I help you gentlemen?' he asked.

'Well,' I said, my relief showing on my face. 'I'm just trying to meet a load of Dave Gormans really. So you've *already* helped me just by existing. But I don't suppose you know of any others do you?'

'Actually, I had a couple of uncles called David Gorman. But they've both passed on now. I could point you to the cemetery, if you like.'

'Er, no, thanks. But thanks. But no thanks.'

'Aside from those guys, well . . . actually, you know, there *is* another guy called Dave Gorman. He uses the same pharmacy as me.'

This was exciting.

'Really? Whereabouts is this?'

'Well, I think *that* gentleman is in Mount Kisco, but I live a couple of miles away in Chappaqua', he said. 'You know Chappaqua?'

He said it as a rhetorical question. In a tone of voice that assumes that yes, of course we know Chappaqua, because *everyone* knows Chappaqua, right?

I looked quizzically at him, 'Chappaqua?'

My tone of voice was meant to ask several questions. Where? What? And am I pronouncing this correctly?

'Chappaqua', he said, confirming my pronunciation, before answering the other questions. 'It's about an hour north of the city by rail. It's where Bill and Hillary Clinton live.'

'I thought that was the White House,' said Danny, and I rolled my eyes at him for not knowing better, before realising that yes, *I* thought that was the White House, too.

'Hillary's running for the senate in New York. If you do that, you have to be resident in the state, so they've bought a place in Chappaqua.'

Wow, DG15 was a neighbour to the President of the United States of America! And he used the same pharmacy as another Dave Gorman! I could only hope that neither of them had an embarrassing complaint – a mix-up in prescriptions could be dangerous.

But the best was yet to come. Our stockbroker Dave Gorman was the key to yet more cultural diversity. New York is the melting pot of the world and it was to prove to be the melting pot of the Dave Gormans, also. Because DG15 was our first Jewish Dave Gorman.

'I don't know, maybe my grandfather was say, a Gordetski or something, then when he gets to America he meets an Irish customs officer who couldn't pronounce his name and says, no . . . your name begins with Gor . . . you're a man . . . hey! You're a Gorman!'

I didn't care how many generations of his family had been Gormans – that was of no consequence to me. Dr. B. David G was probably one of a long line of Gormans, but this relative newcomer was the real deal, a full square namesake, and that was all I needed.

The whole encounter lasted twenty minutes, before his demanding job made its demanding demands, and we made our excuses and left.

I was in the mood for a celebration so on the walk back to the hotel I bought a bottle of champagne. We retreated to my room and I was about to open the bottle when Danny pointed out that there were no glasses. Not to worry, there was a beaker on the side in the bathroom and presumably the same was true in Dan's room. So Dan dashed off to fetch his and I held the bottle under the cold tap.

But then the phone rang.

We were in the lift heading down to the lobby while Dave explained precisely why we were rushing off leaving a bottle of perfectly good lukewarm champagne unopened.

'I had a call, Dan. You won't believe this. There's a journalist waiting in the lobby. And you'll never guess what his name is. . .'

'Oh, I think I can. Would it be "Dave Gorman" by any chance?'

I said, the brainwork required to work it out hardly making me weary.

'Er, no. His name's Ellis Henican.' He looked at me as if I'd just said something that qualified me for insane. 'I just thought it was quite an unusual name that you were unlikely to guess, that's all.'

'Right. How are we going to recognise him?'

'He said he was the skinny man in beige with white hair standing in the lobby under the clock.'

'Will that be enough?'

'I'm sure it will,' replied Dave, too excited to register my sarcasm. 'I got his mobile number off him so we can always give him a call if we can't find him. Listen, this could be really good for us, Dan. His paper gets all over the place. We might be able to launch an appeal. Who knows how many Dave Gormans it could lead to?'

The lift pinged and we arrived on the ground floor. 'Here we go,' said Dave, taking a deep breath.

We scanned the place for any beige skinny blokes with white hair, and, sure enough, exactly where he said he'd be, stood Ellis Henican.

'How ya doin'?' he said, swinging his hand towards us in the most laid-back, Joey-from-*Friends* way.

'Hello,' I said, suddenly sounding more middle class and English than I ever have. Dave, too, sounded quite posh when he said 'Thanks so much for taking the trouble to find us'.

'Not a problem,' said Ellis, evidently a man tipped off by one of the many New Yorkers Dave had rung up and bothered. 'So you guys like food?'

'Very much so,' I said.

'Great – you wanna eat? How about we go to Grand Central? A finer display of humanity you're not gonna find. We can eat and watch the freaks. And you guys can tell me all about this mission you're on. . .'

This was exciting. This man was your stereotypical fast-talking New York kind of a journo. We felt safe in his hands, as he walked us down backstreets, through doorways we never usually would have dared enter, and eventually into Grand Central Station itself.

I suddenly found myself wishing that we'd travelled to New York by train. Grand Central provides an extraordinary and stunning entrance to the city. The huge great hall was renovated in 1998, Ellis told us, something that led to it becoming quite a fashionable place for people to spend time in, rather than just arrive at and leave. The basketball star Michael Jordan even has a restaurant there, but when we walked past he appeared to be neither in the office nor on the tills. We resolved to have another look in a little while, in case he was on a later shift.

'This place good for you?' Ellis asked, as we arrived at a packed Italian cafe on the edge of the terminal. 'This one's on the paper, okay guys?'

We took a seat and while Ellis popped to the bathroom, Dave and I leafed through copies of that morning's *Newsday*, the tabloid-sized paper he writes a column for.

The showbiz news centred mainly around the Tony Awards, happening in the city that weekend but, not being much of a man for musicals, I turned the page. The most tempted I've ever been to see a musical was when I was on the escalators at Holborn tube station after a particularly heavy night of revelry, and I noticed the poster advertising *The Buddy Holly Story*. In bright yellow letters was the slogan *'One Legend, One Stage'*, but in my inebriated state I had thought the words read *'One Legged, On Stage'*, and wandered home thinking that this was a chapter of the Buddy Holly story that had entirely passed me by.

A picture of a sullen-looking man on page 3 caught my eye and next to it was the headline 'Nude Photo Shoot Ruled Legal'. It had taken the US Supreme Court to decide that it would be alright for a photographer to take a photo of dozens of nude friends beneath the Williamsburg Bridge that day, something which the 'nude landscape photographer Spencer Tunick' was obviously very happy about. 'I'm so excited', he was quoted as saying, which provided me with an image of an excited naked photographer I really didn't care for, so I was relieved when Ellis returned to the table and distracted us from such unsavoury tales.

'You know apparently I got quite a fanbase in Aberystwyth?' he said as he settled into his chair.

'Sorry?', Dave said. Of all the words we expected Ellis to say, 'Aberystwyth' wasn't high on the list. It turns out that when BBC Radio Wales decided that they needed an American man to cast a wry eye over world events, they somehow found their way to Ellis, and he'd been pontificating to the Welsh on a regular basis ever since, direct from his New York apartment.

'That's a lot of fun,' he said, and when he asked us to tell him about Aberystwyth, we told him it wasn't entirely dissimilar to New York. No sense in disappointing the man.

'So. . .' he said, after a slight pause. 'Where do we begin with this Dave Gorman thing?'

The next morning I was like an eight-year-old boy going to collect the post on his birthday. Before any thoughts of breakfast
even entered my head, I'd collected Danny up from his room and
dragged him onto the street, borrowed a dollar off him, and
found a copy of *Newsday*. I flicked it open and scanned the contents box . . . there, under 'columnists': 'Ellis Henican, page 6'.

I got to it as quickly as I could, and there, in black and white,
taking up half of the page: 'CASTING CALL FOR DAVE GOR-
MAN'. He'd done it! Ellis had made good on his word and come
up with an appeal for Dave Gormans!

> *IS your name Dave Gorman?*
> *Maybe you know someone named Dave Gorman.*
> *Either way, there's a young British fellow who would very*
> *much like to hear from you. He is holed up this weekend*
> *at the Roosevelt Hotel in Manhattan.*
> *His name, of course, is Dave Gorman.*

This was great stuff. Ellis had done well. At the end of the article, he repeated where we were staying, along with the phone
number of the hotel, and he positively demanded that people get
in touch.

This newspaper was all over the place. Wherever I looked, I
could see it. Someone came up behind us and nudged us out of
the way so that they could buy a copy, too. What if they were a
Dave Gorman? Granted, it was a short Hispanic woman and it
was therefore less likely, but surely it wouldn't be long before a
Dave Gorman – or someone who knew where one was hiding –
rang us at the hotel?

I was happy. I looked at my watch. It was 9am. Dave Gormans
would probably start getting in touch by midday at the earliest.

To keep him quiet, I decided to let Danny play in Central Park.

Central Park is a great place to go if you want to get mugged, we were
told. Sadly, we were told this after we'd already been there. Had we
been made more aware of this a little earlier, it's doubtful that we'd
have gone there dressed the way we were – specifically, in two *I Love
New York* t-shirts – and decided to complete our twatty tourist image
by parading ourselves around in front of the thieves and convicts in
a horse and trap.

We were only wearing the t-shirts because Dave had bought them on impulse from a lady selling them opposite where the cab dropped us off. The *Newsday* article had put him in a great mood, and it had somehow rubbed off on me. I hadn't batted an eyelid when he demanded I pull the t-shirt over the one I was wearing because 'we've got to give something back to the city that's given us so much.'

The shirts had obviously tipped the horse and trap man off that he could charge us pretty much whatever he liked, but it's a good way to see the sights, he said, so we agreed to give him $23 plus tax in return for his knowledge and a trip in his trap.

He was certainly very informative.

'Dat ice rink over there,' he told us, a couple of minutes into our tour, 'well, dat ice rink was de original ice rink used in de hit movie *Home Alone 2: Lost In New York*.'

Dave and I weren't really very interested in that, to be honest, but we politely looked over and played to our touristy image, wowing and goodnessing and generally pretending to be impressed.

'If you look to your left,' our guide said, his Russian accent extending each word, 'dat bench there was used in da movie *Ghostbusters 2* for de character played by Rick Moranis.'

We looked at the bench as instructed. It looked just like an ordinary bench. Neither of us could remember the scene, or, in fact, the film, but we made vaguely interested noises nevertheless.

'If you now like to look to your right, do you see de gate over there, by da kids? Well dat gate also featured in da movie *Home Alone 2: Lost In New York*.'

We didn't bother responding to that one.

Several more points of interest were pointed out to us, each of which corresponded to some unimportant scene apparently contained within either *Ghostbusters 2* or *Home Alone 2*. There was also, if memory serves, a passing reference to one of the latter two *Highlander* films. It seemed our tour guide's main area of expertise on Central Park lay in below-average film sequels. I suppose if we'd wanted to find out about the originals, we'd have to have got an earlier tour.

It was now around half past 12, and we dismounted, paid up, and took a cab back to our hotel. Dave walked straight up to the receptionist and asked if there had been any messages for him.

I already knew there were. Someone had placed a small scrap of paper in the pigeonhole under Dave's room number.

Here we go again.

We headed back to Central Station, but this time we weren't going to dine, or even to look at the freaks.

No, this time we were intending to use the station for the more traditional purpose of catching a train. We were heading to Mount Kisco to meet DG16, the man who presumably shared a pharmacy with DG15.

We arrived at Mount Kisco an hour later, because in foreign countries, trains arrive on time. We were a little early for our appointment, in fact, but the sun was out and there was a patch of grass with a tree to sit under where we could keep a watchful eye out for any potential namesakes who might turn up.

Mount Kisco might only be an hour out of the hustle and bustle of New York but it could be worlds away. It's a small place occupying only three and a half square miles and it's the epitome of smalltown America. From the station there was a good deal of white picket fence to be seen, a small parade of shops and really not much else.

We hadn't been there long before we were approached by a man in his mid-thirties, with pale skin, and a reddish hue to his hair. We were back on course. We shook hands. We exchanged pleasantries. There was a pause.

'Did you know you share a pharmacy with a Dave Gorman from Chappaqua?' I offered up.

'Really?', asked Dave, singularly unimpressed by my inside knowledge. 'So anyway, what do you want to do? Do you want to go somewhere?'

'Anything really. Anything you want to do?'

'Well, I guess we could go and find Bill Clinton's house?'

'In Chappaqua?' I said. But it was a rhetorical question because everyone knows about Chappaqua, right?

'Come on, let's go for a drive.'

The three of us piled into Dave's sporty black car. This was like the coolest school trip ever, as we started the short drive to Chappaqua to find the home of the President. I mean . . . we were going to find the President of the United States! How cool was this?

On the way out of town, we learnt a bit about Dave. In fact, within minutes he'd told us that he was a bit disappointed with his recent foray into computer dating, which seemed like rather a lot of information to divulge to two strangers. Even if one of them *does* share your name.

I knew from DG15 that Chappaqua was only a couple of miles away, so when we'd been driving for 40 minutes or so I started to get a little fidgety. Dave Gorman was playing it off nicely, though. If he was lost, he certainly didn't let on. Not until we'd been down the same street twice did he finally come clean.

'I'm having a little trouble finding this place, guys. . .'

We were driving along the widest roads and between the biggest houses I'd ever seen. And every now and then the car would slow down while Dave would stare intently at a property before shaking his head and driving away.

'Shit, I *know* it's round here somewhere', he muttered at us.

Danny and I shared a concerned look, and then aimed it towards Dave.

'I thought that was it, but it isn't that one. I'm sorry guys. Shit.'

'It's okay,' I said, trying to hide my disappointment, 'it's been nice to see the place. Amazing houses. It doesn't really matter.'

'I've been past there once,' he said through gritted teeth. 'Really I have. Thing is, a friend of mine was driving, and I was drunk.'

It was at that point that I think I finally realised that we were never going to find Bill Clinton's house.

'I'm sorry guys. Son of a bitch! Geez . . . I don't know where it is. I'm sorry. I'll have to give you a ride back to the station.'

We shrugged our shoulders and he began to drive back. It was fine. I'd come here to meet a Dave Gorman, anyway, not exchange pleasantries with a world leader.

But within minutes of turning round and heading back to the railroad station, something very dramatic and unexpected happened. Something that frightened the life out of Dan and me.

The heavens turned black.

There was a deep, terrifying rumbling.

It started to rain . . . but not normal rain.

Violent rain.

Rain in biblical quantities.

A minute later and the wind started to pound the car with twigs at first, then small branches, then pebbles, and stones.

It was the most incredible change of weather I have ever experienced in my life.

'Goddamn . . . that is just denting and scratching the hell out of my car. . .' said Dave, with a sorry, but calm, shake of his head. I looked back at Danny. He was white.

'Well, will you look at that?' said Dave, stopping the car, which was beginning to rock slightly from side to side in the gales. I couldn't actually look at anything, because the rain was falling faster and heavier than the wipers could deal with. Dave turned on the high beams, and I could see brake lights up ahead . . . lots of them. As my eyes adjusted to the strangely refracted view I could make out the shape of a huge tree blocking the road. It was unmistakable.

'What's that?' said Dan. 'A big horse?'

'Shit,' said Dave. 'There's a tree down.'

Dave sounded as though this was the sort of thing that happened all the time. But it had never happened to me before, and I was gripped by fear. There was a fierce wind blowing, it was hammering away at our car, and it had already taken a big tree down. What would have happened to us if our car had been beneath that? I tried to push such thoughts out of my head.

'If our car had been beneath that we'd be dead', said Dan.

I began to panic.

'Do you guys want to get a closer look at that?' asked Dave. This seemed like the stupidest question I could imagine. I mean . . . No. No, we didn't want to take a closer look. We wanted to get away from there as soon as possible. But a mixture of fear and utter incredulity left me silent. He edged the car towards the fallen tree and we took a closer look.

'Oh yes,' I said. 'There it is.'

Dave thought he knew another way to the station, but by now I wasn't too confident. I mean, he thought he knew the way to Bill Clinton's house, didn't he? Maybe he'd been a different route to the train station once before, but his friend had been driving and he'd been drunk. Five minutes later and we were driving at speed down another small road. The wind hadn't let up, and the car was still rocking on its suspension as we made it over the brow of a hill.

'Holy shit!' said Dave, as he slammed on the brakes. 'Another one!'

Another huge tree had been blown down by the winds, and lay before us, a terrifying example of what nature was threatening to do to us.

'I'd like to go back to London now, please, Dave', said Dan. I didn't blame him. We were in the middle of what we would later find out was a 100-mph tornado.

Now, there are moments in life in which we are allowed to be paranoid, and this was one of them. All we had done was try and find the home of the President of America, and now here we were, caught up in the middle of a tornado!

I think I'm entitled to ask: exactly how powerful *are* the FBI?

And what if we *were* to be hit by a tree on this stupid little adventure of ours? What would the authorities think if they found a car with our dead bodies in it? Two men who had never met before, who had no family connections, but who were *both* called Dave Gorman? That shouldn't happen in real life – that's a storyline for *The X-Files!*

I couldn't see very much and what I could see frightened me so for the next half an hour I sat there in silence with my eyes shut instead. Danny did the same. Neither of us cared any more what Dave Gorman thought of us as he drove us back to safety. We just hoped *he* didn't have his eyes shut, too.

The car eventually stopped and we were back at the railroad station in Mount Kisco. The three of us left the car and rushed under the station canopy where we completed our photographic formalities before a firm handshake and a wave goodbye.

I had never been so scared.

One hour later and we were thankfully back within the relative safety of New York City. It may have had more muggers, but at least it didn't have any ruddy great trees.

Dave and I made the short walk from Grand Central Station to the hotel and I noticed that his hands were still shaking from our tornado experience. The weather in the city was fine, but he still wore an expression of ashen-faced fear, so I suppose he must have looked like a man who'd never seen a city before.

'I think, Dave,' I said, 'that we need a drink.'

'I tend to agree,' he said. 'I think that we need a drink more than anything else in this world.'

We walked into the Roosevelt, fully intending to dump our bags and then hit the hotel bar for a Drambuie or two. As we got to the lifts, though, one of the receptionists shouted Dave's name.

We both jumped as she did so, no doubt imaging that any second now a grand old oak would fall through the ceiling of the Roosevelt and finish the job his cousins in Kisco had started.

'There's an envelope here for you, Mr Gorman. . .'

Dave and I walked towards her suspiciously. Inside the envelope were two pieces of photocopied paper, one headed 'To Mr Gorman', the other headed 'To Mr Wallace'.

We exchanged a puzzled glance.

Someone had invited us to a party.

And guess what. This was not just any old party. This was the night of the Tony Awards, and we were at a party being held by the company of the Lincoln Center Theater. And that's not just any old company, either. That's the company that had staged *Contact* – the musical that on June 4th 2000 was to scoop Tony Awards for Best Musical, Best Featured Actor In A Musical, Best Featured Actress In A Musical and, as if that wasn't enough, Best Choreography.

This was the most showbizzy, swanky thing Danny or I had ever attended.

We were somewhat underdressed in our jeans and t-shirts, and I decided to hide out in the shadows and nurse my pint while Danny disappeared to the bar, where he'd talk to fancy people, and generally make a nuisance of himself.

But one thing was puzzling me. Who had invited us? And why? I could only assume that this was the result of Ellis Henican's handiwork. The headline had a theatrical air to it; 'Casting Call For Dave Gormans'. That's the kind of headline that would attract a thespian type. And it had mentioned our hotel, which was only a few blocks away from where we now stood. No doubt someone involved in the party had thought it might be fun to invite the two rather odd Englishmen in the story.

I contemplated this while staring out into space, my concentration broken only by the musical revellers swapping high-fives and hugs all around me. Americans are good at winning.

I took in the scene. Everyone else was suited and booted; dressed to the nines. I took in my own denim-clad legs.

'Excuse me,' came a strange voice interrupting my thoughts. 'But what are *you* doing here?'

A tall man in a swanky black suit towered over me. He was the sort of man who looked like he enjoyed grooming himself, trimming his fingernails, applying moisturiser. He looked like he belonged here. I didn't.

'Erm, I was invited, I'll find it, I won't be a minute.' I started to feverishly rifle through my pockets, looking for the scrap of paper that had led me here.

'Hey, no, I didn't mean that at all', he said, very apologetically. 'Look, this is going to sound a bit weird. I've invited someone and I don't know what they look like and I thought it might be you?'

'Oh. Well, this might seem a bit weird as well. My name's Dave Gorman and I'm looking for people. . .'

'It's you!' he cried. 'I knew it'd be you! Stay there. Stay right there, because I've got a present for you!'

And with that, he scarpered off into the cloak room. He returned moments later with a videotape clamped between his hands. He thrust it towards me. It was called *The Ice Storm*. On the front were Kevin Kline and Sigourney Weaver, looking mysterious. This was interesting.

My hands gripped the video. His hands gripped mine. He locked my eyes with a steady gaze.

And then he spoke.

'There's a Dave Gorman in there.'

I'd left Dave standing in the corner, looking awkward, while I approached the bar. I had somehow ended up talking to a man in a white cowboy hat and white silk suit standing at the bar, waiting to be served a bottle of odd German beer. Beneath his hat was a perfectly smooth head and a film star's set of teeth. Anyway, he claimed to be one of the blokes from the *Dukes of Hazzard*, and that made up the bulk of our five-minute conversation.

'And what are you doing here?' he asked me, towards the end.

I was too embarrassed to tell him.

'I'm a . . . photo . . . maker . . . man.'

They were the first words I found myself able to say, and was a lie prompted by nothing other than one of many flashbulbs going off around the room.

'A photographer?'

'Mmm' I said. 'That's right, yes. Or a 'photo . . . maker . . . man', as we say in Britain,' I bluffed.

This led me to be unwillingly introduced to a 'fellow photographer' (whom the *Dukes of Hazzard* man had actually introduced as a 'photo maker man', which warmed my heart, but confused the other chap), and in the resulting meeting I skilfully managed to avoid any talk of photos or photography, despite the man's best efforts and persistent attempts to steer the conversation that way.

He'd brought with him a woman who designed posters for musicals. From her I was introduced to a lighting designer, then to two dancers, who introduced me to a man called Bernie who writes bad songs, he took me through another two dancers, a Korean theatre director, and a television presenter, and from the television presenter I was finally, gratefully, presented to the very blonde, very bronzed Miss Georgia.

'Wow. So you're a proper Miss Georgia, then?' I said. I thought this was a pretty good opener, myself. I felt I was impressing her already.

'Yes, I am!' she replied cheerfully.

'That's a very short dress.'

'Yes it is! I like your accent!'

'I like yours.'

There was a definite spiritual connection going on here. I wondered what we would call our children, and whether we would spend our summers in Georgia and winters in Britain, or whether it would be better the other way around. Would she mind moving to East London and having to share the marital home with Dave? How would she get on with my girlfriend? As it turned out, I didn't get a chance to ask her any of this.

'Danny,' said Dave, suddenly standing a few feet to my right. 'Hey, Danny. . .'

I tried to pretend I hadn't heard him, and ploughed on with the subtle seduction of Miss Georgia.

'So, is it good being. . .'

'Danny. . .'

'. . . I mean, do you enjoy. . .'

'Pssst. Dan.'

'. . . is it something that you'd always. . .'

'Dan!'

It was no good. Miss Georgia had become distracted by the sound of another British accent, this one becoming more and more agitated.

'Uh . . . I think someone's trying to get your attention?'

I snapped my head round to face Dave.

'Not now, David.'

'I've got a film for us to watch when we get back to the hotel.'

'That's nice, Dave. I look forward to it.'

'So do you like your job?' asked Miss Georgia, flashing me a smile.

'Well . . . I get to travel, and to meet a lot of new people,' I said.

Miss Georgia threw her head back and laughed insanely. I couldn't work out why. She didn't even know what my job was. Maybe this wasn't the girl for me, after all.

'Danny. . . psst. . . Dan.' Dave was acting like a little brother, pulling at my trouser leg. 'Honestly, we have to see this film. I've just been given it by a man. Apparently there's someone in it called Dave Gorman.'

'Why is that important?' asked Miss Georgia, sternly.

'Because that's my name, too!'

'Oh,' she said, and turned to me, confused.

'That's very exciting for us,' I said.

'I see,' she replied, now evidently realising that I probably wasn't the boy for her, either.

'Danny, please can we go back to the hotel, now, please?' Sadly, these were Dave's words, and not Miss Georgia's, and I reluctantly agreed to leave the party so that we could go and watch his bloody video.

'I'm sorry about dragging you away from Miss Georgia like that. I'm just excited!' he said, as we trudged down Fifth Avenue, back towards the Roosevelt. Well, I trudged. Dave was virtually skipping.

'No, it's okay,' I sighed. 'It probably wouldn't have lasted. Georgia sounds too hot. And I can't deal with those long-distance relationships.'

'What, like with Hanne?'

'She's only in North London, Dave.'

'But you're in New York.'

'Yeah, but I don't *live* here, do I?'

'Oh, right, I see what you mean.'

Back at the hotel I rang down to reception to request a video player. They reacted as if this was an odd request at one in the morning, but America is the land of service culture and a video was delivered within the hour.

We must have looked quite suspicious; two blokes in a hotel room with a photograph album full of seemingly random men, a bottle of champagne on the go, awaiting the arrival of a video player, but the young man who delivered it showed great restraint and didn't bat an eyelid.

We watched the film. More importantly, we spooled on to the end to watch the credits. After all, that was the bit I was interested in: I was trying to find Dave Gorman. The credits wound past and we studied the names. Kevin Kline, Joan Allen, Christina Ricci, Sigourney Weaver. It was an impressive cast if you were a movie buff, but not so if you were a Dave Gorman hunter.

I rewound the credits and had another look. No. Still couldn't see our man. I rewound again. And this time I saw him. I hadn't seen him before because I was looking at the actor's names. I should have been looking at the characters. Because this Dave Gorman, it turned out, wasn't real. He was a character played by a man called Larry Pine.

This was incredible. We'd found a Dave Gorman that was . . . *fictional!*

'Well, I guess we have one more job before we head home then Dan', I said, rubbing my hands together.

'Eh? What d'you mean?'

'We have to find Larry Pine.'

'He isn't a Dave Gorman, though. He's a Larry Pine. We don't have to meet Larry Pines.'

'He's played Dave Gorman in a Hollywood film, Dan. That makes him an honourary member of the brotherhood.'

'Eh? Bollocks! So what you're saying is that Dr B. David Gorman – who if I can remind you, actually exists – *doesn't* count because his name's got a letter in front of it . . . but Larry Pine counts even though he's called Larry Pine?'

'Look, he's a Dave Gorman on celluloid, right? You wouldn't understand, I guess. There haven't been any Danny Wallaces on film, have there?'

'Yes, actually. There was Danny Wallace the idealistic young rookie cop unaware of how power and influence have compromised his bosses, in *The Corruptor*, actually. That's a celluloid Danny Wallace right there for you. *And* he was played by Mark Wahlberg, which is someone you've actually heard of.'

'Well, we're not looking for Danny Wallaces, are we? If we were, we'd try and get Mark Wahlberg. That's what I'm saying! But if he'd played Dr B. Danny Wallace, then that'd be different. Just like if Larry Pine had played a fictional B. David Gorman he wouldn't count. But he didn't. He played a Dave Gorman. So he counts. Jesus, Dan, sometimes I worry about you, I really do. . .'

'All I'm saying is. . .'

'Listen, he's in a movie, so I reckon he must live in New York or LA. We've got a 50/50 chance of him being in *this* city right here. Tomorrow morning we are going to try and find him.'

'No.'

'Come on Dan, we're in New York! We're going to find a movie star! We've met *three* real Dave Gormans here, but we can make it four! How much cultural diversity can one city give us? We've met a gay Dave Gorman, a Jewish Dave Gorman, now we might be able to meet a real-life fictional Dave Gorman! COME ON!'

I had gripped Danny by both shoulders, staring into his eyes, challenging him to defy me while I shouted at full volume, like a sergeant major fighting for control. But I was fighting for control of myself. I fell silent, but my hands remained where they were. I didn't know what to do next. There was a pause.

'Alright then', said Dan. 'It'd be nice to meet a movie star. Give me a call in the morning.'

He walked to the door and left.

I didn't sleep that night. Instead, I watched the film. I watched it once through, and then I rewound it and watched it again. And here's the weirdest thing. At no point did anyone *ever* refer to anyone else as 'Dave Gorman'. In fact, in the whole film, no one was ever referred to either as 'Dave' *or* as 'Mr. Gorman'. I'd no idea what Larry Pine looked like, but whoever he was, there was absolutely no reason why his character should have a name of *any* description, let alone *my* name.

What strange twist of fate had led the filmmakers to christen this character at all? We may never know. But this was surely a gift from a higher power.

I didn't sleep that night. I packed my things ready for the next day's flight, and then lay awake, waiting for the phone to ring. Something odd was happening to Dave. Even more than usual, he was turning into what I believe we would at school have termed 'a mentalist'.

With hindsight, my sleeplessness was wasted. The phone didn't ring. There was no banging on the door. I didn't need to throw any of my shoes. I even managed to slip out for breakfast to find no angry where-are-you messages on my return.

I gave Hanne a quick call, telling her that today was the day I'd be getting on a plane home. She said she was looking forward to seeing me again. That it was about time we spent some proper time together. That it was about time I stopped behaving so childishly. I agreed. There comes a point, when you're sitting in a hotel room on the other side of the world and unable to explain why, that you really begin to feel that a return to humanity would be a welcome thing. She was glad I agreed. She said she hoped we could sort everything out. I said I didn't know there was anything to sort. She told me that was the bloody problem, and hung up.

I was watching *The Nanny* on cable when Dave finally rang. It was noon, and he sounded excited.

'Bingo!'

'What?'

'We've got him!'

'Who? Larry Pine?'

'Yep. I spent the morning ringing round a load of agents. I couldn't find Larry Pine's agent, but one of the others told me about Larry. He's very good apparently.'

'I should hope so. You wouldn't want a Dave Gorman played badly.'

'Quite right, Dan. Anyway, he's in a play at the minute; "The Designated Mourner". Apparently, it's a "must see".'

'Yes. Well. We're not seeing it.'

'No, fair enough. But Larry Pine's a "must meet", yeah? I rang the theatre and I left a message. He rang me back just now. We're going to meet him at the venue. Bring your bags, we're checking out. I'll meet you at the lift.'

He hung up.

'Okay.'

It has to be said that Larry Pine looked every bit a Dave Gorman. A tanned, slim, in-his-early-50s Dave Gorman. Whoever was responsible for casting *The Ice Storm* had clearly done a great job on this one. I shook his hand with perhaps just a little too much emotion for a complete stranger.

'So, what's this about?' asked my fictional brethren.

'Well . . . you played Dave Gorman in *The Ice Storm*, I said, as if that explained everything.

'I did?', asked Larry, with wide-eyed incredulity. That was how small the part had been. Even Larry had no idea it existed.

'Yep,' I confirmed it for him, 'and I'm trying to meet as many Dave Gormans as I can.'

'Right . . . well, I guess that means I'm pleased to meet you. . .'

'No, no, the pleasure is all mine', I said, modestly . . . but I knew full well that he was enjoying this, too. I mean . . . imagine meeting someone with the same name as a character you didn't know you'd played and you'll understand exactly what this man was going through. Ever the actor, though he hid it well.

All in all, we were with Larry for about five minutes. I shook his hand, I took his photo. He signed it 'Larry Pine as Dave Gorman' which was nice of him as I don't think he was actually in his DG costume at the time.

'So, that's all you want?' he asked. And then to Danny: 'And what about you, what do *you* want from me?'

'No, I'm fine, thanks. Unless . . . you don't know Mark Wahlberg, do you?'

I cut in.

'No, that's it. Thanks for your time though, Lar. It really is appreciated. You're number seventeen.'

'Seventeen,' he said, as if weighing up the merits of the number. 'Alrighty then.'

Job done. We hailed a passing cab and jumped in.

'JFK please. And we're in a hurry!'

Chapter 10

HE'S GOT A TICKET TO RYDE . . . AND *HE* DON'T CARE

The traffic was heavy on the way back from Heathrow and I had to change down to third gear as the M4 became the A4. For some time I had been deep in thought.

'While you were sleeping on the plane, Dan, I got to thinking . . . about the numbers.'

'What numbers?'

'The Dave Gorman numbers. I just thought, wouldn't it be weird if there turned out to be mathematical connections? So, if, say, all the prime number Dave Gormans turned out to have something in common. Or all the even numbers, or whatever.'

'Right. Yes. I've wondered the same myself.'

'So, for example, if you take the prime numbers, right?'

'Right.'

'That's 1, 2, 3, 5, 7, 11, 13 and 17, so far – East Fife FC, his son, Tooting, Edinburgh, Wolverhampton, Warminster, Highbury and the fictional one – is there any weird connection that separates them from the others?'

'And *is* there?'

'Nope, not a sausage'. I moved out to overtake an ice-cream van. 'Weird if there *was*, though, eh?'

When we finally got home Dan immediately checked the messages on the answering machine. He'd clearly been hoping for a 'Welcome Back!' message from Hanne, but didn't find one. There was only the one message, in fact, and it was left in a plummy, clipped voice that sounded like a wing commander from a black and white war movie. I was actually surprised when it didn't end with the phrase 'Roger, over and out', so I think it's safe to say that Dan knew it wasn't Hanne, pretty much straight away.

In Norway. It's always embarrassing when you arrive
at a party to find someone else in the same outfit...

Dave Gorman (left) meets Dave Gorman (right)

Dave Gorman (left) meets Dave Gorman (right)

Dave Gorman (left) meets Dave Gorman (right)

Dave Gorman (left) meets Dave Gorman (right)

Dave Gorman (left) meets Dave Gorman (right)

Dave Gorman (left) meets Dave Gorman (right)

No need for Directory Enquiries in our house...

I AM NOT DAVE GORMAN ARE YOU?

Welcome to our World of Dave Gormans. (Hey… when we went to visit one of the Daves, Dave took his pet prawn along on his shoulder. Can you spot him?)

Celebrating on the Isle of Wight

Relaxing in Venice

Our youngest DG...

...and our oldest

Dave Gorman, Dave Gorman
in New York, New York

Some men who definitely
enjoy a Big Breakfast…

Our Norwegian DG. And to put your
mind at rest, those aren't our shadows

DAVID
GORMAN

The amazing self-captioning man

Celebrating in Oslo

In the offices of solicitor Charles Gorman. With their deed polls
in hand, the Dave Gormans formerly known as (from top left)
Colin Hurley, David Heffron, Graham Cleminson, Pascale
Beatrice Noele and Kelly Scutts surround one very happy Dave.

'Err . . . hello. . .' it began. 'I'm standing in a car park at Heathrow Airport looking at a sticker on a car that reads, "Are you in the Dave Gorman club?" Well, I'm not sure what that's about but it's bugging me. What is the Dave Gorman Club? Is this anything to do with Dave Gorman? Well, I mean, obviously it's something to do with Dave Gorman, I mean the Dave Gorman I used to work with. At Legal & General . . . he was a bit of a card. Is it you Dave? It's Ken here. What does it all mean? Could you let me know?'

Well, I wasn't the Dave Gorman Ken thought I was. But neither had I met the Dave Gorman he thought I was. Ken had left his number. We had another lead.

My nap, that afternoon, didn't have quite the recharging effect that I'd thought it would. Because, for the first time since I was a kid, I had a nightmare. I dreamt that I was on *MasterMind*, sitting in the famous black leather chair opposite Magnus Magnusson, and I'd selected my specialist chosen subject carefully. . .

MM: Mr Wallace, from East London, what is your specialist chosen subject?

DW: Men called Dave Gorman.

MM: Mr Wallace, you have two minutes to answer as many questions correctly as you can on the subject of Dave Gormans, starting . . . now. How many *Ford Capris* does Dave Gorman from Wolverhampton own?

DW: Three.

MM: Correct. In Swindon, what does Dave Gorman have stacked in his back garden?

DW: Two canoes.

MM: Correct. The brother of which Dave Gorman is a close acquaintance of the Mexican Elvis impersonator, El Vez?

DW: Tooting Dave Gorman.

MM: Correct. In Edinburgh, Dave Gorman is "the account manager *for* technology *within* technology" – why is that bizarre?

DW: Pass.

MM: Which sport does Bromsgrove's Dave Gorman regularly enjoy with his lovely wife, Alexandra?

DW: Can I phone a friend?

MM: I'm afraid all your friends have forgotten you because you've been on the road for months seeking out men called. . .?

DW: Dave Gorman?

MM: Correct.

I awoke with a jolt and realised I needed to get out of the flat before I went out of my mind. I also felt like I should remind some of my friends that I was still alive.

I got up, washed my face, and left another message for Hanne. I'd had a good time in New York but that was the last thing I could tell her.

'Hey Hanne. It's me. I'm back. Didn't have a good time, really. New York's a bit rubbish. Too many Dave Gormans. Listen . . . call me any time. My mobile's on, and I'm . . . just . . . waiting. Bye'.

I put the phone down and chewed at my lip. Maybe she'd call back later. Anyway, I had to get out of the flat.

I walked into the living room only to find Dave sitting crosslegged on the floor in front of the TV. On his lap, there was a big black ring-binder with 'Dave Gormans 1 – 17' written on it, and he was surrounded by glue and sellotape. I think there may even have been a tub of glitter by his foot.

'I'm just off out for a bit,' I said.

'Okay, Dan. I've got a bit of work to do, so I'll see you when you get back.'

I still marvel at how a grown man can call writing his own name in glitter on a ringbinder 'work'.

With the sun on my neck, I headed across Victoria Park to the Royal Inn, where I'd agreed to meet my friend Ian, a man in the then unique position of not being called Dave Gorman, and therefore someone I was very keen to spend some time with.

Ian's a radio presenter, with a late-night phone-in show that attracts a huge listenership of nutters, insomniacs, students and pensioners every night of the week. These he keeps happy with a mixture of controversy, laddish intellect and a voice so radio you can't believe it belongs to a mere man.

'So what've you been up to lately?' he asked, and with a heavy heart I told him.

'Have you thought about moving house?' he said. For a brief

second it seemed like a brilliant idea, until I realised that Dave would be sure to notice.

'No, it's not like that,' I said. 'But I've realised that bets can be very dangerous things. And if not bets, then flatmates. My whole life is Dave Gormans at the moment, you know? It's ruining things with Hanne. She hates what I'm doing. She hasn't returned any of my phone calls since before New York. All because of *this*. Dave's obsessed. I'm obsessed. I'm even dreaming about them.'

'What . . . what kind of dreams?'

'Not those kind. D'you know, Dave even invented a 'miles per Dave Gorman' system to try and keep me interested? Apparently, according to this bloody graph he drew up, we've now travelled 743 mpdg.'

'mpdg?'

'Miles per Dave Gorman.'

'And you're on 743 of these "mpdg"'s?'

'Yes. But Dave reckons we should really be under 500. Something about only lunatics travelling that far to meet a namesake.'

'But haven't you just come back from New York?'

'Exactly. But he rationalises that by saying that when we were there we met *four* of these Dave Gormen.'

'"Gor*men*"?'

'It's the plural.'

Ian put on a thinking face and placed his pint on the table.

'Why don't you make him meet some Danny Wallaces?' he said.

'I couldn't do that to another human being. It's not right.'

'Have you *thought* about meeting any others?'

'No, not really.'

'You should.'

'Why?'

'It might help you deal with all these Daves, psychologically. Unfocus your mind. Make the journey about *you* for a bit. I'm sure Dave wouldn't mind. He'd help you.'

'Oh God, no he wouldn't'. I knew this for sure. To Dave's mind, this would be sullying his project. This would be making it dirty. I would, in effect, be cheating on my flatmate, and my flatmate is not the forgiving kind. 'I think it would hurt him a great deal if I did that.'

'So do it secretly. Listen, I'll help you find some. I'll ask on the show tomorrow for anyone who knows of any Daniel, Dan or Danny Wallaces in, say, London. We're bound to find some.'

'And then what?'

'And then you could meet them. We could make a night of it. It'd be fun.'

'I dunno. What if Dave finds out?'

'How would he find out? And anyway, you're a grown man, you can do what you like.'

'I'm not sure. I feel a bit uncomfortable about this,' I say, and it was true: I did.

'Look, I'll ask anyway. I'll get some numbers. Then you can decide what to do.'

'Okay,' I said, 'But I'm not saying I will.'

Ian stayed true to his word and the next night devoted a small part of his show to a feature entitled 'Are You Danny Wallace'? Approximately eighteen people rang up to inform Ian that there used to be a Danny Wallace who'd played for Southampton and Manchester United.

I drifted off to sleep with the radio on, quietly cursing that bloody footballer as I did so.

In the morning, there was an e-mail from Ian entitled 'Are You Danny Wallace!' and in it, the details of three other Daniel Wallaces in London. My stomach turned over at the prospect. It was exciting because I knew I shouldn't have been thinking such naughty thoughts. I printed off a copy for Hanne; she'd like this little bit of revolution. And then I noticed the PS. I scrolled down to see it all. 'By the way,' it read. 'You're all meeting at The Crown and Two Chairmen, Dean Street, on Tuesday, at 8. Bring your camera.'

My God. It was all arranged. A meeting! What would I tell Dave I was doing? How would I keep this a secret? Should I be playing with fire like this?

And then I thought sod it, and tried to remember where I'd put my camera.

It turns out that Legal & General Insurance headquarters are in a small village called Kingswood, in Surrey. It's through Croydon, but before the M25, unless you're coming the other way, and I feel I must warn you: it's *not* to be confused with the small village of Kingswood, in Kent, which is 40 miles away, just past Maidstone on the M20. That's 40 miles that I would imagine takes more or less an hour to drive.

We arrived at the *L&G* HQ more or less an hour late for our appointment with a Dave Gorman who used to work with a man called Ken who recently visited Heathrow airport and saw the car sticker that had been suggested by Dave Gorman from Warminster. It's nice how life works out, sometimes.

The insurance company's headquarters were huge, and reminded me, worryingly, of nothing more than some massive Soviet monument. It's something of a surprise to find it placed in such green and leafy surroundings, although it's skilfully landscaped within its own extensive grounds.

Dave came out to meet us and we took a stroll outside, walking past the swimming pool and sports facilities that are laid on in this office complex-cum-Stalag-cum-holiday camp.

Dave had an unruly mop of curly black hair that made him look a lot younger than his 40 years. Combine that with a sharp suit that's more Friday night than Tuesday morning, detailed, shiny, buckled shoes and a tie-less, open collar, and he looked more like a man about to get on stage and plug in his guitar than a man who works in insurance. It came as no surprise, then, to learn that he's played in various nearly-made-it bands. He'd be back on stage that weekend, as it happened.

He also had a revelation for me. As a matter of course, I'd asked him whether he knew of any other Dave Gormans. . .

'Well actually, there *is* another one who works for Legal and General. . .'

'Really?'

'Yeah . . . I've never met him. He doesn't work here. Every now and then I get the odd letter or phone call meant for him so I pass them on. He's a salesman. In . . . is it Eastbourne?'

'Eastbourne?'

'Now, is it Eastbourne?'

'Do you think it's Eastbourne?'

'I *think* it's Eastbourne. . .'

We took a couple more strides and then, as one, we said it again, but with a tone of voice that implied it was a word with mystical qualities, a word that somehow conjured up some kind of deep human truth: 'Eastbourne'.

Oh bloody hell. I knew what was coming next. And it was Eastbourne.

By the time DG18 had walked us back to the car park, my mind was made up.

'Right, Dan!' I said, with a clap of my hands. 'Let's go to Eastbourne!'

Dave Gorman was shocked.

'You can't just go to Eastbourne!'

'Why not?'

'Well, he might not be there!'

'But he might be!'

Surely it wasn't too difficult to understand.

'Yeah . . . but he might *not!*'

Clearly it was.

We buckled up, we waved goodbye, and we left.

I wasn't best pleased with this. For one thing, I wanted to get home and make sure everything was okay with my girlfriend. For another, this was Tuesday, and this evening, at a pub in London, four Danny Wallaces were supposed to meet for the first time thanks to the efforts of my mate Ian . . . and I was meant to be one of them.

'Dave . . . we can't really go to Eastbourne, now' I said. 'Sorry.'

'What?', he replied, a smile still on his face from the sheer, free, adventurousness of it all. 'Yes you can. I checked your diary, you're free all week.'

'I don't use a diary.'

'No, but I phoned around, called up your mates, just to make sure you hadn't made any plans. They sounded quite surprised about what you were up to. Hanne especially. She said you hadn't told her about Kingswood.'

'You phoned Hanne? I thought I told you to destroy her number!'

'I did. Well, no, I didn't. But only because I didn't want her to get annoyed with you any more.'

'So you told her about Kingswood?'

'Yes. And she was very annoyed with you.'

We turned onto a main road. We were Eastbourne-bound, whether I liked it or not.

'Look, we're on our way, now. What's so important that you think we can't go to Eastbourne?'

Well, what could I possibly say? He'd go mad if he knew about Ian's plans.

'Nothing. But if we do go to Eastbourne, we'll be back by this evening, won't we? We're not going to stay over anywhere, are we?'

Please please please say no.

'Not unless we get to Eastbourne and decide to drive along the South Coast or something. Y'know . . . seeing as we're almost there.'

Oh no. This was bad. He was already thinking of extending the trip. What was supposed to have been a quick jaunt around the M25 now seemed to have limitless possibilities.

I had to tell Ian. I had to tell him I might be late for the First Annual Danny Wallace Convention. Or, worse still, unable to attend at all. But how did I get the message through? I couldn't just call him up with Dave in earshot. I glanced over at the dashboard. Would we need petrol soon? Would we need a service station? Could I lean out of the window and do it?

And then I remembered the joys of mobile phone text messaging. I had to be quick, though, before Dave could read what I was up to or even ask me about it. I set about typing 'UNABLE TO MEET YOU. I'M ON COAST ALL DAY. AAARGH!', which I thought conveyed the desperation of the situation quite well.

However, being a young man, I was doing it in the way all good style magazines suggest you do; completely without vowels. Consequently, it now read 'NBL T MT Y. M N CST LL DY. RGH!'. I stared at it wondering if *GQ* and *The Face* might have made some kind of mistake, but found myself instinctively hitting 'Send' when Dave coughed. I hoped Ian read the same magazines as me and had a few hours of deciphering time to spare.

Moments later my phone beeped and a text message arrived for me. It must be Ian. It wasn't. It was Hanne. 'STILL LOVE YOU' it said. Thank God. Thank God she still loved me. But, again, I found myself in a difficult texting situation. Having to return affection while a male friend sits only a foot away from me? Difficult. I replied with 'I DO TOO', again dropping the vowels, and hoping Hanne could work out what I meant from the letters 'D' and 'T'.

I looked at it. Clearly, I'd got something very wrong with this vowels thing, so I sent a proper one. I felt bad that I hadn't told her that I was going to meet a Dave Gorman in Kingswood. But I hadn't thought I'd need to. After all, it was only supposed to be a two-hour trip. Now that we were heading for Eastbourne, though, I felt I should come clean. I wrote a very apologetic message telling her what had happened, and sent it off. She didn't reply.

I should have sent another one to Ian, too, but Dave interrupted me.

Danny was playing games on his mobile phone, so I told him to do something useful with it and ring directory enquiries to find a Dave Gorman in Eastbourne. We had our man.

DG19 actually lives about five miles north of Eastbourne, in the town of Polegate. It's the kind of nondescript town that, if *pushed* for a description, even the locals can only manage, 'it's quite near Eastbourne'. Which it is. The A22 took us there in a little over 90 minutes.

We're blessed with good timing, as Dave, a man with silver hair and slim frame, is only home because it's his lunch hour. Although when he explains his daily routine, I am immediately struck with guilt. You see, on a regular day, Dave goes out selling insurance, normally staying relatively close to home. Then, at lunchtime, he pops back and spends the hour with his permanently-smiling wife, Barb. During this hour they play a game of *Scrabble*. Alarmingly, though, Dave refers to the game as 'a challenge match', which one might think is a worrying foundation for any marriage.

After the game, Dave will go back out to sell more insurance, but this time travelling further afield, often not returning until quite late – a process which means that they really do treasure their lunchtime wordplay.

I looked across at the dining table and, sure enough, a game was underway. They'd been going through this routine for twenty years now, and it was the most important hour of their day . . . and here we were, two idiots, interrupting it.

'We don't want to be a nuisance, we can come back later if you like?' I offered

'Oh no, not at all. We'll play again tomorrow', said Dave

'It's just our little game,' said Barb. They looked lovingly at each other. 'We keep all the scores'.

'I beg your pardon?' I asked. I could have sworn I'd heard her say they kept all the scores.

'We keep all the scores'. Barb repeated. And then smiled a silly-old-us smile.

'Oh yes, all of them . . .,' said Dave, reaching down and producing a huge, leather-bound ledger. 'Here we are. . .'.

He opened the book and, yes, there they were. The results of Scrabble games – sorry, 'Challenge Matches' – going back twenty years. Dave flicked through the pages as if to prove they were all there. They were. There was the day when Dave had beaten Barb by 342 to 279. There was the day she had beaten him 303 to 297.

'That must have been a nail-biter', said Dan.

This was the most amazing document of a marriage I had ever seen. A love letter written daily between man and wife. And yes, it might only contain numbers, but you'd be hard pushed to find a more loving testament to holy matrimony.

I looked my namesake in the eye; I was impressed. He returned my gaze and I knew what he was thinking. He was thinking, 'Oh yes . . . you might well have come "all the way" to Polegate to meet a man that shares your name . . . but this, this book here, this twenty-year-old record of absurdly irrelevant facts . . . this is *truly* obsessive. You, sir, are a mere amateur. . .'

When we were sat back in the car I slipped his polaroid into the album. I gazed at it in awe. I felt inspired by the man's tenacity.

'Right. Dave. Back to London, now,' said Dan, at his most chipper. 'If we head off now, we'll probably beat the worst of the traffic. Can I get out near Oxford Street?'

'Did you learn nothing in there, Dan?' I said, sternly. 'Nothing at all? That man is an inspiration, my friend. Did you see that Scrabble book? It pisses all over this photo album at the minute.'

'What? No it doesn't. It's just different . . . can we go, now?'

'My point is, that wasn't a man who does things in half-measures. And what's more, he's a Dave Gorman. He's made me proud to be one too. And from now on, I'm going to be more like him.'

'Fine. We'll play Scrabble when we get home. . .'

'We're going to find some more. We start now.'

I reversed out of Dave Gorman's drive, and, much to Dan's annoyance, took the south road, laughing in the face of the north one as I did so.

I'll be honest. I was upset. It really wasn't looking as if a Tuesday night return was going to be possible. Mainly because it *was* Tuesday night, and we were sitting in a poorly heated B&B in Eastbourne. Dave had been around me ever since we'd left the Scrabble man's house, and so it had made any attempts to phone Ian and cancel the Danny Wallace evening impossible. Not without risking violence from a jealous Dave, at any rate.

At least I'd managed to sneak a text message through, though. He's an intelligent man, Ian. He knows about vowels and stuff. Surely he'd been able to understand it and postpone the meeting for some-time more convenient?

Well, no.

And so it was that a man called Ian Collins spent a Tuesday night sitting in a pub with three men with *my* name, but *I* spent it on the south coast of England looking for men who share my *flatmate's*. Something wasn't right with the world.

The elderly lady who ran the B&B offered to make us some hot chocolate, something to which we eagerly agreed, and as Dave regaled her with tales of the day we'd just had, I tiptoed over to the payphone in the hall and dialled Ian's mobile.

'Ian, I'm so sorry, I ended up in Eastbourne against my will,' I said.

'Not a problem, Dan, that's how most people get to Eastbourne. When you didn't show I tried Hanne's phone and she suspected something like that must've happened.'

'Oh, God, she didn't sound angry, did she?'

'Yes.'

'Oh.'

'She sounded fairly annoyed about the Danny Wallace convention, too.'

'Great. You told her about that.'

'Didn't you?'

'No.'

'Oh. But the Dans and I had a really good night.'

'Did you? Seriously?'

'Yeah – they were all great blokes. They really wanted to meet you. One guy in particular, whose PE teacher used to bully him at school because he had the same name as that Southampton player.'

'What – Danny Wallace?' I say.

'That's the fella. That's both of them, in fact.'

'So you're not angry with me, then?'

'No. A bet's a bet, and if you had to go, you had to go. The more you meet, the sooner it'll all be over. I had a bit of a job explaining why I'd brought those three Danny Wallaces there, though. I think they thought I was some kind of really specific murderer, at first. But we had a good night.'

Well, that was a relief. We said our goodbyes, and I felt less bad about the way I'd spent my day. After all, Ian had an odd experience he can talk about on his show, I met some nice people, and a couple who spend their time the way married couples should spend their time. Tomorrow wouldn't be so bad. We were on the coast. We could go paddling. Life was good.

I looked at Hanne's text message again. 'STILL LOVE YOU'. She couldn't be that angry, surely? I gave her a ring. Her phone was off. I left another message.

I drank my cocoa, ate a sandwich and went to bed happier than I thought was possible, given the circumstances.

Over breakfast I revealed my plan. We were going to work hard, but with military precision we could make this work. From Eastbourne to Brighton, from Brighton to Portsmouth and then . . . well, I had a treat for Dan. But best not build him up too much. Best to keep that one up my sleeve for now. He'd love it, though.

We were greeted in Brighton by the always welcome sight of sea and sand. Well, sea and pebbles, but that's quite welcome too. Had we also been able to see the sun behind the thick charcoal-coloured clouds, I dare say we'd have forgotten all about this Dave Gorman nonsense and simply spent the afternoon running around on the beach giggling like girls.

As it was, we only had twenty minutes until we were supposed to turn up at Dave Gorman's house, so we decided, quite sensibly, to park the car and entrust ourselves to a taxi driver's local knowledge. Was that what Dave meant by 'military precision'?

We parked near the *Grand*, a fine, old-fashioned hotel so posh many of the rooms actually have doorbells. We flagged down a taxi and moments later we were on our way round to Old Shoreham Road.

'Right, then,' says Dave, as we step out of the cab and watch it speed away. He checks the front door. 'This is the right number isn't it?'

We ring the doorbell and when a tall, bespectacled man answers the door, we grin inanely and do everything but step forward and hug him. 'Hello!' says Dave, rather loudly. 'We made it!'

It turns out that although this man lives at the right number on the right road, this is not the right house and this is not the right man. Because it turns out that Old Shoreham Road is a very long road. And whoever is responsible for numbering houses in Brighton decided, for reasons best known to themselves, that once you'd got up to number four hundred and something, you were better off starting again from '1' and carrying on. Now personally, I'd rather be the only person living at number 1500 Old Shoreham Road than the 3rd person to live at a number 55. But in Brighton they obviously like to confuse the postman. So, there are two other houses on the same road that share the same address. One of them was a couple of miles away. The other was no doubt four miles away.

We ask the bespectacled man for directions. A stupid question that got the answer it deserved: 'It's on this road. Only much further.'

We finally arrived at Dave's house (after unsettling the woman who lived at the same number, two miles away) and we were ushered indoors by his wife, who immediately put the kettle on while we watched Dave watch the telly. He turned out not to be the chattiest man in the world, but this was more than made up for by his wife, who took a great interest in our recent travels. At one point, she looked at the ceiling and wistfully said, 'I wish I could do it myself'. I don't think she'd thought it through, to be honest, but in fairness, she'd got all the equipment she'd need: including one Dave Gorman and a car. Maybe I should have offered to swap places with her. She could have gone off with my Dave Gorman and I could have stayed watching TV with hers.

Anyway, before she took the chance to pack a bag and make off on a weekend of Dave Gorman hunting, we forced her husband to have his picture taken and to tell us a little about his life. We found out that Dave Gorman number twenty is a carpetfitter who enjoys watching football and buying DVDs for his elaborate home entertainment system. But while he was explaining that carpet fitting was 'alright', his wife hadn't let go of the idea. In fact she'd popped out and visited her father in law and returned carrying a very frightening tome.

'Here you are, Dave' she said, proudly, although I'm not sure which one she was addressing. 'Take a look at this: "*The World Book Of Gormans*"'.

Oh my God. Were Gormans really as obsessed with their name as they seemed to be? Within this red, embossed, leather-bound book was Gorman upon Gorman upon Gorman, and a few of them . . were Davids.

'Wow . . . I'm . . . amazed . . .' said Dave, as Mrs Gorman stood above him, beaming with pride. She had done a very good thing, according to Dave. My side of the story is slightly different, but then that's doubtless something you've become accustomed to by now.

Dave made some notes about a couple of leads he said he'd like to follow up, and Mrs Gorman looked delighted. So delighted, in fact, that she offered us a lift back to the car. On the way back into town she asked if either of us had a girlfriend and whether we still expected to by the time all this was over, and showed great sympathy for Hanne when she heard about Venice, New York and just about every other trip that meant I'd been late or missing. Or nearly killed by a tornado. I couldn't help thinking that I, the idiot who was being dragged along on this oddest of odysseys, was more deserving of her sympathy, but I was grateful for the reminder as I'd forgotten to give Hanne a call with my whereabouts. Again. What if she was out searching for me in Eastbourne while I was mucking about in Brighton? And how would she know where I'd be in two hours' time?

As Dave got back into the car with the map and his notes from *The World Book of Gormans*, I walked up the promenade with my mobile and tried Hanne's number once again.

She didn't answer. I left another message. This was all very odd.

The vagaries of Brighton's house numbering system had cost us 30 minutes. We were behind schedule, and I was eager to get on the road and make up time. But Danny was holding me up. When Batman had a crime to solve, do you think he had to sit there with the Batmobile engine turning over while Robin went for a walk on Gotham prom chatting on his mobile phone? I doubt it. I honked the bat-horn, the Boy Wonder jumped in, I pointed the car at Portsmouth, we hit the A27 and I put my foot down.

Waiting for us as we arrived at The Portsmouth War Memorial was Dave Gorman of Portsmouth. A shortish, jolly man with a proud belly and a cute, lovable, bearded face, I remember thinking he would make an excellent Santa Claus at Christmas time.

It was now a very, very windy day, and the fact that we were situated on the vast expanse of totally exposed seafront made it hard to perform activities that most people take for granted. Like walking, or putting your jacket on, or breathing without inhaling a lungful of sand. So DG21 suggested we move somewhere more secluded.

'So what is it that you do?' I asked.

'I work just down the road,' said our new DG. 'I work as a. . .'

And in all honesty, this is where he lost me. What I do know is he started to give a very technical and inordinately detailed description of whatever it was he did. Every so often I'd catch a word I understood, like 'the' or 'it', and would nod my head to show that I'd picked it up. Danny, I think, was just as lost as I was.

It was a reasonably short meeting, mainly because Dave and I lacked the necessary code books to crack this man's vocabulary. His job had something to do with water, if I'm right, and I think at one point the word 'goggles' was mentioned. Perhaps he was a swimmer. After he gave us a lift back to our car, in which time he'd nearly come to the end of trying to explain exactly what his job was, we decided he was probably a Marine Scientist. It's just easier than imagining Santa as a professional swimmer.

'Okay Dan, we've done well', I said. 'So, out of the goodness of my heart, I've got a treat planned for you.'

'Really?'

'Really. As a reward for all the hard work, I'm taking you on another overseas trip.'

Dan's jaw dropped.

'No Dave, absolutely not. I've *got* to get home today. I'm worried about Hanne. I mean, it might sound like a nice idea but . . .'

'Whoa cowboy. . .'

'Hang on. Did you just say "whoa cowboy"?'

'Yes. Sorry. Look, we're going home today, okay? Rest assured, we'll be back in London this evening. Ring Hanne right now. Book a restaurant. Buy her a Babycham. Take her to the disco.'

'You haven't had a girlfriend in quite some time, have you, Dave?'

'I promise you we'll get back tonight. We *are* going overseas. But only five miles overseas! We're going to the Isle of Wight!'

We looked out across the Solent, and inhaled another lungful of sand. Where we were, it was windy, with a spitting rain. But in the distance – ah, the distance – there appeared to be an oasis of sunshine. Dan smiled at the sight. I tried to encourage him a bit more.

'We can hit the beach'. His smile broadened. 'I'll buy you an ice-cream'. It became broader still. 'And . . .'. I took a deep breath. 'There are absolutely no Dave Gormans there'. It became broader than I ever thought possible.

'Okay. Let's go.'

I'd got him. It was good to see him happy. And I only felt a *little* bit guilty. Far less guilty than I *should* have felt, given the lie I'd just told him. . .

We were actually having fun. Together. Two mates, having fun. Now, I'm not saying that I hadn't had fun before on this stupid quest. I'm not going to deny that there had been moments of pleasure along the way. But it had never been the ultimate purpose behind what we were doing. This, though . . . this was fun for fun's sake. Dave bought two tickets from Portsmouth to Ryde and we boarded the Seacat.

I'd never seen Dave in such a light mood. The very moment we set sail he launched into an almost unnecessarily lively vocal rendition of 'Ticket To Ryde', much to the annoyance of everyone else on board. It seems the Great British Public aren't nearly as keen on a sin-galong as you'd have thought.

Now, I can assure you that I haven't received a kickback from the Isle of Wight Tourist Board, but I can faithfully report that in that five-mile hop, we were transported to a different, happier, sunnier world.

I stepped out onto Ryde pier and gulped down the healthy sea air, pleasingly absent of sand.

'Right, what shall we do first?'

'We'll find some fun, Dan,' said Dave. 'Hang about, I'll ask that chap over there'.

He strode past me, towards an older man, leaning on the pier looking out to sea. He had a white, wide-brimmed hat tied around his head, and a labrador waiting patiently by his side. Why Dave should think this was the man to ask about fun I couldn't work out. I watched as they chatted, shook hands – and I was surprised by how convivial it all looked. Dave returned to me with a grin.

'You'll never guess what, Dan!', he said, with eyes the size of saucers.

'What?'

'That man there . . .' He pointed back at the old gent who returned the gesture with a military salute. 'That man there goes by the name of Dave Gorman!'

My eye began to twitch. I had been tricked.

'I can't believe it!' said Dave. 'I mean, it's almost *beyond* belief!'

I wondered what Dave expected me to say. 'Well, what an amazing coincidence!' perhaps. Or 'Goodness, they're everywhere, aren't they?' In the end I settled for 'You shit.'

'What?' he said, desperately trying to maintain the illusion. 'I don't understand what you mean!'

'You heard me. You're a shit. Did you really think I'd fall for that? Of all the people in the world, the man you randomly approach on a pier in the Isle of Wight that you've oh-so-kindly brought me to just happens to be yet another bloke called Dave Gorman!'

'Keep your voice down, Dan, he'll hear you.'

'I don't *care* if he hears me. Hello Dave Gorman!' I waved at the confused-looking man and his confused-looking labrador. 'And your dog!'

'Look, we're here now,' said Dave, angrily. 'He wants to show us his house; it won't take long. He's an old man, we can't let him down.'

We stared at each other in a tense silence. I felt like belting him one. I think Dave sensed this, and quickly returned to his namesake, number 22. They started to stroll off down the pier. I wanted to turn around and walk the other way, but I was also on the pier. If I walked the other way I'd get rather wet. So I waited a while, gave them a considerable head start, and then began an angry amble after them.

DG22 was a jovial man, and had a colourful hue about him. Despite being at least 30 years my senior, he set a brisk pace that left me feeling short of breath while trying to listen to his life story. His voice had a kind of military precision that had almost destroyed his Brummie accent – but it still hung on in there, as Brummie accents always do. His mouth was cocked at a jaunty angle that suggested he was smoking an invisible pipe, and if I'd been asked to guess, I'd have said he was a naval man. He wasn't, though. He described himself as 'a semi-retired lighthouse technician'. I have no idea what that involves, but I can say without a shadow of a doubt that it's my favourite job title of all the Dave Gormans I've met.

His house was a ten-minute stroll away. Eight minutes if you marched. We were there in five.

Dave Gorman's house was a lovingly-restored Victorian two-bed end-of-terrace with a fancy nameplate on the front. Inside, he revelled in showing us a mass of 'before' and 'after' photos of the building work he'd done. It's the subject of a preservation order, his place, but few would go to the lengths this man has in tracking down and using authentic paint colours of the period. This seemed to lend weight to the theory that there might be some kind of special 'obsessive' gene in the Gorman DNA. The Ford Capris, the Scrabble scores, the *World Book of Gormans*, the spectacular level of detail involved in restoring this property, and, I am forced to admit, my own search, all pointed in this direction.

We sat in the front room and Dave offered to make some tea. We gratefully accepted, and he left the room. Danny scowled at me. I felt too awkward about the lie I'd told, and left him there, scowling. I wandered through to the kitchen to keep our latest Dave company.

'It's teabags, I'm afraid', he said. 'But that's how people make it these days, isn't it?'

I smiled at what seemed like an unnecessary politeness. That's how tea's been made all my life. It was more the kind of sentence *my* generation might say to *his* by way of apology for our uncouth modern ways. It seemed odd coming the other way.

Over tea he showed us yet more photos and it was fascinating to see a man's life unfold in snapshots. But one thing leapt out at me as he flicked through various photos: the number of women. Different women. Different, leggy, glamorous women. With shiny mascara and flamboyant clothes. Or shiny mascara and almost no clothes.

'If you don't mind me saying so, you appear to be a bit of a ladies' man', I said.

'Oh yes', he winked. 'Of course. . .'

He sighed a sigh of reminiscence and looked skywards.

Dan coughed. Evidently he found this a little embarrassing.

'I promised Dan we'd go to the beach, Dave,' I said. 'So I hope you don't mind if we don't hang around.'

'Not at all', he said. 'I'll walk down with you; I could do with the exercise. I'll bring the dog.'

And so it was that this spry old rogue of a man walked us down to the beach and waved us goodbye while we two youngsters were left short of breath, put to shame by his unwavering pace, waving back and trying to remember if we'd ever used that gym membership we'd taken up last Christmas.

I bought Danny his ice-cream, as promised, and, because there was nothing else in the shop vaguely resembling a treat, I also bought him a kite. Yes. A kite. I handed my gifts over with a conciliatory look. He took the ice-cream, and then looked at the kite with suspicion.

'That's a kite,' he said.

'I know. It's the best thing they had. I'd have bought a frisbee but that's more of a two-man activity. I think you're in a bit of a mood with me, so I didn't think you'd be up for games. So I got a kite.'

'You got a kite?'

'I'm sorry about lying to you. I mean it. If there's anything I can do about Hanne, just ask.'

'I think it's best if you don't get involved, there.'

'Okay.'

'Thanks for the kite.'

'It's just a kite.'

I think because he knew it was a heartfelt gesture, Danny decided to play with the kite anyway. It was his way of accepting my apology. Off he ran, like a free spirit, dragging the kite behind him. No doubt it would have been a pretty spectacular thing to play with back in Portsmouth, where the wind was unrelenting and vigorous. Here, in the sun, it wasn't quite so satisfying. I watched, smiling, as my flatmate dragged his kite through the sand. He was happy.

When we returned to London later that day I could see Dave was happy. He'd had an exhilarating couple of days. We'd started on Tuesday morning, heading off for a quick meeting with one man, and we'd ended up travelling for two days and meeting five.

We were up to 22; something in which Dave took some pride. After all, it now meant he could referee an all-Dave-Gorman football match.

'Who would you pick first?' he asked. 'I mean, if you were choosing your first eleven?'

'The East Fife Football Club Assistant Manager, obviously,' I said. 'He's getting on a bit, but experience and know-how go a long way on the football pitch.'

'Okay, I'll take Wolverhampton, he coaches kids, presumably he's a bit handy.'

'Fine. I'll take East Fife's son, the policeman. It's in his family.'

'Good one . . . tricky . . . I'll take Ladybank, young lad, seems fit. . .'

'I'll take Tooting.'

'Really?'

'Just joking.'

We laughed. But what was I doing? I was happily chatting away as if this was the most ordinary thing in the world. Dave was trying to suck me into his evil game again. And that wasn't on. Not when I had deep, personal issues to sort out.

Halfway up the M3 I'd developed an uneasy feeling about things with Hanne. By the time we were in the capital my stomach was in knots. As we drove closer to home, and reality, I began to wonder why she hadn't phoned me. Why she hadn't returned any of my messages. I needed to sort things out with her. I *didn't* need to pick a Dave Gorman XI. I snapped out of it as Dave was deliberating over whether or not to pick Bromsgrove over Swindon for goalkeeper, and I decided to tell him how I felt.

'I think something's very wrong with Hanne and me.'

'Do you? Really?'

'Yes. Deeply wrong.'

'Hmm. Well, I'm not surprised, Dan. I mean, you've been running around all over the world meeting your flatmate's namesakes.'

The cheek.

'Yeah, but only 'cos *you* made me!'

'I didn't *make* you, Dan. It's for a bet. Hanne's probably feeling a bit ignored.'

'Oh, hark at you, the great master of female psychology. Of *course* she's feeling a bit ignored. She's feeling a bit ignored because you insist on carrying out your side of this stupid bloody bet. Why didn't you tell me you thought she was probably feeling a bit ignored?'

'I didn't think it was my place to comment.'

We got home, and Danny immediately rushed off to his room to call Hanne. He wasn't happy. I did what all good flatmates should do in this situation, I made him a cup of tea. Gingerly, I knocked on his door. He shouted 'come in', and I nudged it open with my elbow. I put the tea down on his desk. He had both his mobile and the regular phone out.

'I'm trying her mobile on this line and her home on this line', he said, blushing slightly. 'She's not answering either of them.'

'Maybe she's still at work?'

'I'll check my e-mails.'

'Don't log off, I need to check mine as well'.

Hanne hadn't rung me, she hadn't e-mailed me and there were no pigeons on the window sill with messages strapped to their tiny ankles. I was very, very worried.

When Danny had ceded the computer to me, I could tell without asking that Hanne hadn't been in touch. So when I found the news in my inbox, I tried not to be too excited.

I read the mail through. 'Dear Dave, A friend told me that you are looking for other people called Dave Gorman. Well I have good news for you!! I work with one. He's from New Zealand!'.

No! *New Zealand?* My heart sank. I could never afford something like that. For the first time since I started looking, I might actually have to turn a DG down. How upsetting was this?

But the e-mail continued: 'But he now lives in London.'

Manna from heaven!

'Our office is near Victoria but his home is in Northwood.'

Northwood? I knew that – it wasn't far from Harrow, our old stomping ground. Northwood, that was easy. I took down his number and his address, and started trying to work out how I would broach the subject with Danny. This wasn't going to be easy, given his current mood, and where his thoughts were lying.

I went back to his room. The door was open and he was putting his jacket on.

'Where you going?' I asked

'Hanne's house.'

'You spoke to her then?' I said, relieved.

'Nope. She's not answering. I'm going round there. It's the only way.'

My news could wait.

'Do you want a lift?' There was a pause. 'It'll be quicker. I mean . . . obviously, you'll have to tell me where she lives, though. . .'

I had nothing to lose. Nothing to lose except my girlfriend.

'She lives in Kenton,' I confessed. There. I'd said it now.

'What . . . as in the Kenton near Harrow which is near Northwood?'

Dave was smiling.

'How long does it take to shake a man's hand and take his photo?' he asked.

We snagged ourselves a Kiwi DG; large, cheerful, photography-loving family man – our quickest yet – and then we drove to Kenton. Rain was beginning to spit down out of a moody grey sky.

'You stay in the car,' I said to Dave.

'No way!' he said. 'I want to see what Hanne's house is like.'

'This is a very sensitive situation.'

'I'm a very sensitive guy!'

I rang the doorbell and waited under the canopy, with Dave trying to peer through the living room window.

'She's got a TV!' he said. 'You never told me that.'

Someone began to unlock the door from the other side, and it opened, cautiously. It was Hanne's flatmate, Janne.

'Hello Danny,' she said. 'Hello . . . Dave, I suppose?'

'Hello there!' said Dave, smiling. Janne didn't smile back at him.

'Janne, can I come in? I need to speak with Hanne.'

'Danny. . .'

'She hasn't been returning my calls. Is she okay? I got a text message but that's it.'

'Danny, Hanne's not in.'

'Right. Well . . . can we come in and . . . wait for her?'

'I don't know when she'll be back.'

Janne looked sad.

'Ah. Okay. Can we wait anyway?'

'We could watch TV,' offered Dave. Janne ignored him.

'Danny, listen. You know that Hanne loves you.'

'Yes.'

'But you've kind of been a bit . . . busy . . . lately. I mean . . . *Venice*, for God's sake. What was all that about? I thought you'd always promised to go there with *her*.'

'And I will, as soon as this is all over, we'll. . .'

'And then New York. You know how she'd have loved to have gone there with you. Her boyfriend. And yet you go with your flat-mate.'

'That's me,' said Dave. 'And for your information, we found *two* Dave Gormans from the Venice trip.'

'What if she'd done that to you, Danny? What if she could never see you because she was travelling all over the world meeting people with *my* name. Like, "Oh, sorry, Danny, I can't meet you this week-end because I'm in bloody Aberdeen meeting people called Janne Bjøernæs?". Wouldn't you think that was stupid?'

'That'd be quite an interesting challenge, actually,' said Dave. 'I wonder how many. . .'

'Shut up, Dave,' I said. 'Look, Janne. . .'

'Danny'. She moved closer, angling her shoulders to cut Dave out and speak to me more privately.

'Hanne has gone back to Norway for a while.'

The words hit me hard.

'What do you mean "for a while"?'

'She wants to sort her head out. I think you should try and do the same.'

Janne smiled gently, said she was sorry, and closed the door.

I was stunned. Dave put his arm around my shoulders and we walked back to the car.

The sun that was now peering through the clouds was lying to me. Because this was now a very black day indeed.

Chapter 11

HAWAII HO HO

I hadn't seen hide nor hair of Danny all day. His bedroom door remained firmly shut, and on the one occasion when he opened it to pick up the cup of tea I'd left, the blinds were down and the lights were off. I was worried about him. I've been in similar situations myself and I know how inescapable it can all seem. Every book you open, every soundbite you hear on TV and every song on the radio seems to be about you and your situation. As I walked past to go to the bathroom, though, I heard him listening to a downbeat acoustic version of 'I Am The Walrus', which was perhaps a blessing, because unless he was on some pretty hard drugs, I think it's safe to say that Danny's relationship with Hanne wasn't what The Beatles had in mind when they wrote that. Mind you, I'll check with Tooting Dave and get back to you.

'Dan,' I whispered outside his door. I heard him mumbling. I pressed my eye against the crack of the door. He was on the phone.

I had spent my day under a cloud, but had finally managed to get Hanne on the phone. She was indeed back in Norway, at the family home, on top of a mountain in the small village of Fagernes. It's the kind of village that you don't think it's possible actually exists in the world. It has a heart-breaking natural beauty, from top to bottom, with wonderfully clichéd views of fjords, Tipp-Exed mountain tops, and acres of green firs hugging the hills that, the last time I had my photos developed, prompted the man on the other side of the counter to beg me to tell him where I'd just been. It's the perfect place to go when you've got some thinking to do.

When Dave whispered my name, I was only an hour into what was to become a very long conversation with her, in which she'd apologise for running off to Norway, and I'd apologise for making her.

'So where is it you've been this time?' she said, sternly.

'We were in Surrey. And then we went to Eastbourne. And then Brighton and Portsmouth. And then Dave lied to me and made me go to the Isle of Wight. Oh, and Northwood, when we were on our way round to your place.'

'Hang on. He *lied* to you?'

'He knew I needed to get back to you, and that I wouldn't want to go to the Isle of Wight, so he lied to me.'

'I hope you're not going to let him get away with that,' she said, which is a very Hanne thing to say, and I told her I had a few plans of my own. She laughed. This was good. She was getting more into the spirit of things than she'd been able to when she'd been in London. But she also whipped me raw, verbally. She remembered every detail about every sufferance I'd made her go through. The dinner I'd missed because of staying late with Swindon Dave. The film I couldn't go to with her because I'd been too knackered after Wolverhampton and Bromsgrove. The meetings I'd cancelled, that after-work drinks do of hers I couldn't make, the Sunday lunches I'd had to forego, the friends who'd continually asked after me, the times she'd lied about my whereabouts because she was too embarrassed to tell the truth, and the list went on.

'At least I didn't forget our anniversary,' I said.

'When is it, then?'

Er. . .

'Listen, are you going to come back here soon?' I said. There was hope in my eyes. It was a pity she couldn't see them.

'I think I'm going to stay over here for a little while. I'm back at my old job for a couple of weeks.'

Hanne was working on the Norwegian phone system dealing with directory enquiries; she was Norway's equivalent of a 192 girl. Fagernes just happened to be one of the places the country relied upon to take care of that.

'Okay. But you *will* come back? I promise to try and deal with this Dave Gorman nonsense.'

'Listen, I think you should come over here, Danny. I think we need to see each other to get over this. I think you should come to Norway soon.'

I took in her words. I knew she was right. And I really should be the one making the effort. My stomach told me I was again as nervous as I'd been when I'd dialled Hanne's number in Norway.

This time, it was because I was going to have to tell Dave I needed to stop.

As soon as I'd seen that Danny was on the phone, I left him to it. Well, I tried to listen for a bit, realised I couldn't make the words out, and *then* I left him to it.

It was good that he was sorting things out with Hanne. Maybe then I'd have him back, and we could get on with the very serious business of completing the bet.

I mixed myself a cocktail and sat in the lounge, watched a little cable TV, and bounced a small ball on a bat. Dan still hadn't come out of his room, and it was getting late. I was bored. I went to my room and sat down in front of my computer.

With nothing else to do, I decided to check my e-mails. I had four. Only one of them, you will be surprised to hear, was from a Dave Gorman. It was more than enough to make *me* happy.

More specifically, it was from a *Davey* Gorman. Fantastic, I thought. We hadn't met a Davey yet!

My excitement was set to double by the end of the e-mail.

Dear Dave,
I understand you are trying to meet people called Dave Gorman. I was christened David Gorman. Do I count?

Well . . . yes. He might not be the sharpest knife in the box, but that wasn't a problem. Dave Gormans should come in all varieties, young and old, clever and stupid.

My great grandfather was also called David Gorman, but sadly he is no longer with us. I was born in the Boston area, but I now live and work in Hawaii.
Interested?
Sincerely,
Davey Gorman

I shot out of my chair, sending it flying backwards, and had to grab hold of my mouth with both hands to stop myself from shouting. I was giggling uncontrollably – Hawaii! This was the best news I'd heard all day.

I couldn't tell Danny yet, but boy, what a treat was waiting for him when he'd finished on the phone. Hawaii! That'd cheer the little idiot up!

It was nearly midnight. I'd ring a travel agent first thing in the morning. For now, I just stared in wonder at the e-mail. Then I noticed something odd . . . something very odd . . . and my wonder turned to suspicion. It may have been late, but I decided to ring my mate, Gareth.

The conversation was coming to an end at about a quarter to one. We'd talked about anything but Dave Gormans for the last half an hour, opting instead for topics less likely to cause an argument, such as war and religion.

We'd agreed that we needed to see each other to make amends, and I was to tell Dave in no uncertain terms that I was ending the bet, in order to sort out the things in life that really mattered. He could win. I was emotionally shattered, and I just didn't care any more.

But I'd told Hanne that this was the most I could do for now. I couldn't fly to Norway because the money to get there, and then to make the trip to Fagernes, just wasn't in my account. Not if I was going to make this month's rent, at any rate. Hanne had suggested I ask Dave for the money, but he's a friend, and what's more, he's a friend who was very nearly blind to the deep financial trouble he was getting himself into, and as such was not someone I was willing to borrow money from to satisfy my own selfish needs.

I promised her I'd try and sorts things out, and apologised profusely for not being able to fly to Norway to apologise in person.

'I understand,' she said, and despite the sadness in her voice, I think she did.

'Gareth,' I said. 'I need you to come round to my house and look at my computer.'

'Who is this?', he said.

'It's Dave. I need you to come round right now.'

'Dave who?'

'Dave Gorman.'

'Dave Gorman? Hello mate! I haven't seen you in . . . blimey . . . two years?'

'Do you still know about computers and stuff?'

'Well, yes. . .'

'Can you come round?'

'It's nearly one in the morning!'

'When *can* you come round?'

'Look . . . what's all this about?'

It was about suspicions I needed confirmed. When I'd taken another look at the e-mail from Davey Gorman, I'd clocked his e-mail address. It was davey_gorman@hotmail.com. And that rang a little bell with me. Because I thought back to that day when Danny and I had sent out 4,000 e-mails on the recommendation of Dave Gorman the author from France.

Now, I was damn sure we'd tried Davey Gormans, and I knew for a fact that if we'd sent one to a davey_gorman@hotmail.com it would have been rejected, because all the ones we'd sent to Hotmail addresses were. Which meant that someone had registered the address in very recent times. Which was suspicious. Was it a Davey Gorman? That's what I wanted Gareth to find out.

So when Gareth came round early the next morning I watched with fascination as he sat before my screen and went to work.

He analysed Davey Gorman's e-mail. He browsed through the menus and selected complicated sub-menus, and picked among things like 'View,' and 'Source', and with each click of my mouse he came nearer to a conclusion of some sort.

Every computer, it turns out, has a special ID number attached to it, and if you send an e-mail, that number goes with it, whatever e-mail address you're using at the time. If you take that number and cross reference it against all the other e-mails you've received, and you find a match, even if it comes from a different address, then you know it was sent from the same computer. So, in theory, you can find out which computer it was sent from and, in turn, who sent it.

If you're Gareth.

After four hours, and plenty of tea, I heard Gareth yell: 'Eureka!' Well, he actually yelled, 'I've got it!', but you know what I mean.

Dave burst into my room at nine o'clock in the morning, and pinned me down in my bed.

'You tit!' he shouted, before giving my nipples such a ruthless tweak that I thought I was going to pass out.

'Aaahhhww! You freak! Get off my nipples!'

'No! You deserve it, you little tit!'

He tweaked again, with twice the ferocity.

'Aagh! Get off my arms!'

'Never, Dan!' He had me in his mercy. 'Or should I say . . . "Davey"?'

'What are you on about?'

'Shut up! You're Davey Gorman, you little bastard!'

'Yeah, so what if I am? You lied to me about the Isle of Wight! You nearly cost me my girlfriend!'

'So you thought you'd try and blag a free trip to Hawaii out of me?'

'Yes!'

'How could you?!'

'Easily! Ow ow ow ow ow! Stop it with the nipples!'

'Er . . . I'm going now,' said Gareth, standing at my door.

'Bye Gareth, thanks,' said Dave.

'Bye Gareth,' I said.

We waited until we heard the front door click shut, and then continued.

'So what would you have said, Dan? "Oh, looks like Dave Gorman's not in, Dave – let's go to the beach then?"'

'Precisely! And then I'd have ended this stupid bet there and then!'

He went in for another tweak but I wriggled free and managed to push one of my hands up into his face. He jabbed at me with his fingers, firing off little bullets of pain, and I waved my hand vigorously in his face, clipping his nose as I did so. He moved his head back and I freed my other arm, reaching out across my side table for any kind of weapon. His finger jabs continued as I fumbled for something to use and I batted my thumb against his chin until I found an errant sock with which I whipped him. He leapt off the bed, and I held the sock in front of me, as if it were a knife.

'I almost bought two tickets to Hawaii because of you!' he said, his face bright red.

'Good. I'm glad. Because this has all got too much for me. It's *over*, Dave, okay? *Over*.' I wiped the sweat from my forehead with the sock.

He stepped closer.

'Ah ah ah,' I warned, holding it out in front of me again.

He pointed a finger at me.

'You haven't heard the last of this,' he said, and walked out of my room.

I exhaled for what seemed like the first time that day and sat back against the wall.

Dave's arm appeared around my door again and he blindly threw a tennis ball at me.

The phone rang.

That bastard. Imagine doing that to your flatmate. This was the kind of thing that would earn him three months of washing up duty, if he wasn't careful. It certainly wasn't a fitting way to repay someone who, not two days before, had bought him a kite.

I knew Danny was at the end of his tether with the bet. He'd been pretty down about it lately, and I knew I shouldn't have lied to him that day. I'd thought it was the only way. But that had been a real turning point, for him. And all this stuff with Hanne . . . I'd wanted to avoid thinking about it before, because I couldn't handle the thought, but . . . maybe this really *was* where the bet would end.

I cooled off in the kitchen with a glass of milk while Danny answered the phone.

Minutes later he joined me in the kitchen in his pants. These were the pants Hanne had bought him as a present from Norway. Much as I tried not to look, I couldn't help but notice the smiling, cartoon elk on the front of them. I'll be honest – it was very hard to look elsewhere. I hope whoever drew this cartoon elk takes it as a compliment when I say that his eyes seemed to follow me around the room.

'That was Hanne,' he said. 'She broke the rules at her work and searched on the computers through the entire population of Norway.'

I didn't understand. It wasn't like Hanne to break the rules of anything. What had she done that for?

'She's found a David Gorman in Norway.'

I stepped forward and hugged Danny. I looked him in his eyes – his human eyes, not his elk ones – and smiled.

'Then we must prepare.'

Hanne was to be admired.

She knew the only way I'd be able to get out to Norway was if Dave signed on the dotted line and put the trip down to just another leg of his mission.

So she'd done something she really didn't want to do. Something that she'd taken a forceful stand against a long time ago. She'd aided and abetted the Great Dave Gorman Hunt. She'd kept the bet alive just when it looked like it couldn't continue any more.

She'd saved our relationship in the process. I think she may even have saved my friendship with Dave.

My nipples were fucking killing me.

Chapter 12

NORVÈGE UN POINT

Our plane touched down in Gardermoen Airport in Oslo, a futuristic vision of brushed metal, modern sculptures and wooden flooring stretching out as far as the eye could see. It might have stretched even further, but I couldn't be arsed to walk all that way just to check.

Hanne had managed to find Norwegian Dave's mobile number and Dave had had a brief chat with him to let him know we were coming. The Norwegian had been somewhat relaxed about the whole thing; as if this were the third time this week a fellow Dave Gorman and his flatmate had offered to fly out to Scandinavia to shake his hand.

For Dave, it was one of the most exciting trips we'd made. I mean, it'd been unusual enough to track down Dave Gormans in France and Italy . . . but Norway? This just wasn't the sort of place you'd expect to find a namesake.

At the airport we hopped onto a sleek, silver, bullet-shaped train with tellies that talked to you and teams of super-efficient female ticket collectors in smart designer jackets with pocket computers. We travelled at lightspeed, and twenty minutes later we were at Oslo S train station, right in the heart of the city. We could see our hotel from where we were standing, and so we decided to check in and dump our bags.

'Right,' I said. 'I'm going to call Hanne and tell her we're in Norway and arrange to meet her tomorrow. You still up for that?'

I had made it part of the conditions of coming to Norway that we'd travel up to Hanne's little village after we'd bagged our man. Dave happily agreed. After all, she'd given him a Dave Gorman. The least he could do was give her her boyfriend back.

'Okay. I'll go to my room and take a shower or something.'

But I didn't do that.

If there was one Dave Gorman in Norway, there could be two. Or even three. Maybe that had been why Dave hadn't seemed all that surprised to hear from me. Maybe he was bumping into Norwegian Dave Gormans left, right and centre. The thought got my blood pumping.

I'd learnt a lot from Ellis Henican and his *Newsday* article. If we were going to find another Dave Gorman over here, we were going to need publicity.

I ran downstairs and bought a sample of Norway's newspapers from the kiosk on the corner: the *Aftenposten* and the *Dagbladet*.

The *Aftenposten* appeared to be Norway's equivalent of the *Times*; a serious, nicely-set-out broadsheet with a traditional-looking logo. On the other hand, the *Dagbladet* appeared to be their equivalent of the *Sun*; a brash, colourful tabloid, with huge, black headlines and exclamation marks sprinkled liberally over the page. These would do, I thought.

Back in my room, I rang the *Aftenposten* first, as they looked as if they'd appreciate the seriousness of the quest.

The man on the newsdesk, however, wasn't too impressed. His name was Simen and he was very polite.

'Well . . . yes . . . it is a nice story you have. However, it is not really for us. But I wish you and your housemate all the best with your journey and I hope you have a nice time in Norway.'

I put the phone down, disheartened. Never mind, I still had the *Dagbladet* to go. I spoke to a man called Anders.

'Well . . . yes . . .' he said. 'It is a nice story you have. However, it is not really for us. . .'

My hopes were dashed, and my heart hit the floor. But Anders continued. . .

'But I would like to help you . . . could you maybe . . . *spice it up* a little. . .?'

Spice it up? How could I spice it up? My mind raced, trying to uncover spicy angles. Would it be wrong of me to imply that the Norwegian Dave was a stripper?

'Because the story just needs a little more . . . *spice*. . .'

I have no idea why I said what I said. I didn't want to, and I didn't mean to. I could feel the words welling up in my throat, collecting together and forming into a sentence. Even with the benefit of hindsight I am unable to explain why this sentence formed in my head and why I couldn't prevent it from emerging.

'We've got some t-shirts.'

Great. Really bloody spicy. He wants spice, I give him t-shirts.

'What *kind* of t-shirts?' said Anders, immediately.

Well, I was thinking on my feet.

'Er . . . "Stop Me If You're A Dave Gorman" t-shirts.'

'And you wear these all the time?'

'Yes.'

'Okay. Quickly, what hotel are you staying at?'

He said he'd be straight over. Well, this was intriguing. I sensed I had discovered something vital about Norwegian journalists here. So I phoned Simen at the *Aftenposten* again.

I said 'By the way, did I mention the t-shirts?'

'What t-shirts?'

'The "Stop Me If You're A Dave Gorman" t-shirts?'

'No, you didn't. What hotel are you staying at? I'll be around tomorrow morning – don't tell the *Dagbladet*!'

Somehow, unwittingly, I had successfully tapped the spicy vein of Norway. It was as simple as this: *in Norway, t-shirts are spicy!* The only problem was, we didn't have any. And Anders from the *Dagbladet* would be here any minute. . .

After making arrangements with Hanne, I had switched on the television in my hotel room to find an episode of *The Golden Girls* just beginning.

Someone began to thump at my door just as Rose was saying something quirky about St Olaf, and I waited for the punchline before swanning over to the door and opening it.

Guess who it was.

'Danny, we have to get some t-shirts right now! I lied to the Norwegian press and I seem to have accidentally caused some kind of media frenzy. A journalist is on his way round and we need to be wearing t-shirts when he gets here.'

I stared at him, blankly. He continued.

'We need to get some "Stop Me If You're A Dave Gorman" t-shirts, right away!'

'Do they sell those here?'

'I've no idea. It's unlikely. We're going to have to get some done specially.'

'Where?'

'There's a shopping centre opposite.'

Twenty minutes later we were the proud possessors – and slightly embarrassed wearers – of two green, "Stop Me If You're A Dave Gorman" t-shirts.

'Remember, Dan,' said Dave, back in the hotel. 'We wear these all the time on our travels, just in case.'

'Fine. But how long do we have to wear them today? I feel a bit of a berk. We look like American tourists on a really weird package holiday.'

'We only have to wear them while Anders is here. And tomorrow again when Simen from the *Aftenposten* arrives. Although I might keep wearing mine. I don't know why we didn't do this ages ago.'

The phone rang. Anders was in reception with a *Dagbladet* photographer.

'Wow, just look at those!' said Kris, immediately taken in by our ruse. 'You wear these things all the time?'

'Oh yes,' I said. 'You never know when you're going to bump into a Dave Gorman.'

'This is great.'

Clearly, they were trying to paint me as an obsessed nutcase. I thought I'd play along.

We'd been standing in the lobby for all of 30 seconds before Anders suggested we take a little drive, as he wanted to make sure that no one else got onto the story.

'Sure,' I said. 'Where shall we go?'

'I don't really want to say out loud in here,' he said. 'The car is outside.'

Anders drove us at speed through the wide, respectable streets of Oslo to Vigelandsparken, an open-air commemoration of the sculptor Gustav Vigeland, but, more importantly, 'a big open place where you can see people coming and it is much tougher to be spied upon.'

Novelty t-shirts are big news in Norway.

We stood beneath the obelisk in the centre of the park, surrounded by smaller granite sculptures of pot-bellied toddlers and, in the distance, frowning, growling bronze figures.

Once Anders felt safe, he began his interview, while Kris took picture after picture of Dave and me looking cheery with our t-shirts. They loved the things. So much so that they had failed to notice that they were clearly brand, spanking new. Dave's even had a 100 kroner price tag hanging off the back. But we got away with it, and the *Dagbladet* boys dropped us back at our hotel, urging us to keep them abreast of further developments. We waved Anders and Kris goodbye, and as soon as they were out of sight, I put my jacket on, keen to hide my ridiculous new apparel.

We'd had a nice time with Anders and Kris and I felt happy as we returned to the hotel. We'd only been in the country a couple of hours but the media campaign was already well underway. We'd call our established Norwegian DG on his mobile, arrange a meeting, then spend the evening celebrating in Oslo.

But as soon as we walked into the lobby, a man and a woman sitting on one of the sofas stood up, studied us, exchanged a few words with each other, and began to approach.

'Uh-oh,' said Dan. 'What's all this about?'

'Excuse me,' said the man, a shortish chap with glasses. 'Are you Dave Gorman?'

'Yes,' I said. 'How did you know that?'

The man and the woman looked at each other and then back at me.

'Your t-shirt.'

'Oh!,' I said. 'Yes. Right. I wear this all the time. Yes. So *that's* how people always know it's me, is it? Right.'

'I'm Simen from the *Aftenposten*.'

'I thought you were coming tomorrow,' I said.

'I was, but decided we should move on this. This is Katrina, my photographer. I was trying to call you at the hotel this last hour but you were not in. Where were you?'

'We went to . . . a . . . place,' said Dan, cleverly covering up the fact that we were in the company of the *Dagbladet*.

'Which place?' said Katrina.

'I can't pronounce it, I'm afraid.'

Dan was clever. Katrina seemed to accept this, and Simen continued.

'It's no problem. I checked your story out and I got through to the Dave Gorman you are set to meet in Norway. He said you hadn't arranged a time to meet yet, so I took the liberty of doing so. It's all arranged. But we have to leave now.'

'Where are we meeting him?'

'I don't want to tell you in here,' said Simen, his eyes scanning the room. 'The car is outside.'

Simen had arranged to meet this Dave Gorman in the small town of Sandvika. It was a twenty minute journey by car, although the route we took made it closer to 50, so keen was Simen to make sure we weren't 'being followed'. Plus, we were meeting Dave at the train station; not because that was particularly convenient for him, but because Simen thought it would be safer to meet somewhere totally random and neutral in case 'the TV journalists become aware of progressing developments'.

I wasn't sure how Simen would feel when he opened the *Dagbladet* up in a couple of days to find pictures of me and Dave grinning like fools by an obelisk in central Oslo. Perhaps we could tell him they were done with a long lens by some fiendish paparazzi, and just hope he didn't read the lengthy interview we'd done. It seemed silly to warn him now that he'd gone to all this effort, so Dave and I kept quiet and looked guilty in the back of the black *Aftenposten* Mercedes.

We arrived at Sandvika train station, parked up, had 50 or 60 pictures taken looking happy in our ever-popular t-shirts, and, once Simen had scoped the area to his satisfaction, we were allowed to go and stand under the big clock, as arranged.

It was quiet. Perhaps too quiet for Simen's liking. Standing with him and Katrina, who nervously looked at their watches and jabbered quickly to each other, all the time making sure that there were no rival photographers perched on the roof of the train station or dictaphones buried in the bushes, I realised that I didn't really know much Norwegian. I can say *øl*, which means beer, and I can say *takk*, which means thank you, and *skål*, which means cheers. Oh, and *buktaler*, which means ventriloquist. I think that's four words we should all learn in any language. One day you might get drunk with a Norwegian ventriloquist and you'll thank me.

Danny is far more accomplished in Norwegian than I am.

I can say *'flink jente, gå i sakkosekken!'* which means 'bad girl, go to your beanbag'. This is particularly handy if you own a dog, or, as in my case, have a Norwegian girlfriend, and a beanbag for her to go to.

I can also sing the songs *Mil Etter Mil* and *La Det Swinge*, the master-pieces entered into the Eurovision Song Contest by established singer-songwriter Jahn Teigen in 1977 and happy-go-lucky girl group Bobbysocks in 1985. It is not often I get to use these skills or recount these facts, so, as you can imagine, this was a very exciting day for me.

Katrina's grip on her camera became more tense every time a different, potential Norwegian Dave Gorman looked like he might be about to approach us. Perhaps this was her first big scoop, and she was nervous of missing out on the all-important photo that could launch her career. Perhaps the bosses at the *Aftenposten* had decided that as of today she was ready for the major league stories like this one, and this was her chance to show them what she could do.

But she suddenly raised her camera to her eyes and started clicking away. A young man was walking purposefully in our direction. He raised his hand to acknowledge the camera and grinned. Simen started to scribble in his notebook. Danny and I looked at each other and smiled. This was him. This was our Norwegian Dave Gorman.

'Hei!' he said.

'Hi,' I said back.

'Hello,' said Danny.

'Hei,' said Katrina.

'Hallo,' said Simen.

'Hei,' said Norwegian Dave, again.

There was a strange, awkward pause, while everyone stood around looking at each other. Katrina took another picture and then lowered her camera. Simen stopped scribbling and looked up.

'So . . .' said Norwegian Dave.

'Yep. Nice to meet you,' I said.

Simen wrote it down.

Another pause.

'You just do whatever you normally do,' said Simen. 'Imagine we're not here.'

'Well, that's it, really. We've met him, now.'

I looked at Danny and he shrugged and nodded. Katrina looked at Simen, who also shrugged and then said something in Norwegian. She took another picture.

'I know!' said Danny. 'Let's go somewhere and have a chat about the whole Dave Gorman thing.'

There was an audible sigh of relief from all concerned, and everyone agreed that that was a great idea. We could get to know Norwegian Dave, tell him a bit about the 23 of his namesakes we'd already met, Katrina could take more pictures, and Simen could write some more stuff down.

I patted Dan on the back, gratefully.

We made our way to a small cafe behind the station called Egon's, and I got my photo album out and began to learn a little about Dave Gorman the Norwegian.

Well, that's the first thing. Although he considers himself to be Norwegian, has lived in Norway since he was two, speaks better Norwegian than he does English, and even *dreams* in Norwegian, Dave's Irish-born. Now eighteen and preparing for university, his parents moved from Ireland to Sandvika because of the oil industry, and he'd joined us today after finishing his shift at a nearby kiosk, where he worked selling cigarettes and lottery tickets.

'I've got a brother called Alan David Gorman. You could meet him if you like.'

'No thanks.'

'Well, I've a cousin in Ireland called David Gorman. But I've only met him once, when I was very little. I can't remember where he lives exactly. I'll try and find out and get you the details.'

'Great. I think a trip to the place where it all began might be necessary soon.'

'How do you mean?', asked Dave. 'Because you know the name *isn't* Irish, don't you?'

This was the first time I'd heard these words. Could it be true that the Gorman surname wasn't actually Irish?

'It's actually a Norwegian name, originally. I mean, this is just a theory, but the name "Gorman" sounds exactly the same as the Norwegian word for "farmer": *gårman*. Now, when the clan moved to Scotland hundreds of years ago, the Scottish didn't have the special letter "å", and so they just changed the name to "Gorman". That's what I think, anyway.'

This was interesting. More than likely wrong, but interesting nevertheless. It filled me with renewed hope that the *Aftenposten* article would uncover some more Dave Gormans over here for me. But when I turned round to tell Katrina and Simen, they'd gone. They'd left separately during the meeting, according to Danny, Katrina to develop her film, and Simen because he had to file his copy.

We talked some more and then Dave offered us a lift back into town. He'd borrowed his girlfriend's grandfather's car specially. Back in Oslo, I shook his hand vigorously. It had been great to meet him.

Now it was time to celebrate.

Our spirits were high, and what better way to treat them than to drown them? We'd had a very exciting day, what with our dealings with the Norwegian media, and celebrity status in the Scandinavian territories was now more or less guaranteed.

Unfortunately, beer at our hotel worked out at around £5 a pint. In the pub next door the prices were the same. In the bar around the corner, the price was just as ludicrous. Norway is not a place that treats its beer drinkers well.

It was decided that if we were to spend our money wisely, we would have to invest it in spirits. We walked into a bar called *Nichol & Son* on Olav V's gate, the walls of which were decorated with nothing but huge, black and white pictures of Jack Nicholson. The barman, who admitted to us that he'd never actually seen a Jack Nicholson film, suggested we try *aquavit* – something that we'd have flatly turned down had we realised it was a kind of Norwegian tequila. Tequila, as we have already taught you, is evil.

We drank litres of the stuff.

I can remember dancing. And a lot of singing.

Our celebrations, after the bar, had taken us, joyful and raucous, past the Royal Palace, up Karl Johans gate and the *Domkirke*, and through Oslo town centre. We stumbled into another bar, this one by the name of *Stravinsky* (a fact I can only relay to you thanks to a pack of matches I found in my pocket some time later), and then into a club on Rosenkrantz gate called Head On. It was there that, if my somewhat hazy recollections are to be believed, Dave and I attempted some impromtu, *aquavit*-fuelled breakdancing to '70s funk, much to the delight of the gathered Norwegian spectators.

This would certainly explain why, the next morning, when my watch bleep-bleeped loudly in my ear, I awoke on the floor of Dave's hotel room with two very bruised elbows and a bad ankle. I also had a small can of Heineken digging into my hip.

My head was pounding in much the same way it had pounded as I sobered up and found myself on a train heading for East Fife a month or two before; savagely, and with a ferocious sense of regret.

I looked up at Dave and tried to make my voice work. He was lying in a ridiculously awkward position on the bed, and if I hadn't known better, I'd have thought his arms grew out of his head. He was drooling and he seemed to have a black eye.

'Dave,' I said, before clearing my throat and actually saying it out loud. 'Dave!'

He stirred with a grunt, looked me in the eye and for one split second he appeared to be fine. Then the headache began.

'Oh . . . my . . . God . . .' he croaked, looking at me in desperation. 'Water . . . please . . . Dan . . . water. . .'

I stood myself up as best I could and walked into the bathroom, poured some water into a glass, downed it, poured some more in, and brought it to Dave, now sitting up on the bed trying to remove an odd yellow stain from his shirt.

'How did *that* happen?' I asked.

'We must have had a kebab, or something.'

'No. I mean your black eye.'

His hand instinctively reached up to his face, and he touched his eye. The bruising seemed to rub off on his hand. I studied it.

'Mascara?'

'Eh?'

'How did you end up with mascara on your eye?'

'Well, *you* can talk, Johnny Hotlips.'

I walked back into the bathroom and looked at my face. I was wearing bright pink lipstick. I washed it off before people started to talk.

'How did my elbows get so bruised?' I asked him.

'I don't know. Mine hurt, too.'

'We should get some alkaseltzer, or something. And some breakfast. We're on a bus to Hanne's house in. . .'. I looked at my watch. 'An hour.'

'Can't we just stay here? Can't you just phone her?'

'No. Come on. You've got your Dave Gorman. And the headache to prove it. We'll spend a quiet evening in Fagernes, okay? Now let's get out of here, this room stinks.'

'Fine. Let me just wash my face.'

Dave hobbled into the bathroom and applied water to his mascara. I couldn't be sure, but I think he might have been wearing a bit of blusher, too.

I straightened myself up, chewed on a mint, and tried to find my shoes.

'Dave, where are my shoes?'

'I dunno, Dan,' he called from the bathroom. 'Have you checked you aren't wearing them?'

'Of course I have'. I checked. 'I'm not.'

'Well . . . under the bed?'

I looked.

'No.'

'Er . . . in one of the drawers?'

'Why would we put our shoes . . . okay, hang on, I'll look. . .'

They weren't there. And it wasn't just my pair. Dave's were nowhere to be seen, either. We tore that room apart looking for our shoes. We checked under the bed three or four times. We shook the duvet down. We ran to my room. We looked under my bed three or four times. We shook my duvet down. Nowhere. That's when it struck Dave.

'The mini-bar!'

We quickly pulled the door of my mini-bar open. It was empty. We ran back to Dave's room, and checked his mini-bar. It was full of empty bottles. We winced at the surprise expense. But not one, single shoe was to be found, anywhere.

We sat in our socks in the lobby of the hotel, all checked out and ready to go, but with an air of puzzlement still hanging over our heads.

'Dave,' I said. 'I think we must have sold our shoes for booze.'

He sighed.

'I think so too', he said, before joining me in a smile. 'We must have had a *great* time.'

We only had twenty five minutes before we were supposed to be on a bus to Fagernes. We needed a shoeshop. And breakfast.

We walked out of our hotel and into the Europa shopping centre opposite.

'I'll get us some shoes, Dan, you get us some food and headache pills.'

'I think I should come with you for the shoes, Dave.'

'There's no time, is there? I've got the credit card, I'll get the shoes, you're size 10, right? You run to the supermarket and get us some food for the journey.'

I watched Danny jog, his socked feet slapping against the marble flooring, into a *Kiwi Minipris* shop, and I set about finding us some respectable shoes.

When I'd come out of the *Kiwi*, Dave was nowhere to be seen. In our slightly below-par state we'd forgotten to agree on where to meet. I'd assumed it would be where we'd separated. That was what common sense dictated, after all. Time was ticking away, and we now only had twelve minutes before we had to be sitting on a bus, pulling out of Oslo station.

So I remained where I was. Surely that was the sensible thing to do. After all, he'd seen me go in here, he'd know what to do. I looked through my plastic bag full of shopping. Bread, jam, a big block of *Norvegia* cheese, headache pills, two big bottles of water, chewing gum, and two extremely expensive Mars Bars. Oslo seems to treat its chocoholics with the same contempt it has for those who like beer.

I scanned the place for my flatmate. Plenty of Norwegians, but not one Dave. This was typical behaviour. I looked at my watch. Time was against me. It would take perhaps five minutes to run to the bus station. More if you're running with bags of shopping. Even more if you're not wearing any shoes.

I began a quick march around the shops nearest the *Kiwi*, licking the sweat off my upper lip as I nervously studied the window displays to see if I could see any shoes, or any Daves trying them on.

If I missed this bus because of his tardiness I would be in big trouble once again. Hanne was expecting me this afternoon – she'd be waiting at the village bus stop – and if I didn't show, well . . . I didn't like to think what she'd do to me.

I looked at my watch. Six minutes to go. I made an instant decision. I had to get that bus, whether Dave was with me or not. He'd know what had happened. It was his own fault. I'd get a message to him later.

I ditched the bottles of water and ran through the shopping centre, over the bridge, through another shopping centre, and continued along those lines until I met the big sign saying *Oslo Buss-stasjon*.

I was already sitting on the bus waiting for Danny as he came into view, his ankle clearly causing him as much pain as the cobbled area near the entrance to the bus station was causing his thinly-covered feet.

He didn't seem at all pleased to see me sitting at the window as he got closer. But that's just selfish. He knows I hate the aisle seat.

We were just pulling out when he banged on the door and the driver allowed him on board.

'What the hell are you doing on here?' he said as he clambered up the steps, his face red and flustered.

'This is the *Valdres Expressen* bus. We're going to Fagernes, aren't we?'

'Well, yes . . . but I could have missed the bus! I had to run!'

'You should have left earlier.'

'You left me at that supermarket! You never said you wouldn't be back, did you? What would you have said to Hanne if you'd turned up in Fagernes without me? What would *I* have told her if you'd turned up in Fagernes without me?'

'I'm sure she would have seen the funny side of it.'

The bus finished reversing out of our parking space, and we were on our way.

Dan sat down and exhaled heavily. He was very sweaty.

'You shouldn't run without shoes on. It's bad for your feet,' I offered. Someone has to look after Danny, sometimes.

'Then give me my shoes. Here's your bloody food.'

He threw the plastic bag down on my lap.

'Did you get water?'

'No,' he said.

'You look like you could do with some, after your run.'

I knew what would cheer him up. I picked up the box I'd placed beneath our seat and opened it, proudly presenting Danny with his brand new shoes.

He stared at them.

'What the hell are those?'

'They're *lobber*.'

'They're what?'

'*Lobber*. Come on, Dan, they're traditional.'

'Look at them!'

It had been a bit of an impulse buy, admittedly, but I'd brought back two pairs of grey shoes, made of felt, with blue plastic soles, and tips that rose and doubled back on themselves.

'They look like shoes an elf would wear!'

'They're traditional.'

'You said that.'

Danny didn't seem too happy.

'They're all I could find.'

'I don't believe you. This is twenty-first-century Oslo we're in. Not some kind of medieval Norwegian village. What, did you have to barter with a minstrel down the market for these? I passed a *Footlocker* on the way here, why didn't you go there?'

I thought about it. 'They're traditional!'

The bus journey from Oslo to Fagernes is a three-hour, 300-kilometre drive through the mountains. It's about an hour from Lillehammer, and we intended to spend one evening there – just long enough for me to make amends with Hanne before travelling all the way back to Oslo for our morning flight home.

At a place called Nes i Årdal – which I would be tempted to say was a town were it not for the fact that it seemed to be just a petrol station – we took a ten-minute toilet break.

'This is exciting,' said Dave.

'People are staring at our shoes' I said.

'They're *lobber*,' said Dave, sounding bored with my protestations. 'And they're traditional.'

'We look like tits. And sod the fact that they're traditional. If a Norwegian man visited London and dressed up in full Morris Dancing gear, would you think "oh, look how traditional he is", or would you think "oh, look at that tit"?'

'I like them. I want to be the first person in the East End to wear them.'

'I don't think that'll be a problem. I dare say you'll also be the first person *killed* in the East End while wearing them.'

'That'd be cool.'

It's a curious fact about Norwegian petrol stations that they also double as sausage shops. Dave and I joined the back of the queue while every other person from our bus ordered their sausage and applied their own unique measurements of dried onions and spicy mustards. We all then marched onto the bus, sausages in hand, and munched them down while the driver – who was first in the queue – finished his off. Everyone on board, satisfying moustaches of mustard on their upper lips, we set off again.

The road that takes you into Fagernes drags you past Strandefjorden, a fjord that stretches for miles and lies beneath a mountain that's missing its top. A troll pushed it into the water many years ago because he was a bit angry with it. That's what the Norwegians believe, anyway, and who were we to argue with them?

We arrived in Fagernes in the middle of the afternoon, and were a little surprised to see most of the village gathered around a marquee on the edge of the lake, near the village hotel.

'What's going on here?' asked Dave, stepping off the bus behind me.

'I'm not sure.'

Hanne was waiting by one of the trees near the bus stop, making full use of the sun. I jogged to her and hugged her.

'I'm so sorry about all of this,' I said. 'But thanks for . . . y'know . . . finding that Dave Gorman. . . .'

'I see you brought Dave with you', she said, nodding to where Dave was standing, surveying the crowd.

'Yeah. I couldn't really leave him in Oslo. *Someone* has to take care of him. Do you mind?'

She smiled.

'No. It's okay. Well, I mind a bit. But it's fine.'

Dave started to walk towards us. Hanne noticed his shoes.

'Oh, Jesus, what is he wearing now? Are those *lobber*? What is he thinking?'

'Well . . . they *are* traditional,' I said.

'Yeah, but he might as well wear a bloody Viking helmet with them.'

'Hello Hanne!' he said. 'We're in Fagernes!'

'Yes, you are. And you're wearing *lobber*!'

'Oh yes. Do you like them?'

'Er . . . yes. They're very . . . traditional.'

'See, Danny? Told you. Danny didn't want to wear his at first, but I think he's getting to like them.'

Hanne flinched. She looked down at my feet and took in the whole, ghastly, but *very* traditional, sight.

'You are *both* wearing *lobber*?' she said, as if trying to cope with the concept by enunciating each syllable and posing the result as a question.

She sighed.

'And that is fine with me.'

Hanne had clearly been doing some anger management since she'd been back.

Danny and Hanne sloped off for a coffee and a cosy chat. It was good that they were going to sort this out.

I was standing by the side of a beer tent, trying to work out what was so important that an entire village was standing around a marquee drinking bottles of *Ringnis* and babbling excitedly. I bought a bottle myself – hair of the dog – and was minding my own business when a man in a stars and stripes t-shirt left a group of his friends and approached me. He appeared slightly drunk.

'Det er sjelden å se en voksen mann ha på seg lobber disse dager . . .' he said. 'Du må være litt rar. . .'

'I'll stop you there if I may,' I said. 'I'm English'.

'You are? Hey, hello and welcome in Fagernes!', he said, in an accent more than a little affected by years of watching subtitled *Seinfeld, Starsky & Hutch* and *The Golden Girls* on TV.

'Thank you very much', I said.

'What are you doing here?' he said, followed by a little burp.

I thought it best not to recount the whole story.

'My flatmate is visiting his girlfriend. She's from here.'

'Okay. I thought you were here for the *Mannsfestival*.'

'What's that?'

'The *Mannsfestival*? It's a celebration of manliness. It's something we do every year in this village. All the men of Fagernes compete.'

'A celebration of manliness? That sounds great. Me and my flatmate are big fans of your Norwegian ways. Look at my *lobber*.'

I indicated my feet, cheerily.

'Yes. I noticed. Just look at those. You are actually wearing them.'

'Yes.'

'Out, in front of other people.'

'Yes.'

'Well. You are a better man than I.'

'And thus I win the *Mannsfestival!*'

Hanne and I spent a lovely hour talking in the sun by the village pond and eventually we came to a good-hearted agreement. She was enjoying being home, seeing her friends, seeing her family. But she wanted to come back to London. She'd only do this, however, when I stopped acting like 'a mental'. But, crucially, I could continue. For a little while, at least. Until either Dave, or myself, lost the bet. Within reason.

'A month would be pushing it,' she said. 'Do you understand? I don't want to come home and find that you're always away again. Always catching more Daves. I'm coping with it better now, but don't push me.'

I assured her it would all be over by the time she got back. Dave would give up sooner or later, surely. We couldn't keep this pace up. There was no way. She smiled, and said she was banking on that, but that it was nice to be back in Norway for a little while.

But this was good. I now had at least a month to prove Dave wrong, before Hanne started to get annoyed again. And he still had another 30 Dave Gormans to meet. He couldn't do that; I'd seen his credit card bill. I smiled as I thought of my victory, the pressure of keeping Hanne happy gone. For the time being, at least.

We wandered, hand in hand, from the pond, past the village hall, and back to where we'd left Dave. For some reason, he was bouncing from foot to foot.

'What are you doing?' I asked.

'I'm limbering up.'

'Oh no,' said Hanne. 'Oh please, no.'

'What is it? What are you limbering up for?'

'I was joking with a drunk man. I told him I was manlier than him because of my *lobber*, and now he's made us enter the *Mannsfestival* because of it!'

'What do you mean, "us"?'

'It was all very jovial and jokey, but then the man actually put our names down for it.'

'Hang on – you're talking as if I'm entering this competition too.'

'He put *your* name down as well.'

'Eh? How did he *know* my name?'

'He put your name down as "that other *lobber* fool", or something.'

'Yes,' said Hanne, pointing at a blackboard set up on the grass. 'There it is: *"Den Andre Lobbe Idioten"*.'

And so it was that, despite Hanne's best attempts to get my name taken off the scoreboard, Dave and I entered the *Mannsfestival 2000* in the tiny Norwegian village of Fagernes, witnessed by an audience of several hundred.

I would love to be able to tell you that we performed admirably, and were carried aloft on the shoulders of the assembled crowds, as they chanted our names and made us their new Kings. But sadly we came second and third from last, saved only from the humiliation of actually being the least manly men in the place by a sixteen-year-old boy who appeared to weigh less than an apple.

I did fairly well on the Tobacco Spitting, and Dave did himself proud on the Leg Wrestling. Hanne was annoyed when I dropped her during the Wife Carrying Race, though – a competition which Dave had had to enter using Hanne's little brother, Eirik.

Eirik, incidentally, ended up considerably higher on the final scoreboard than either of us two. My place in that family is far from assured.

We had a great evening in Fagernes. After the competition – which I still maintain I won – we ate barbecued elk steaks and reindeer, drank Ringnis and Hansa, we sang songs, and we oohed and aahed at the pretty fireworks. And then Danny, Hanne and I all went back to her house, where we sat in the garden and looked at the mountains. It stays light and warm until nearly midnight in the summer in Norway. It wills you to stay there.

The next morning Danny kissed Hanne goodbye and we got back on the bus that would take us to the airport.

Once there, Danny disappeared for a minute and I bought a copy of the *Aftenposten*. I was pleased to see that not only did our story take up all of page 3 of this fine Norwegian newspaper, complete with substantial photographic evidence documenting our meeting, but we were also a front-page selling point. We'd done well. Simen had printed my e-mail address, and told Norway to spread the word. If another Dave Gorman were anywhere to be found in the entire country, we'd find them off the back of this, for sure. I checked my internet account at the airport internet cafe. There was nothing Norwegian. Yet.

Danny returned with new shoes on.

Chapter 13

WILL THE REAL DAVE GORMAN PLEASE STAND UP

On our way back from Norway a strange thing happened. I was busy looking at the in-flight meal trying to work out where the plastic ended and the food began, when I suddenly became aware that I was being stared at. Across the aisle I met the gaze of a curious, elderly, female passenger. She waved at me coquettishly, then turned away smiling, before turning back and waving again.

'Dan', I said. 'I think that lady is waving at me.'

'Which one?' he asked, not looking up from his in-flight magazine.

'The one who's waving. At me.'

'You're probably right then. She probably is waving at you. I expect she's noticed your *lobber*.'

'My feet are under the chair.'

'Maybe you should show her them then, and she might stop waving at you.'

'It's freaking me out. . .'

'Oh, let me have a look at her', said Dan, looking up for the first time in the conversation.

I turned back to look across the aisle and found myself pointing at an empty chair.

Dan smirked.

'Are you imagining Scandinavian beauties who find you strangely fascinating again?'

'No I'm not . . . to be honest, she looked like a right old bat.'

There was a tap on my shoulder. I froze momentarily before turning to find the inevitable. There, smiling broadly at me was the 'old bat'. It seemed she did find me strangely fascinating.

'Excuse me', she said, waving a copy of the *Aftenposten* under my nose. 'Are you Dave Gorman?'

In the days to come I would look back on that moment and it would prove to be a moment of huge importance and inspiration to me.

The trip to Norway had been a huge success for both of us. While Dave had met his 24th namesake, I had managed to enter into detailed negotiations with my girlfriend which I hoped would ensure my relationship with her wasn't about to crash and burn in the bonfire of my flatmate's insanity.

It was nice to see that Dave was excited by what the *Aftenposten* article might yield. I was hoping it would turn up another Dave Gorman in Norway, too, to be honest. Hanne was going to stay over there for a while, and if I was going to see her sometime soon it'd be because there was a Dave Gorman involved.

And besides, while I still wanted to win the bet, I may as well come clean and tell you that a part of me was now quite happy to see Dave win. At least that way it would all be over.

Back in the East End, Dave ran off to check his e-mails and I filled the kettle. Five minutes later, tea on the table, he returned.

'Anything from Norway?', I asked. If there was, I wanted to be on the next flight out there.

'Nope,' said Dave, looking slightly confused. 'Not from Norway. . .'

I had fully expected to receive a couple of e-mails off the back of the *Aftenposten* article. This was, after all, one of Norway's biggest newspapers.

And sure enough, that day we returned, and in the two days that followed it, I did indeed receive e-mails as a result of it. Twelve of them. None of them turned out to be much help to the quest, but they were all linked by one, odd, common bond.

They were all from Denmark.

A typical example reads:

Hello Mr. Dave Gorman. My name is Jeppe Frandsen. I am from Denmark. I am sorry my name is not Dave Gorman. Good luck with your search. Goodbye.

Now, I found this very odd. Why Denmark? Why not Norway? Who were all these Danes and how did they hear about the journey? Could news of the t-shirts have spread that fast?

So I wrote back to Mr Frandsen and asked him how he'd heard of my search. He wrote back to inform me that he had read about it in the newspaper. But not the *Aftenposten*. Nor the *Dagbladet*. No, Jeppe, and millions of other Danes like him, had read about me on the front page of the *Berlingske Tidende*. And this, I am reliably informed, is one of Denmark's biggest daily papers.

Somehow – and don't ask me how – we had become front page news in Denmark . . . and we hadn't even been there. What in God's name was on page 7 if the fact that two men in t-shirts had been to Norway qualified as front-page news?

I was about to relate our new-found international celebrity status to Danny when the phone rang. It was my agent, Rob, a man possessed of a cheeky barrow-boy charm and a staccato delivery that manages to miss a lot of words out while still, somehow, making sense.

'Dave? Rob,' he said, which I think should have at least started with a 'hello', had an 'it's' in the middle, and ended with a 'here'. But I knew what he meant.

'Hello Rob, how are you?'

'Good. So, Edinburgh?'

'Edinburgh?'

'Festival?'

This was Rob's way of asking me if I planned to do a show at that year's Edinburgh Festival.

'I don't think so.'

'Why?'

'I'm really busy at the moment, Rob. It's a bit complicated, really. I'm trying to find other Dave Gormans. I've not really got time to think of anything else. I'm not sure I've got the time this year!'

There was a pause. He was trying to calculate the minimum response. Eventually he plumped for 'Okay. Bye.' The phone went down.

I stared at my feet for a moment, deep in thought. I'd forgotten about the festival this year. I never do that. It's usually the highlight of my year. I stared at my feet some more, and an idea started to form. We had appeared in newspapers in New York, Norway and Denmark so far. But only one of these articles had led us to a new Dave Gorman. I didn't think it was a coincidence that this had happened in the English-speaking country. Surely we were missing a trick here. We were wasting our time trying to get into the Scandinavian press; they operated in countries where Dave Gormans were thin on the ground, expensive to meet, and even more expensive to celebrate.

Surely we'd be better off trying to get some interest out of the British media? I knew that they were more sophisticated – a simple t-shirt would never make the story spicy enough for the Brits – but maybe there was another way of getting their attention? I suddenly decided that I *was* going to take a show to Edinburgh, after all. I rang Rob. His response was clinical: 'Sure? Okay. Bye.'

I figured that a stage show about the search for Dave Gormans might interest the press and it might even encourage new Dave Gormans to come forward. The elderly Norwegian lady from the plane had already given me the perfect title: 'Are You Dave Gorman?'

I figured that if I saw an advert for a show of that name, I'd think to myself, 'yes, I am' and go along to find out what it was about. I had every reason to believe that other Dave Gormans would feel the same.

Rob was concerned that non-Dave-Gormans might not be that interested in it as an idea, but it didn't matter if *they* came did it? Dave Gormans were what I was after. They were my target audience, after all.

I whisked Dan off to the greasy spoon café opposite the flat. We ordered two all-day breakfasts and proceeded to make them last all day while discussing how to turn what had happened so far into 'a show'.

Rob had immediately booked a venue so there was no turning back. For the month of August I would be 'performing' this 'show' every night in a 'theatre'. Not a real theatre, mind. It was a room that normally formed part of Edinburgh University Students Union, but with the help of some scaffolding and copious amounts of black cloth, it would, for the purposes of the festival, be masquerading as a theatre.

After two or three days of thinking, playing the cafe's remarkable *On The Buses* themed fruit machine and clogging our arteries with full English breakfasts, we decided that the best way to relate this story to an audience was to just, well, to just tell it to them.

The only thing I needed to organise was some way of showing

everyone the photos of our travels. I paid a visit to Anand, an acquaintance of mine who can be found developing photos in a wardrobe-sized shop in the middle of Piccadilly Circus tube station. He converted all our snaps into photographic slides that I could project onto a large screen.

I figured that would be quicker than passing them round.

Dave was seriously going to go through with this. He was going to go on stage in front of members of the public and tell them what he had done and what he had made me do. I had imagined this situation before now, but somehow I'd always seen it happening within a courtroom setting.

But the prospect of basing the bet in Edinburgh for a month didn't bother me at all. I'd spent every August for the last six years working up there, and so it felt natural to be going back for a seventh. And I could see Dave's point. Millions of people from all over the world go to the Edinburgh Festival every year. I suppose *some* of them must be Dave Gormans.

Crucially, this also meant staying in one place for an entire month, rather than sitting in a car for hours on end driving from town to town meeting slightly bewildered men. That I wouldn't mind at all.

I made calls to a couple of people and found work at the festival. A few features here, a couple of articles there, and I'd have as much time as I wanted to go and see shows. That's the good thing about the festival – you're never short of a show to see. In the course of my duties over three weeks in 1998, I saw 51 shows. The year after, I saw 63. Maybe this year I could go even further.

'Of course, you'll have to be there every night,' said Dave.

'Oh, yes. I'll be there, waiting in the bar for you.'

'No, I mean at the show.'

'What do you mean, "I mean at the show"?'

'If a Dave Gorman turns up, you have to be there. Otherwise I could be making him up.'

'Er . . . no. I'll believe you, it's okay. I think I know you well enough by now.'

'No no. You need to be there to document the meeting. And also, I think it'd help motivate people. I want them to help me prove you wrong. You'll be a hate figure! It'll be brilliant!'

'I don't want to be a hate figure, Dave!'

'Oh, don't worry. I won't hate you. It'll just be the general public. Hey, you might get beaten up and make front page news – a Dave Gorman would be bound to turn up if that happened!'

'Are you going to have me beaten up, now? Is that what you're saying?'

'I'm just saying that you getting beaten up would be good for the cause.'

'You make it sound like a religion, Dave.'

I watched his eyes glass over as he contemplated the idea, as if considering whether creating a Dave Gorman religion might be the next step forward for us.

'Dave. Come on. I'm not sitting there every night for a month to hear the same story, which will never be new to me because I was actually there for the whole thing anyway, and which I've already heard you recount to people dozens of times, and which I myself have also recounted dozens of times to dozens of people . . . it'll be very boring.'

'No it won't and yes you are. It's for the good of the bet.'

It suddenly seemed like I *would* see more shows than I'd seen in any previous year. The problem was, they would all be the same one.

As the festival got nearer, Dave started to get a little nervous. I can't say that I blame him; he was planning a month of daily confessions to his own obsessive-compulsive disorder. He decided that before we headed back up to Scotland, the sensible thing would be to 'test the story out' on some people in London.

The Riverside Studios can be found in Hammersmith. Remarkably, around 70 people found them one night in July and decided to watch a show they knew nothing about, other than its title: 'Are You Dave Gorman?'

Rob had sent a fax to *The Guardian* asking them to put the starting time of the show in that day's theatre listings, and Danny and I had printed up a small notice and put it in our local post office window. So word was out.

I told those 70 people the story with all the earnestness it deserved.

I told them about the trip to France that had almost ended in failure but which had been rescued by a trip to Greenwich. About our unplanned trip to Eastbourne which had resulted in uncovering Daves all along the South Coast. About gay Dave

Gorman, and Jewish Dave Gorman, and the Dave Gorman senior who presented us with Dave Gorman junior. I told it honestly, and I told it straight. And they stayed in their seats to hear all about it. That was a good sign.

But after I'd told them about meeting Norway Dave, I had something very important I had to make sure they understood.

I needed them to know that this wasn't primarily a show. This 'show' was just something I was doing to try and find more Dave Gormans. I still had some way to go. I was still 30 short of my target. I began to sweat profusely as I asked them to do their best to find me new Dave Gormans. I tried to look deep into as many eyes as I could, trying hard to convince them of the seriousness of my quest.

Coming up now was the crucial moment. A final, vital part of the evening that had taken the best part of an hour to get to. This is what the whole evening had been in aid of.

I took a deep breath.

'Ladies and gentlemen, you know how seriously I take this,' I said. 'You know the lengths to which I will go to find another Dave Gorman. I now have to ask. . .'

Another deep breath.

'Is there anyone here, in this room, tonight. . .'

I scanned the room.

'. . . who is called Dave Gorman?'

A silence.

I watched as various audience members turned their heads left and right in search of any sign of a Dave Gorman. I searched with them. But nothing.

I was about to move on but there was a gasp somewhere to my right. My head turned in slow motion to the source of the gasp. It was a woman. She was looking behind her at a man. He was wearing a stripy blue shirt and had his hand in the air. More people gasped as they turned and registered the sight. Still seemingly in slow motion, I clapped my hands together and made some unrecognisable noise of surprise. The audience fell into a hush.

'You're a Dave Gorman?' I asked. 'Really?'

His response was slow in coming. He was working the crowd.

'Yes,' he finally said.

There was uproar. The room exploded into a cacophony of cheers and claps . . . I was stunned. It had worked! The show had found us a new Dave Gorman! A 25th! We were onto something –

something that had made this man's wife drive him all the way from Enfield to see a show she'd simply read the title of in the small print of *The Guardian*. I assumed it was *The Guardian* she'd seen. It seemed unlikely she'd have read about it in our post office.

I called Dave up onto the stage to take a bow, lost in my own bizarre little world. Danny stepped forward and took the now standard picture to record the meeting and I became dizzy with the emotion. But my sensible head took over; I asked Dave for identification and, when he satisfied the room that he was indeed a Dave Gorman, the audience cheered him once more, with double the vigour. A collection of strangers was cheering a stranger for having the same name as another stranger. That's not something that happens too often.

It was then that I remembered I was still on stage.

This was all very odd. Odd . . . but exciting. This was the first time a Dave Gorman had come to find us. I sat back in my seat, camera in hand, and tried to make sense of it all.

I promised to speak with Dave a little later and then tried to wrap up the show as planned.

We'd come up with one idea that we thought might attract the attention of the press, and thus land us some more Dave Gormans. It was certainly more 'spicy' than the t-shirts.

I was going to offer people £200 if they would change their name by deed poll to Dave Gorman. I mean – fair enough. No one would actually *do* it, because it's not exactly a life-changing amount of money. Most people who win a million quid immediately say, 'I'm not going to let it change my life', so you wouldn't expect anyone to actually change their life for one five thousandth of the sum, now, would you?

But that wasn't the point. The point was, it was an angle. And papers love angles. I wanted to get the story into a paper where it could be read by a real, live, willing-to-meet-me Dave Gorman.

I scoped the room for any potential journalists. One man had brought a hat with him, so I reasoned that if it was going to be anyone, it was going to be him. This was the bit where Dave was going to flash some cash and see whether or not the Great British Public could be persuaded that being a Dave Gorman was actually something quite pleasurable. Which it might well be. It's sharing a flat with one that's the problem.

'So,' said Dave, sweating and happy. 'We've got a real live Dave Gorman in the audience tonight . . . but the rest of you can still help me.'

I glanced at the people sitting on the front row. They looked like they actually wanted to help.

'I am offering £200 to anyone here, who is prepared to change their name, legally, to Dave Gorman. . .'

If it's possible, the room fell even more silent than it had been. Someone giggled. Then, from right behind my seat, a voice pierced the darkness.

'*I'll* fuckin' do it!'

I span round to see a man with a shaved head and his hand proudly raised. The audience erupted into a cheer, but Dave looked confused. . .

I didn't know what to do. I was stunned. I hadn't been expecting anyone to say yes.

I looked deep into the potential Dave Gorman's eyes.

'Will you really?', I asked.

'Yes.' He said it quickly and clearly. This was a man who had made his mind up. The audience cheered louder still.

'What's your name at the minute?' I asked.

'Colin. Colin Hurley.'

'Colin?'

I considered his name versus mine.

'You're doing a wise thing,' I said, and shook his hand.

Uh-oh. Dave shook Colin's hand. What had he done that for? That was virtually a legally binding contract – a legally binding contract made in plain view of witnesses. *Plenty* of witnesses. Witnesses that were cheering, clapping and whooping. One of those witnesses stood up. His friends on either side of him joined him. Soon more people were standing, shouting the praises of this man called Colin. He had become their hero. They loved him.

Dave and I packed the car and prepared for the seven-hour drive up to Edinburgh. The show – and again, 'show' is perhaps too strong a word – it was more of a talk, a lecture, or a presentation of sorts – ran for 27 nights at the festival.

We didn't know what would happen while we were there. But what did happen surprised and delighted us both . . . because it achieved precisely what we'd hoped it would. . .

● Word was spreading like wildfire – the story of our journey was discussed on several TV shows, from the heavyweight arts discussion of BBC2's *Edinburgh Review* to throwaway fun pop TV like *Top of the Pops @ Play*. I appeared on several cable TV shows, and even Sky TV's One o'clock News to try and get the message spread across the land.

● I made an overnight trip back down to the East End of London in order to appear on Channel 4's *The Big Breakfast* to do an interview with the idiot-savant otherwise known as Richard Bacon. He thrilled me by introducing me to three brand-spanking new Dave Gormans that the programme's researchers had found.

● We were visited at the theatre by Dave Gormans 1, 4 & 5, all of whom were greeted with huge ovations from audiences purely for sharing my name.

● One new Dave Gorman, also living in Edinburgh, attended the show. We were delighted to meet him – as were the audience – even though his heavily-pregnant wife declined my kind offer of 'financial assistance' should they choose to make the newborn Gorman a 'Dave'.

● Six more people volunteered to change their names – David, Iain, Dan, Graham, Pascale and Kelly. When you read that list, you might notice that two of those names are unisex in quality. There are Pascales and Kellys in the world of either gender – but these two were both quite definitely female. We hadn't expected anyone to say yes to this request, let alone seven of them, let alone two girls! We took their details and 'promised' to get back to them about it at a later date.

● A producer asked me if I would tell the story to an audience in their theatre every night for a week. The Comedy Theatre was designed in 1881 by Thomas Verity. It seats nearly 800 people in the stalls, dress circle, royal circle and balcony. It has a lot of red velvet and gilding knocking about the place. It's in the heart of the London's West End. In short, it's a 'proper' theatre. It was a chance to spread the news yet further and uncover more namesakes. I said yes.

● As hoped, another new Dave Gorman attended the Comedy Theatre show. As did a Dave Gurman and a Dave O'Gorman. Both close, but no cigar.

Now, all this was very exciting indeed – by the end of it all, thanks to Dave Gormans in Hammersmith, Edinburgh and then the West End, as well as three being delivered on a *Big Breakfast* plate, we had added six new namesakes to the tally. We were up to 30.

And while we'd been in Edinburgh, not one day had gone by without a stranger approaching one or both of us in a bar, cafe or on the street and promising to aid the search as best they could. Teachers were promising to search their schools for Dave Gormans. Prison warders were promising to search their prisons. And anyone with access to e-mail at work promised to send a message out to the entire company staff list asking any errant Dave Gormans to please come forward.

A wealthy American theatre producer asked if he could buy the rights to the story with a view to turning it into a lavish, virtually all-male Broadway musical. But he didn't want to use the name Dave Gorman so we turned him down.

A pair of budding screenwriters asked if they could use the story as the basis for a film about a serial killer intent on bumping off people who shared his name. They *did* want to use the name Dave Gorman so we turned them down. Well, Dave did. I thought it was a great idea.

I was happy with what we'd achieved in Edinburgh. I was sure that we'd sown some important seeds, and that we'd soon see the benefits. Two more factors, in particular, couldn't fail to help.

For a start, the nation's journalists were suddenly on our side. Reviews and features appeared in *The Sun, The Mirror, The People, The Express, The Sunday Express, The Mail, The Mail On*

Sunday, The Guardian, The Observer, The Times, The Sunday Times, The Independent, The Independent On Sunday, The Scotsman, Scotland on Sunday, The Herald, The Sunday Herald, The List, The Daily Telegraph, The Financial Times and even *Insurance News.* Crucially, most of these encouraged new Dave Gormans to come forward and contained my e-mail address.

The *Sun* even used our journey as their main Page 3 story, and we were honoured to share that hallowed spot with the semi-clad Jo, 21, of Leicestershire.

The people at *The Sun* chose to illustrate the story with photos of some of the Dave Gormans – which means that at long last I am able to legitimately claim to girls that I am a Page 3 photographer.

Another ambition realised.

The other vital factor that came into play was the promise of pure, undiluted People Power.

Over the course of the run, more than 7,000 people had walked through the doors of the theatre in order to hear our tale. Every single one of them took a solemn oath, which we'd prepared for them in the cafe opposite the flat, and which we hoped they would take as seriously as we asked them to. I watched, night after night, as hundreds of people swore to do their utmost to find us new Dave Gormans, and it filled my heart with hope.

Before the festival, we were doing this on our own. Now we had recruited a private army of 7,000 researchers who were all searching with us.

We'd upped the game. We couldn't fail.

Chapter 14

A NEW DG AT THE BBC?

Hanne phoned from Norway with two pieces of news. She'd been browsing the internet and had made her way to the news pages, where she was surprised to see the names Dave Gorman and Danny Wallace in an article.

Some cheeky so-and-so had decided that Dave and I qualified for inclusion in what they called their 'Silly Season Top Ten'. Our tale was at number 2, directly between a contribution from *Carp World* magazine about a 47lb carp called Bazil who'd been caught by fishermen 59 times, and the story of a Russian gangster whose bid to sneak into Slovakia failed when his fake ears fell off at border control.

We were becoming an international laughing stock.

Her other piece of news was that she was planning to come back to London.

'When?' I asked, urgently.

'Saturday. For my birthday. I thought we could spend it together.'

Saturday. Brilliant. Just one problem. Saturday was the final night of the show in the West End. Curse this infernal search! Hanne would hate me forever if I couldn't meet her on her birthday of *all* days, and the fact that she'd decided to come back from Norway just to spend it with me was a milestone move in our relationship.

Could I get out of being there? Could I ditch Dave and risk not being at the theatre when a new Dave Gorman might be? Every Dave Gorman I met was one closer to the end of the search, after all . . . but would Hanne understand that?

I had to decide.

'Because it's your birthday,' I said, 'I'm going to take you to the theatre.'

'Great!' she said. 'What are we going to see?'

'It's a surprise,' I said.

And it bloody well would be.

When Hanne turned up I was surprised to see that she wasn't looking very happy. It seemed odd, seeing as it was her birthday.

On stage, I was very aware of her presence in the front row that night. And, maybe because of that, I was hit by a revelation. As the words came out of my mouth, I slowly began to understand what I'd been putting Danny and Hanne through these last few months. I was just explaining the trip to Vicenza and the early morning phone call to Hanne's house that had dragged Danny away to Italy for the weekend when it all suddenly made terrible sense to me.

The poor girl. What had I put her through? No wonder she was sick of hearing about Dave Gormans.

I stopped talking as my mouth dried up. How, in my heart of hearts, could I stand here and ignore what I'd done to her? I looked down from the stage at Danny and Hanne. The audience stared at me.

'Ladies and gentlemen,' I said. 'I would like to take this opportunity to apologise to Hanne.'

You'd be hard pushed to get a more public apology than this.

'It's her birthday tonight and . . . well . . . I'm really sorry for taking Dan away so often. I'll try and behave from now on. Hanne's here this evening, and I think it would be nice if everyone could wish her a happy birthday.'

'On the count of three . . . one . . . two . . . three. . .'

'Happy birthday Hanne', they said, as one. Well, they probably said, 'Happy birthday Hannah', but you know what I mean.

I glanced down to see that Hanne was blushing. Crucially, though, she was also smiling. I think she knew that I was sincere. Maybe that's all she'd needed all along – an apology. A concession that we realised what we were doing was putting her out. A bit of attention.

Dave seemed to strike a nerve with Hanne. I'd apologised to her countless times, but maybe this is what had been missing all along . . . an apology from *Dave*. For the next few minutes, as he got back on track, she held my hand, she laughed in all the right places, and she rested her head on my shoulder. Suddenly I knew that everything was going to be all right. Dave did too. I smiled at him, and he relaxed and got on with his story.

So I told the audience about Vicenza, and then about Warminster, and tea and cakes in Swindon, and travelling to the Highbury doctor's surgery. . .

And then I told them about New York – so much to tell them, there. Jewish Dave in his Fifth Avenue offices . . . Gay Dave and his Hawaiian shirt . . . Ellis Henican and the help that *Newsday* would turn out to be . . . Mount Kisco Dave and his sports car . . . the hunt for Bill Clinton . . . the tornado . . . The Tony Awards party . . . Danny chatting up Miss Georgia. . .

Oops.

I stopped dead in my tracks.

Danny. Chatting up. Miss Georgia.

Bastard.

I put my hand to my mouth and stood on the stage in silence. I'd been carried away in the excitement of it all. I could hear nothing but the gasps of one audience member after the other, each one realising with horror what I'd just done. I have put my foot in it before, but never so spectacularly and certainly never so publicly. I had just put *both* my feet in it. In fact, I was up to my neck in it. And I had dragged Danny into it even deeper.

I could feel the blush as it filled my face. I looked down at the front row. I saw a very purple Danny. And Hanne. My God, just look at Hanne.

It is worth inventing the word just to say that Hanne was looking even purpler.

'Hanne, come back to the flat,' I said, on the street, after the show. 'Dave didn't mean it – I *wasn't* chatting her up. I didn't get the chance to, because Dave wanted to go off and watch a video.'

'Oh, so you didn't get the chance? Poor you. But you *wanted* the chance, didn't you? When are you going over to Georgia, then? To be with *her*?'

'I'm *not* going to go to Georgia, Hanne, I can promise you that. And anyway, she lives in New York, she's got a penthouse.'

'Oh, so you know where she lives, then?'

'No!'

It was no use. As far as Hanne was concerned, Miss Georgia and I were married.

'Thanks for that, Dave,' I said, in the pub opposite the theatre.

'Where's Hanne?'

'She's gone.'

'Back to Norway?'

'No, no. She's back in London, now. But she might as well be back in Norway. I don't think I'll be seeing her for a while. . .'

'I'm sorry about that, Dan. But if you *will* chat up Americans. . .'

'I *wasn't* chatting her up! Stop saying I was chatting her up!'

'The Norwegians are a curious race, Dan. She'll come round. Imagine how happy she'll be when all this is over.'

'Yes, Dave, but how many Dave Gormans have we met in the last couple of months?'

'We've been doing the show. . .'

'Yes yes . . . but how many have we met?'

'About . . . six.'

'Six. Yes. And we've been doing the show for. . .'

'Six weeks, all in all.'

'Right. So that breaks down as . . . ooh . . . one Dave Gorman a week. We've got another 24 to go, unless you give up. At this rate, that's another six months precisely. I can't do it, Dave. I can't do it at all.'

The thought of giving up didn't seem to register with Dave in the slightest. But the next day, after he received a phone call from his ever-more-exasperated agent, I felt sure it finally would. . .

'Dave? Rob.'

'Hello mate, how are you?'

'Good. BBC woman. Myfanwy. Wants to talk. You and Danny.'

'Really?'

'Tuesday?'

'Okay. . .'

'3 o'clock?'

'Okay. . .'
'Yorkshire Grey?'
'No problem.'
'Right. Bye.'
The phone went down.

The Yorkshire Grey is a nice little pub tucked around the corner from BBC Broadcasting House. As such, it's frequented by many a familiar face, and even more familiar voices, from the world of broadcasting. I saw Roy Hudd and Frank Bruno in there once, on the same day. They didn't talk to one another, though. It was as if they didn't know each other. Celebrities can be funny like that.

Dave and I were sitting in the corner by the fireplace when the lady who'd summoned us there, Myfanwy Moore, appeared. It turned out that she worked on the television side of things at the BBC, and she had a very interesting offer for us.

'I saw the show', she said. 'I loved the bit about "Hanne's birthday" – very funny.'

'Yes,' I said, scowling. 'That was *very* funny, wasn't it.'

'Have you thought about turning the show into a TV programme?'

Dave and I looked at each other. A TV show! Blimey! I knew exactly what he was thinking. At last – here was something which could justify the months of madness. Here was a *reason* for the idiocy. This woman from the BBC had brought us the perfect solution: a TV show. We'd make some money! And, more to the point, it would end the bet! Right here, right now, in this pub in the West End. It was brilliant. We'd *both* be winners. And it seemed easy – Dave had already told this tale to thousands of people. Now all he'd have to do was tell it once more in a TV studio.

I could read Dave's face like a book. He knew this would mean that he could pay off his debts. He knew it'd mean Hanne would forgive us for everything. He knew that, after one final push, we could return to our relatively normal, namesake-free lives.

I wanted to reach across the table and hug Myfanwy. Hell, from now on I'd call her 'Myf'. She didn't know it, but she was my saviour, offering us both a dignified way out of this stupid bloody way of life. Here was something I could finally offer to Hanne as something positive that had come out of all this. A glamorous ending! It was perfect.

Finally, Dave spoke.

'The thing is, Myfanwy,' he said, and I immediately froze. 'We haven't actually finished yet, so there's not much point in a TV show.'

Had I been holding my pint I would have dropped it. I looked at Dave. Myfanwy looked at Dave. I looked at Myfanwy. She looked at me. We both looked at Dave.

'I mean, we've only met 30 so far,' he said. 'I'm still 24 short.'

'Er . . . listen, Dave, I think 30's probably enough for a TV series. Don't you, Myfanwy?'

'Absolutely. I mean, that's about seven a show, and. . .'

'Nah. You see, we're trying to meet 54.'

'I don't mind stopping, Dave,' I said.

'Well, I *do*,' he said, firmly.

Myfanwy looked puzzled. She wasn't used to dealing with Dave.

'I thought that all that 54 stuff was . . . you know . . . a *show*. . .'

Dave and I shook our heads silently while she took in the horrible truth.

'We're trying to meet 54, and if we don't do that then we'd be making a TV show about me losing a bet. I don't like that.'

'You don't have to *mention* the bet,' said Myfanwy.

'Of course we do!' said Dave. 'If people believed I'd dare this for no reason whatsoever they'd think I was a complete lunatic!'

Myfanwy looked at Dave, clearly thinking he was a complete lunatic. She looked over at me, horrified. I closed my eyes and nodded. She was only just beginning to understand my pain.

'Thanks for the drink Myfanwy,' said Dave. 'When I win this bet, and I *will* win this bet, then it will be a pleasure to talk to you again.'

And with that, he downed his rum and coke, stood up and left. I raised my eyebrows. Myfanwy did too. Raised *her* eyebrows, that is, not mine. That would be assault.

We sat in silence for a moment.

'Er . . . they do an odd Bavarian lager called Ayingerbräu here,' I offered, more out of embarrassment than anything else. 'It's got umlauts over the "a".'

'Right,' said Myfanwy. 'I'd better get back to the office.'

I watched her wander out of the Yorkshire Grey, looking like a very confused television executive indeed.

'Dave? Rob.'

'Hello mate. . .'

'Shut up. What have you done?'

'What. . .'

'Shut up. Myfanwy. Rang me. What have you done?'

'I just. . .'

'Shut up.'

'Then stop asking me questions.'

'What have you done?'

'I just. . .'

'Shut up.'

The phone went down.

Rob clearly wasn't very happy. Danny wasn't happy. He'd phoned me up to tell me what he thought of me, too. Hanne wasn't happy. She hadn't called, but I could imagine what she'd have said if she had. My bank manager was *far* from happy. I thought it best to avoid his calls altogether.

The situation wasn't making *anyone* very happy.

Maybe I should put a stop to it. Maybe I should do what Danny wanted and end the journey here and now. This required deep thought. And deep thought required a cup of tea. I wandered through to the kitchen.

Danny was there. He had a knife in his hand but I doubt it was sharp enough to cut through the atmosphere that descended as I entered the room. I tried to ignore it.

'Hi Dan', I said. 'What you doing?'

'I'm making a bloody packed lunch, what does it look like?'

'That's a lot of sandwiches. You and Hanne going somewhere?'

'No, Hanne and I are not bloody going somewhere. Hanne are I are going bloody nowhere, thanks to you. These sandwiches are for you and me. You like ham, don't you?'

'Yeah.'

'Well we haven't got any.'

'Where are we going?'

He put the knife down and turned to me.

'Look. We've got 24 more Dave Gormans to meet. Right?'

'Right.'

'You've been getting loads of tip-offs since we went to Edinburgh, right?'

'Right.'

'So it's time to put them to good use. I want you to win the bet, Dave. I've decided. I have had enough. My life is in tatters because of it. The hatred my girlfriend has for me compares only with the hatred she has for you, and I want this to be over. Quickly, safely and with minimum risk to the public. Which means that tomorrow, we're going to go Gorman-hunting. You've got the information – you look after that side of things. I'm making the sandwiches and bringing the *Um Bongo*. It's a big day tomorrow, so go and get some rest.'

The next morning there was a new urgency about the whole thing. I went over the maths again in my head. Six weeks for six Dave Gormans really wasn't good enough. We'd been slack. Dave had taken his foot off the pedal, metaphorically speaking, and now it was time to put his foot back on – both figuratively and literally, if his driving this morning was anything to go by.

We had to get a bloody move on. It felt like we were running out of time. Eventually something would give – and it would most likely be our friendship. Neither of us wanted that.

In little under an hour we were straight up the M1, off at junction 11, and into the town of Dunstable where we soon found the end terrace house that belonged to our 31st Dave Gorman.

He was wearing a bright red jumper and an even brighter smile. He had a sing-song Irish voice, a mischievous glint in his eye, and a head of grey hair that looked suspiciously like it might one day have been a quiff.

He's a retired man, although I suspect he's more worn out by his duties as a father, having sired eight kids along the way. Perhaps this would explain why his wife was wearing a neck brace.

Although they offered us exceptional hospitality, we were men on a mission, and we couldn't stop for long. We had more Dave Gormans to find today, and a very tight schedule to keep.

From Dunstable, we headed back onto the M1 and further north. Near Daventry is the little village of Braunston. It's just up the A45, about 45 miles from Dunstable, and it took us precisely 45 minutes to get there.

Dave Gorman 32 cracked open a beer for himself and one for Dan, and started to regale us with stories. I got the impression that for this particular Dave, every night was like a stag night. I also learnt that in Daventry, the name 'Gorman' carries a certain amount of cachet as it is, apparently, home to a particularly hard and well-known family of Gormans. Men who, if the stories were to be believed, still lived by the family motto 'First and Last in Battle'.

There was a small model car in the living room – something red, sporty and with the roof down. He caught me looking at it.

'I've made one like that,' he said.

'Really?' I tried to sound impressed, but to be honest, it was only a model car. It can't have taken long.

'Would you like to see it?' he said.

He sounded so proud it would have been rude not to.

'Of course', I said. 'Who wouldn't?'

Danny caught my eye. He indicated that time was getting on, that we had to be making a move pretty soon. But Dave was walking off to show me his model car so I followed.

We walked out to the back of the house and then through a side door to the garage. There, gleaming, spotless and cherry red, was a life-size car just like the model in the living room. I was instantly transformed into an eight-year-old version of myself, fascinated by the Boy's Own fantasy vehicle before me.

'Wow!'

I actually said the word 'wow'.

'Can I sit in it?'

I actually asked if I could sit in it.

'Of course', said Dave, with a look that told me he'd seen this reaction in grown men before now and he was expecting to see it again. I sat in the car.

'Wow!'

I'd said it again.

'Built it myself,' said Dave, beaming with pride. 'Took me years.'

DG32 is divorced.

Not long after setting off from Braunston, we passed a road sign saying 'Royal Leamington Spa – 15'.

On spotting it, I amazed both Dave and myself by muttering the word 'bastard' under my breath, quite involuntarily. When had I started to care so much? Probably about the same time I realised I didn't have a life any more.

We were heading for Peterborough. Most of Britain's motorways are fine for travelling north to south, or even the other way round (they're really rather flexible that way), but very little goes across the country on the east-west axis. We were heading east and making very slow progress, stuck behind wagons, tractors and even, at one point, a couple on a tandem that insisted on riding in the middle of the road so as to cause as much inconvenience as possible. They appeared to believe they were still living in an era in which motorised vehicles were expected to travel behind a man on foot carrying a flag.

It took us well over two hours to travel around 75 miles, but once safe and well in Peterborough, we met Dave Gorman 33. A quiet, portly young man with slicked-back ginger hair who worked in computing. He offered us some apple juice, but we were slipping behind schedule now, so we couldn't hang around sharing pleasantries with this one. We'd met him, we had to go.

Two hours later we'd been straight down the A1 and into London and round the North Circular Road for Tottenham. A quick call to Dave Gorman 34's mobile and we established which pub he was in.

DG34 had a clean-shaven head that made it impossible to guess his age, but there was mischief in his eyes . . . in fact, a little bit of mischief was leaking out of every inch of this man's being. Here was a rogue.

I'd parked the car on the kind of street that made me worry about the chances of ever finding it there again, but Dave gave me the impression that he was probably the man most likely to steal it, so as long as I was with him it was okay. Then he laughed. And his mates laughed, so we laughed.

He posed for the traditional photo by whipping his false teeth out, holding his ears out, and gurning like a jug-eared freak.

We drove home. Now this was more like it. This was precisely the kind of day we needed. We'd found four in one day. Another five days like this and we'd have met the final twenty we needed to get this over and done with.

One long working week and all this would be behind me forever. For the first time in months, I felt blessed with a certain sort of optimism. I could smell my freedom at long, long last.

Chapter 15

OH BOY DANNY

I was enjoying Danny's newfound sense of urgency. We had met four DGs in one day and it felt good. It felt right. Whereas before it had been a source of constant friction, the adventure had now become a collaboration of sorts. United by Dave Gormans, Danny and I were now working to the same agenda. We both wanted the task to be over. It was no longer about who was right and who was wrong, this was a noble quest and we were both responsible for it's completion. No longer would I have to feel awkward about approaching him with news of new Dave Gormans. Because now he was positively encouraging me to do so.

I went back to my computer and searched through the many e-mails I had received full of Dave Gorman related information. I found a treat for Danny.

'Dan, we're going on another trip,' I told him.

'Okay, who have you found?'

'Dave Gorman. From Georgia.'

'Please say you mean Georgia in the Russian sense of the word.'

'No . . . Georgia, USA.'

'Ha ha', he said, flatly.

'No, seriously. Georgia! There's a Dave Gorman in Georgia!'

'You must be joking,' he said, suddenly very stern indeed. 'No.' He definitely meant it.

'No. No. No. No. No.'

See?

'Absolutely no way. Not Georgia. Of all the places in the world, not Georgia. After the trouble you caused me with Hanne and your bloody Miss Georgia story, I can never go there. She'd kill me. I know that Miss Georgia is in New York, but try explaining that to

Hanne. If I go to Georgia she'll think I've set up a secret assigna-
tion with the State's latest beauty queen and that'll be it; over. No
way. Not me, not ever. Not Georgia, no way. Besides, it's too far
to go. Ha! Have you thought of that? No, you haven't, have you?
We'll go all that way and find one, it'll take us three days minimum, and all that time just to find one Dave Gorman? We can do
better than that. We found *four* yesterday. That's more like it.
Besides, you can't afford it. You can't afford it financially, I can't
afford it personally. I'm your friend, I won't let you, you're my
friend, you shouldn't make me. That is it Dave. Absolutely no
way.'

He stopped and took a deep breath. I smirked.

'Don't you bloody smirk at me, Dave, I don't like it when you
do that, and you know I don't like it when you do that. This is
not like the other times, you can't laugh it off, and assume I'm
coming. You can't do that. I don't care if you've already bought
the tickets, you shouldn't do that, it's not right. You should ask
me, we're in this together now, we plan it together, we do it
together, we get through this together. I will not be blackmailed
into going to Georgia. I won't do it. I won't do it to me, and most
importantly, I won't do it to Hanne.'

Another deep breath. I smirked some more.

'Stop it with the smirking, Dave, this is a no smirking zone
from now on, alright? We are not going to Georgia. In fact, from
now on, no foreign travel, I've had enough of it. It's not even like
we get to see anything when we're away. My passport says I've
travelled the world, but all I've seen is bloody Dave Gormans.
From here on in, we look close to home and we look for them in
bulk. One man in Georgia is neither of those things, so we're not
going.'

And breathe.

'And another thing, Gorman is an Irish name; we haven't even
been to Ireland yet, which frankly makes you an idiot. We're not
going to go to Georgia when we haven't even been to the actual
bleedin' birthplace of the Gorman name yet. If it was up to me,
I'd suggest we go to Ireland, Dave, because I've got a bit of sense,
but not you, you're all up for a trip to America, because you're a
berk. What do you think you're doing?'

'Do you mind if I speak now?' I said. 'It seems to be all you,
you, you at the minute.'

Given everything that had occurred over the previous few

months, and with the benefit of hindsight, I think I was probably pushing it with the 'you, you, you' bit, but you know what I mean.

'Okay, have your say, but we're not going to Geor. . .'

'We're going to Ireland.'

'Aha. Good. A bit of sense at last.'

'Dave Gorman from Georgia will be there. He's going to Dublin. We'll meet him there and I bet we can bag a few others.'

'In Ireland?'

'Ireland.'

'Good idea. That's what I'd have done as well. Ireland.'

I was pleased. I felt sure this was the most sensible move – if we were going to reach the target, then Ireland would certainly help us get there. How could it not? So far we'd met five Dave Gormans in London – I reckoned there must be even more than that in Dublin. So we bought two tickets and headed out a day before we needed to. After all, the Dave Gorman we were heading there to meet – Detective David Gorman of the Dekalb County Police Force, Georgia – wouldn't be arriving at the airport until lunchtime the next day. We'd lucked out with this one – a link to a website someone had sent us showed us that Dave was an Irish-American cop who'd organised a trip for other Irish-American cops back to the old country. And that was where he would meet us.

Our plan was to be at the airport when he landed. But that was tomorrow. Today, we'd use our time wisely, bag a few new Dave Gormans, get closer to a conclusion of some kind.

We based ourselves in a hotel in the Temple Bar district of the city. For the uninitiated, the area has more bars than temples, and despite the fact that it's on land which used to belong to the Augustinian order, it owes its name not to friars and monks, but to its seventeenth-century owner, William Temple. I found that slightly disappointing. I'd have preferred it the other way, but then I'd prefer the McDonald's in Glasgow to owe its name to a proud clan of Scotsmen rather than to a red-nosed American clown called Ronald.

Right. We'd been in the hotel five minutes. It was time to get a move on. I looked around the room, and in one drawer, I found the Gideon Bible. In the other, I found what was to be our bible: the Dublin Phone Book.

Danny phoned me about fifteen minutes after we'd arrived in the hotel and got me out of the shower.

'Okay, Dave,' he said. 'Let's get on with it.'

'You're keen,' I said.

'Yes I am. Keen that we should get out there and get some Dave Gormans under our belt. This is a good chance to make some real progress, Dave. We're going to have to work hard, leave no stone unturned.'

'You sound like me.'

'Yeah, yeah. Listen, there's a man from *The Irish Times* on his way round. His name's Robin and he's agreed to send out an appeal.'

'Really? When did you. . .'

'Hurry up and get dressed. I'll meet you in the lobby in five minutes.'

It was time to stop messing around. Robin from *The Irish Times* turned up a few minutes late, which Dave didn't mind but I thought was bloody inconsiderate given the rush we were in.

'Relax, Dan . . . this is Ireland. This is where everyone is supposed to be chilled and calm.'

'I don't care, mate, there are Gormans out there and we've got to meet them. Lots of them. Just waiting for us. We can't sit around all day being laid-back. . .'

'Dave Gorman, I presume?', said a tall man dressed in black, carrying a tape recorder. He smiled at me, knowingly.

'No. That's him,' I said, 'I'm Danny. Take a seat. Let's crack on.'

The interview was confusing. Normally, whether with Ellis Henican, the *Dagbladet* boys or any one of the numerous Edinburgh scribes, every question was met by either an enthusiastic answer from me, or a dry, semi-cynical answer from Danny.

But this was different. I think Robin walked away from that interview wondering which one of us was most keenly engaged in our task. I was slightly confused, too.

'I think Robin thought you were me,' I said to Danny.

'Eh?'

'It was like you were utterly obsessed with my namesakes. That bit where you lectured him about it being his "duty to the people of Ireland that he do his utmost to find us some Dave Gormans"? And that bit where you quoted some sub-section from the Journalistic Code of Practice about a newspaper's "moral obligation to publish public appeals"? You got quite aggressive. . .'

'I thought it might help.'

'I think he got scared.'

'I thought it might help.'

'I'm sure it will. Lunch?'

'Nope. We're going out.'

'Where to?'

'Get your coat.'

I'd ordered a taxi for 11 o'clock and at four minutes past it arrived. Jesus, what was wrong with this country?

I dragged Dave into the cab and off we went. Ten minutes and a speedy journey through Dublin town centre later and we were at the offices of accountancy firm *Gorman Quigley Penrose*.

I pushed Dave down the path – he was just being too slow, today – and opened the door for him.

'Go on, get in.'

The last time I had met an accountant at his office, he charged me by the minute, so in some ways I was relieved when, after we'd finished our coffee with our new Dave Gorman, Danny tapped his watch and said we really needed to get a move on.

While I got Dave to sign his polaroid for us, Danny called a cab and five minutes later we were on our way back to the hotel.

'That was a quick meeting,' I said. 'One of our quickest, surely?'

'Yep,' said Danny, sternly, 'but we can get quicker.'

Dan had the air of an army man about him. A great general, taking charge of the situation. I wasn't used to it.

'More to come. These . . .', he said, handing me a piece of paper, '. . . are the numbers of two more Dave Gormans in the Dublin area. Give them a call and get them to meet us this afternoon.'

'Right. Yes. But I can't help feeling a little. . .'

Strange. I felt strange. Everything was happening so quickly today.

'I studied the phone book, Dave,' said Dan, looking like he was letting me in on an unbelievable secret. 'This is a hotspot. An absolute hotspot. Dublin alone holds riches beyond your wildest dreams. We'd be fools not to take advantage of it, Dave. Fools!'

I kept my mouth shut and did as he said. The next Dave Gorman volunteered to meet us at our hotel, and this made Danny happy, as it showed greater efficiency from someone who clearly understood our cause. Dave Gorman 36 turned up at around 2 o'clock and all three of us immediately hit it off. Despite the fact that the drink disagrees with me it seemed rude not to join Dave in a few pints of Guinness. He told some tales, and we learnt all about Dave's life. He's hugely friendly, a part-time drummer in a band, someone important at *Hewlett Packard*, and about to move to America. I'd love to tell you lots more details about him, but Danny looked at his watch, realised how long we'd been talking, and clapped his hands together.

'Right. Well, we've got to get on. . .'

And we did. We'd only talked to the press and met two so far today, and it was already 3.30.

Dave got on the case and summoned the next Dave Gorman to our hotel. He only worked around the corner, as a stockbroker, and he turned up in dapper clothing and happily obliged our every whim – a handshake, a photograph and a pint, but only the one this time – and that was that. DG37 went on his way and we had another cele-bratory Guinness.

I was beginning to feel a little ill by now. The rushing around, the stress, the unexpected pressure from Danny, and most of all the Guinness, was starting to make me feel queasy. But it was then that I realised we still hadn't had lunch. Or, in fact, break-fast. Maybe that was why my energy levels were so low, and why the Guinness was having a worse effect than normal.

'Dan, can we get some food, now?'

'We need to crack on, Dave. We need to get at least one more today.'

'No, Dan, I need some food. I'm feeling odd.'

'You can have some crisps on the way to the next one.'

'The next one? No, come on, Dan – that's three today! And Detective Dave from Georgia in the morning! And tomorrow that *Irish Times* thing comes out, as well, and we'll find another one off the back of that, surely? Let's have a meal, have a rest.'

I couldn't believe it had come to this. I was turning the idea of meeting another Dave Gorman down. I looked at Danny. I could tell I was letting the side down. Letting him down. Letting Dave Gormans everywhere down. He didn't want to stop. He couldn't get enough.

What had I done to the poor lad to make him act like this?

Please see chapters 1 – 14.

'Okay,' he said, finally. 'We'll have a meal and see how you feel after that.'

'Thanks, Dan.' I said. Thank God, I thought.

Right opposite our hotel was a restaurant by the name of Mongolian Barbeque, where, after you've decided upon what slab of meat you want, the chef cooks it right in front of your hungry eyes. Quite how this makes it more of a Mongolian barbecue than an Irish one I struggled to work out – especially considering the chef was Irish and we were in the middle of Dublin. Perhaps he was cooking llamas, or something.

After our meal we took a stroll around Dublin. This was an unusual thing for us to do. Usually, on our foreign travels, we were never anywhere long enough to just take a quiet moment and look around. But by forcing Dave to up the pace I had bought us some free time and we could indulge ourselves with a little sightseeing. We were doing things my way from now on, we'd meet more Dave Gormans, but we'd meet them quickly and efficiently and if I wanted to take a stroll round Dublin, well, that's exactly what I'd do.

Dublin is a young city – that's the first thing I noticed. I didn't get to see them all, but over half of the 1.5 million people who call it home are under 25. It's probably for this reason that not one of the many pubs we passed as we wandered through Temple Bar was less than packed. This was where the Dublin low-life of the eighteenth century used to congregate amongst the dingy bars and brothels . . . now it's the first stop for weekenders from London who traditionally would have clogged up the streets of Amsterdam on their weekend away, so, on the surface at least, I suppose it's really not all that different from the old days. Apart from the brothels, I'd imagine.

'Right, you've had your food,' I said. 'Let's get cracking.'

I really didn't want to find another one today. It was getting too late. I was feeling too ill. Too tired. Too worn-out. But there was a voice in my head telling me that Danny was right. 'Come on Dave', it was saying, 'come on!' Then I realised it wasn't a voice in my head. It was Danny.

We walked to find a taxi which would take us the fifteen miles south of Dublin, into County Wicklow, to the small town of Bray. There, in his living room, we met our next Dave Gorman. The fourth of the day, the 38th so far.

He's a tall chap, lanky even, and he was looking healthy and happy. Unlike my flatmate. He welcomed us into his living room where we were greeted by his smiling wife. I was just taking in the surroundings, exchanging a few pleasantries with this new Dave when my Dave suddenly spoke up. What he said shocked me. It wasn't offensive in any way – it was just that, even for Dave, it established a new level of inanity.

'I see you're wearing a blue shirt,' he said.

As an opening gambit for a conversation it would be hard to find anything so lacking in profundity.

'Yes,' said Dave, who couldn't really deny it.

'Most of the Dave Gormans we've met have been wearing blue shirts.'

What? What was he on about?

'What?' I asked. 'What are you on about?'

'Most of the Dave Gormans were wearing blue shirts', said Dave delving into his rucksack and producing the photo album. He flicked through the polaroids totting them up.

'Eighteen of them to be precise. Out of 38. That's nearly half of them. Quite a significant percentage when you think about it.'

I looked at Dave, aghast. It might very well be a significant percentage when you think about it, but why was he thinking about it? I tried to change the subject.

'So, how long have you been married?' I asked DG38.

Before he could answer, Dave had launched into another one.

'And you're wearing glasses as well', said Dave.

'Yes', said Dave, once again, unable to deny it.

'That's . . . eleven! Out of 38!' said Dave flicking through the album again. 'That's more than a quarter. Again, quite a significant percentage compared to the population at large.'

'Really?' asked DG38.

'Six of the blue shirts were wearing glasses,' said Dave, 'which is pretty much what you'd expect when you consider that around half of the Dave Gormans wear blue shirts and eleven have glasses. You'd expect something near to five and a half, so six is about right.'

'Really?'

'Yes.'

I was going mad. I was sitting in a living room listening to a Dave Gorman tell another Dave Gorman how his appearance matched up statistically against a population of other Dave Gormans. Just as I felt I had caught the madness creeping up on me it stopped creeping and began to gallop. In the corner of my eye I could see the word 'Gorman'. That couldn't be right. I blinked and shook my head because I'd learnt how to remove imaginary images from watching cartoons. I opened my eyes and it was still there. I turned to face it and there on the TV screen were the words, 'O'Gorman's People'.

'What's that?', I was pointing at the screen but asking no-one in particular.

'O'Gormans People', said DG38, who must have thought this was some kind of answer-the-obvious-question convention, 'it's a big RTE show. A fella called Paddy O'Gorman travels around Ireland meeting people and chatting to them.'

'Who does he meet?' I asked.

'Anyone really. Just people.'

'What . . . so they're not all Paddy O'Gormans?'

The gallop had become a stampede.

'No.'

'Well . . . what's the point in *that* then?'

In the taxi back into Dublin, I was leaning dog-like out of the window. I was feeling queasy, I wanted my bed and I wanted air. Danny was talking but the wind in my ears meant I couldn't hear a word.

After a while, he was looking so animated that curiosity got the better of me. I leant back into the car.

'Sorry Dan', I said, 'I missed all that.'

'I'm worried, Dave.'

'What?'

'Today. It's all been a bit weird.'

'It's been a good day Dan. We met four. That's as good as we've ever done in one day.'

'But you didn't want to do the fourth one.'

'I'm not well, mate. I've had five pints of Guinness too many, that's all. I'm not feeling myself.'

'Maybe you're not feeling yourself because you're not yourself. Maybe I'm you. I wanted to meet a Dave Gorman and you didn't! I made you go. When I saw Paddy O'Gorman it didn't make sense to me, because I couldn't see why he wasn't meeting other Paddy O'Gormans . . . that's how you think. I've met too many Dave Gormans. I'm turning into a Dave Gorman.'

'This is nonsense Dan. It's been a long day.'

Danny grabbed me by the lapels.

'I'm wearing a blue shirt!', he screamed, 'AND I'M WEARING GLASSES!'

I needed to calm down a little bit, after my day-long identity crisis. There was something deeply wrong with the world.

'C'mon, Dave, let's go out and have a pint.'

'No, Dan, I'm feeling too tired. Maybe tomorrow, yeah?'

'Dave, we met four Dave Gormans today – you should be over the moon! Four of them!'

'I know, Dan, and that's really nice. I'm really pleased for you, but I've got to go to bed now.'

He just didn't understand.

I decided I'd have a little walk before bed, and left Temple Bar over Ha'penny Bridge, making my way down the wide, heavily-statued O'Connell Street to clear my head. I ambled towards a newish-looking statue surrounded by a fountain. It was, I read, a statue that represented James Joyce's Anna Livia, the personification of the River Liffey – the same river that now ran behind me. I had to admit, they didn't look much alike. But perhaps this Anna bird was what rivers looked like in Joyce's day – I'm no historian.

I had a drink in a nearby pub and the man behind the bar asked me if I'd seen 'the floozie in the jacuzzi'. It was lucky I *had* just seen it, or I might very well have wondered what kind of pub this was. I took great pleasure in the barman's nickname for the statue, though – so much so that he let me in on another nickname the locals have for her: 'the whore in the sewer'. Not the most charming or magical image, I have to be honest, but at least in a Dublin accent it rhymes.

It was getting late and so I made my way back to Temple Bar, this time crossing over O'Connell bridge, and walked towards our hotel. My new route meant that I was approaching the hotel from behind, and caused me to walk past the nightclub that someone apparently decided would make a handy addition to it. Staying there meant we'd been given free tickets, and at the bottom of my pocket I found mine. I looked up at the club. It looked big, and it was packed with bouncers who eyed my trainers suspiciously but who, when I approached, stepped aside and welcomed me in. Well, why shouldn't I go in? I was trying to forget the day before, after all.

It was an impressive sight. A huge lighting rig with constantly revolving lights flashed in perfect timing with each track put on by the DJ in his dancefloor booth, and massive speakers lined the walls, making any type of conversation more or less impossible. Smoked black glass hid the VIP room, high, high above the dancefloor, and chrome-lined staircases with purple neon lights formed a high-tech spaghetti junction around the club. There was acres of space, plush velvet seats, and designer beers by the crate load. Literally. It was loud, it was new, and it was brash. This was what the city was now all about, I decided. Forget the Georgian architecture, or the cathedrals, or the works of Joyce, Swift or Shaw – this club represented the core of a new, European, party-obsessed Dublin.

Fortunately, it seemed I was actually the only person in the entire world who thought this, because, as it turned out, I was the only person standing in this club. Yes, there may have been a DJ, a dozen barstaff, and what looked like even more bouncers, but at a quarter to 12 on a Tuesday night, the club was mine and mine alone. It was all slightly embarrassing.

I decided to leave.

'Are you not going to have a dance?' said the barman, as I began to walk away.

'Er . . . I don't think I will, no.'

I smiled at him, thinking he was having a bit of a joke with me.

'Ah, come on,' he said. 'It's the DJ's first night. Just have a little dance. We've had no-one in here since we opened.'

I looked around. It was still just me.

'But I'm on my own.'

'He won't mind. He's dead keen, but he lacks confidence. Just have a little dance over there – just for a little while.'

'I'm not going to go over there and dance on my own.'

'Ah, come on, now. There's no one here to see you. Just Richard the DJ and myself. It'll mean the world to Richard.'

I scanned the club. He was right and wasn't giving up.

'Look. I'll give you a free drink if you do. One before, and one after you dance. How's that?'

He reached for a glass and poured a shot of vodka.

'Just make him feel like he's not wasting his time – will you do that for us?'

I looked over at Richard, glumly leafing through his CDs for the next track he'd put on for the benefit of precisely no-one. I felt guilty. Ah, what the hell, I was in a great mood, it was a couple of free drinks, and this time tomorrow I'd be back in London. I took the drink.

'Okay.'

The barman yelled out at Richard and gave him two thumbs up, and Richard shot out of his chair, delighted. He reached for his headphones and cackhandedly mixed one song into another. It was Britney Spears. Brilliant.

I swayed from side to side on the dancefloor, moving my arms from left to right but hardly moving my feet at all, and tried to look like I was enjoying myself. I saw the barman smiling over at me as he raised my glass to the optic and fired off what looked like a double. He put it back down on the bar while I continued my little dance for Richard – my prize awaiting me.

Richard started to clap his hands as I got more into the music and the barman joined in with him. Hey – I was being a Good Samaritan here, so I decided to try and get more into the spirit of things. I attempted a little breakdancing, before remembering what had happened in Norway and putting a stop to it. Then I did a little disco, and, when Britney was coming to the end of her wailings, I actually considered staying on for another.

Until I looked above me and saw that six burly Dublin bouncers had lined the staircase above the dancefloor and were now heartily applauding my solo efforts. I raised my hand in appreciation and walked, red-faced, back to the bar, where the barman handed me my drink with his thanks.

I got out of there as soon as I could. I was determined that this would remain a private embarrassment; Dave didn't know I had gone there that evening and I certainly wasn't going to tell him anything about it.

I awoke the next morning and realised something that got me up and out of bed in an instant. Our next Dave Gorman – Detective Dave – was to be our 39th.

This was more significant than you might think.

We'd been running around all over the world trying to collect one Dave Gorman for every card in the deck. Finding a 39th would mean that we had effectively completed three suits. We'd then have met one for every spade, every diamond and every club in the pack. That would leave just one suit to collect. And the jokers. This really would be the beginning of the end of the bet. After Detective Dave, it'd feel like we were doing everything for the very last time.

For a while I'd been content with the way it had all been shaping up. I'd been happy to casually collect Dave Gormans, all the time moving slowly towards my target. But now I was determined. Now I was focused.

Refreshed after my sleep – which had only been broken once, by the sound of a Britney Spears bassline thumping through the walls of the hotel from the club next door, accompanied by a strange, uneasy feeling that came with it that I couldn't quite put my finger on – I got dressed and went downstairs for breakfast where I met Danny.

'What time's his plane arrive, again?' asked Dan.

'Ten past 11. It's about half an hour in a cab so let's just eat our breakfast and go.'

'Right. We may as well just stay at the airport then.'

Our flight back to London was at 1.30pm. We'd meet Detective Dave, have a spot of lunch, and then fly home. I was looking forward to it. Dave had left from Atlanta, Georgia the day before and would arrive in Dublin with all his policeman buddies to the sight of Dan and me standing in the arrivals lounge, looking welcoming.

Only I had no idea what he looked like. How would we recognise him? How would he recognise us?

One hour later, Dan and I were standing in the arrivals lounge, and I was holding a cleverly-crafted sign I'd made myself, bearing the words 'David Gorman'.

This was the only thing I could think of which would help ensure we found our man. But it left me feeling slightly uncomfortable. I've got friends who live in Ireland. What if one of them had walked through Dublin airport that day and seen me holding a sign with my own name on it? Surely this was the very definition of showing off.

'Oh, look at you,' said Dan. 'The amazing self-captioning man!'.

'Hold this for a bit, will you?' I said.

'No. He's your namesake, you hold it.'

'I look stupid.'

'No one else knows your name is Dave Gorman, Dave. No one else thinks you look stupid. You only look stupid to me.'

I looked at my watch to see that Dave's plane really should have touched down by now. He would be walking through those doors at any moment. But another ten minutes went by, and then another, and there was still no sign of him. I looked around. I could see priests – which people always say when they're in Ireland, but it was true, there were several of them wandering about the place, bumping into things – and I could see crowds of other expectant people . . . but I couldn't see a group of police-men.

'Danny . . . can you go and check the arrivals board? I've got an odd feeling about this.'

I found the font of all knowledge that was the arrivals board. Sure enough, Dave's plane had been delayed. By an hour and a half. Usually, this would be annoying. Now, it was a crisis. I could feel a sweat break. His delay meant he'd be landing at 12.40pm. Our plane was supposed to leave Ireland at 1.30pm. We'd have to meet him, photograph him, and say our goodbyes in an incredible hurry, before rushing to our departure gate before it closed and trapped us in Ireland – and all that was only if Detective Dave could make it through customs in time. I really didn't know whether we'd be able to manage it, and jogged back to Dave to tell him the bad news.

He was standing, sign in hand, talking to a middle-aged woman in a suit.

While Danny had been checking the flights, I'd been approached by a lady who'd seen my sign.

'Excuse me,' she'd said. 'I see your sign says you're waiting for Dave Gorman. . .'

'Yes,' I said, 'He should be coming through any minute now.'

'Yes, he's here today, isn't he? In Dublin, I mean.'

'You know him?' I asked, wide-eyed.

'Well . . . it is the pilot Dave Gorman you're after?'

'No. . .' I said, my jaw beginning to drop. 'I'm after the American Policeman Dave Gorman. . .'

'Oh,' she replied, and looked confused. 'Only the pilot, he'll be in the pilot's lounge about now. . .'

It seemed that I had stumbled upon fresh quarry. Just by standing in a public place with the words 'Dave' and 'Gorman' written on a piece of card I had found another Dave Gorman! I should have used this technique months ago.

Danny arrived just as she was leaving.

'What was all that about?', he said.

'We've found another one, Dan! Another Dave Gorman!'

'Eh?'

'There's a pilot – he's in the pilot's lounge . . . we've got to move fast. He might be flying anywhere! What are we going to do?'

'We've got 90 minutes before policeman Dave touches down. His flight's delayed.'

'Brilliant!' I said. This was a real piece of luck. And I couldn't believe how easy our work here had been. It seemed like every time we turned a corner there was another Dave Gorman waiting to meet us. It was like shooting fish in a barrel.

We picked up our bags and ran to the information desk.

'We need to find the pilot's lounge,' I said. 'We need to meet a pilot!'

The woman looked very worried indeed, and cast an eye to her colleague, who shrugged back at her.

'His name's Dave Gorman,' said Danny. 'He's in the pilot's lounge.'

'What airline is he with?'

'We don't know,' I said. 'But it's very important that we see him before he flies away. . .'.

A thought struck me. Gorman is obviously an Irish name. Surely the chances were he'd be flying for an Irish airline?

Twenty minutes later and we'd bagged our 39th Dave Gorman – a First Officer with Aer Lingus who oddly, was not Irish, but Canadian. He reminded me a little of Luke Skywalker with his clean-cut, chiselled Hollywood face and his north American accent. We took his photo, shook his hand, and left him to fly a planeload of businessmen to Birmingham – each of them likely to be five minutes late for whatever meetings awaited them thanks to our insistence that their First Officer have his picture taken both with and without his hat on.

We toasted our good fortune with a hot chocolate and a biscuit in the cafe at the end of the airport, and then, at 12.30, ambled back towards the arrivals area to await Dave Gorman from Georgia. Dave got his sign out again and we resumed our position.

Eventually, we could sense his imminent arrival. It sounds terrible to say it, but the people coming through the door just started to get bigger. We instinctively knew that, whether it was the one we were waiting for or not, a plane from America had quite definitely landed in Ireland.

I looked at my watch. 12.49. This was going to be tight. Very, very tight. If we were going to make our flight back to London, we were going to have to be quick.

'There . . . look!' said Dave.

I looked, but I didn't know what I was looking for.

'Look at what?'

'That woman, there. The blonde one. She saw my sign and pointed at it. See – she's talking amongst her friends. And look how big they are!'

These were Americans alright. They were about a foot taller than most of the other people walking through the gate, very well-fed, and they were wearing shorts, baseball caps and huge trainers. Crucially, they were also talking in American accents. These were our people, all right.

'What's the time, Dan?'

'12.50.'

'How far's our gate?'

'Not far. We can meet him and leg it. Providing he's one of these people.'

Suddenly, a man in a white shirt, pushing a heavily-laden trolley in front of him, walked through the doors. The group we'd had down as his friends cheered him as he did so, and pointed to where we were standing. He read his name, waved at us, and walked happily towards us, friends in tow.

'12.51,' I whispered at Dave.

'Okay.'

'Hiya buddy, how you doin'?' said our latest Dave Gorman, as he thrust his hand into mine. His accent was a strange one – not a typically American one, it has to be said.

'I lived over here until I was sixteen,' he said, 'and then I moved over to the States. Hey, you should come over sometime, I'll give you a ride in the car, it'll be fun. . .'

'Sounds great!' I said.

'Here . . . this is my card, my numbers are on the back, just give me a call and we'll make sure it happens, how's that for you?'

'That's great!' I said.

'My group's keen we should get a move on, we've had a bus waiting for us because of the delay, and we've had a hell of a journey, but listen, here's something for you. . .'

He reached down into his bag and brought out a sew-on police badge, which he handed up to me while still searching for something.

'Wow,' I said. 'Look at that! Great!'

'Here,' he said. 'Here's another one.'

I now had two police patches from Dekalb County, Georgia. I was very pleased.

'Great!'

'Hey . . . here's a toy NYPD motorcycle for you. . .'. He handed up a boxed, metal toy bike to me. I didn't know quite why I was getting all these presents – in particular this toy motorbike – before we'd even had a proper chat, but I didn't mind it one bit.

'This is all so great of you,' I said.

'It's not a problem at all . . . in fact . . . here. . .'

He pulled out a huge bar of American chocolate from the side panel of his bag and handed that to me too.

'Chocolate!' I said, before trying to find a word other than 'great' to describe his unusual generosity.

'Great!'

12.53.

'Could we take your photo to add to my album?' I asked him.

'Sure, buddy,' he said, which made me feel rather good. He posed for the traditional photograph, while his group of friends took pictures of Danny taking the picture.

Dave was keen to move on. He'd had a long flight and was clearly suffering from it.

12.54.

'So give me a call when you guys get to Georgia, okay?'

He began to move off when a thought struck Danny.

'You don't happen to know *Miss* Georgia, do you?' he asked.

'I don't.'

'Well, if you ever see her, say hello from Danny, will you?'

This was a bit like the way an American might assume that all British people are bosom buddies with the Queen and Tim Henman, but it made Danny happy, so I let it go.

Dave and his group of Irish-American cops waved goodbye, and we picked up our bags and legged it as fast as we could towards our departure gate. We still had a few minutes before the gate closed. We ran and ran and ran.

But it was then that a very important thought struck me.

'Danny!' yelled Dave. 'Stop for a second!'

'What is it?' I shouted. 'We've got to run!'

'No, no . . . hang on . . . this is important!'.

We stopped running. My head was pounding and I was out of breath.

'What? What's so important that you're risking missing the flight?'

'We've met forty Dave Gormans!'

'I know – I was there!'

'No, no . . . this morning, when we got up, we thought we'd leave Ireland having met 39! But we haven't – we've met forty!'

'Yes?' I said, still trying to catch my breath.

'Don't you see? We've completed three suits! We've done all the spades, all the diamonds, all the clubs. And because we met the pilot we've now started the hearts! A new suit! The final suit!'

'I suppose we have, but. . .'

'I say we stay in Ireland another day. What harm can it do? Let's fly back tomorrow – this place is a hotbed of action for us. We're bound to meet more here. It makes more sense than flying back to London where we've already met all the Dave Gormans we can!'

I glanced down at my watch. We had approximately 60 seconds left before our final chance of getting on that plane evaporated.

'Dave. . .'

'The final suit, Dan! This is the home run! The final stretch!'

I'd been conditioned throughout my life, by family holidays and constant deadlines, to never miss a plane. It wasn't right. It's not what you're supposed to do. It's a waste. But now I realised that leaving Ireland behind would be a waste. An even greater waste. We'd hit a rich seam in Dublin that we were yet to fully exploit. One more day might let us do that.

We stood, sweaty, out of breath, in the middle of Dublin airport, considering our options. I dropped my bag.

'Fine. One more day. Let's see what we can get.'

We smiled a smile of quiet agreement and walked slowly back, pausing only to rearrange our flights for the next day, and to buy a copy of *The Irish Times*, in which Robin had done what he'd promised and put the word on the street. We got a taxi back to the hotel where the receptionist who had checked us out that morning checked us back in without blinking.

Dublin must surely be the world's most populous city as far as Dave Gormans are concerned. Which made it the most marvellous city in the world for us. Another day in Dublin was an opportunity and a half. The accidental discovery of Pilot DG was just too much good fortune . . . we couldn't just walk away from this city. Maybe this was the luck of the Irish? Granted, I'm not actually Irish, but my eyes are blue, my beard is ginger, and my name is Gorman, so it seems reasonable to assume that there's *some* Irish blood coursing through my veins.

Tomorrow we would see who else we could find, but for now, we would celebrate our good fortune.

We had a meal and a stroll and before too long it was evening.

'Come on Dan', I said. 'Let me buy you a drink. I'm feeling a lot better tonight. I'm in the mood for dancing, romancing, I'm having a ball tonight.'

'Eh?'

'It's a song. You know, The Nolans. *They're* Irish, as well.'

'As well as what? As well as Dublin? Or do you mean as well as you? Because you're *not* Irish, Dave. You're from Stafford, you know that, don't you?'

'Come on, there's a nightclub attached to the hotel.'

'Er . . . is there?'

Danny didn't sound too sure. I couldn't believe he hadn't heard the racket the night before.

'What say you and I go and sample "the craic"?'

'No. I'm, er . . . I'm not really in the mood', he said. 'And for the last time, you're not Irish.'

'Aw, come on . . .' I tried. I'd never known that fail with Dan. If he ever refused a drink, a quick 'aw, come on' usually did the trick.

'No Dave. I'm really not in the mood. You go to the nightclub,' he said, 'I'm sure it'll be brilliant in there and you'll have a marvellous time with all the people of Dublin.'

He smiled – almost laughed, really – and bid me goodnight.

I didn't fancy another night dancing for the sole pleasure of Richard the DJ, and found dancing with Dave for the sole pleasure of Richard the DJ less enticing still.

I went to my room, where I would later run a bath, fall asleep, wake up, find my bathroom flooded, turn the taps off, empty the bath, have a shower, mop the floor and go to bed.

Entering any nightclub for the first time is a lottery. You never know what to expect, but as a hotel resident I was entitled to a free ticket in this particular lottery.

I walked down the stairs and discovered an impressive sight. A huge lighting rig with constantly-revolving lights flashed in perfect timing with the music. Massive speakers were strewn all over the walls, and chrome-lined staircases with purple neon lights formed a high-tech spaghetti junction around the club. There were plush velvet seats, and designer beers by the crate load. Literally. It was loud, it was new, and it was brash.

And it was full. Packed. Rammed. Even though the bar was crowded, it was efficiently staffed and I was served in less than ten minutes. I stood there feeding off the energy that buzzed through the room. The dancefloor positively throbbed with a mixed bag of dressed-up, good-natured people having a good time together.

I finished my drink and started weighing up the odds. I was enjoying myself but I was alone. Should I have another drink, should I have a dance, or should I call it a night? My mind was about to be made up for me. There was a tap on my shoulder. I turned to my right. I expected to find Danny. Instead, I found a short man with reddish hair and a beard, smiling at me. I looked at him confused for a moment. I recognised this man, but I couldn't quite work out where from. Who did I know in Dublin? Then it came to me. This man didn't live in Dublin. He lived in Edinburgh. He worked at The Royal Bank Of Scotland, where he was the Account Manager *For* Technology *Within* Technology (which is a bit bizarre), and he was the fifth Dave Gorman I had met! Wow.

'Dave!', I yelled.

'Dave!' he yelled back.

'Dave Gorman!', I yelled.

'Dave Gorman!', he yelled back.

I was amazed and delighted, here of all places, to see a friendly face. A friendly Dave Gorman face at that. We bearhugged each other like two . . . well, like two bears, I suppose, but two bears who really liked each other and hadn't met in a long while.

'What are you doing here?'

'We're on a stag do,' he said. 'What about you?'

'We're looking for Dave Gormans.'

'I should have known,' he grinned. 'How are you doing?'

'We've met 40 so far', I said, still shouting to be heard over the music. Dave clearly approved as he gave me a double thumbs-up.

'I'm telling you Dave, Dublin is Dave Gorman Central! There are loads of us here. This is our city!'

And for the rest of the night we treated that city as if it was our own. We had a great time. We talked and laughed and sang and danced and drank the night away.

This was Dublin. We were Dave Gormans. We belonged here.

At breakfast I waited for Dave to join me. I felt slightly guilty about the amusement I'd found in imagining him swaying akwardly from side to side to the sounds of Britney and for the benefit of no one but Richard the DJ. And six burly bouncers, too, pissing themselves laughing on the staircase, hopefully.

He didn't know that I knew that particular hell from first-hand experience, so I was looking forward to hearing him relate his version of events.

He turned up looking a little the worse for wear.

'What happened to you?' I asked, although obviously I already had a pretty good idea.

'I went to the nightclub.'

'Oh yes?' I asked, smiling. 'And how was it?'

'I had a great time. The place was rammed.'

'Really?'

'Chocker.'

'Mmm. . .'

'Plus, you'll never guess who I bumped into. Little Dave Gorman from Edinburgh! He was in there with a bunch of his mates. Great bunch of lads, you should have been there.'

'What?'

'Great club, great night. Honestly, Dublin is amazing, there are Dave Gormans everywhere I turn – old ones, new ones. Oh, and I checked my e-mails this morning. . .'

'Hold on,' I interrupted. 'Go back a bit.'

'What do you mean?'

'The nightclub. It really was fun? And you met little Dave Gorman from Edinburgh? Dave Gorman number 5?'

'Yeah.'

'So Dave Gorman from Edinburgh just *happened* to be in Dublin last night and of all the nightclubs in town he just *happened* to be in the same one as you?'

'Yeah.'

Dave was clearly making this up. Whatever had happened to him last night was obviously too embarrassing to reveal so he'd been driven to concoct this flimsy cover story instead.

Much as I would like to have embarrassed him further, it would have been difficult to do so without revealing the full horrors of my own awful nightclub experience, so I tried to ignore his obvious deception. I couldn't help the fact that I was smirking, though.

'So,' I said, biting my lip. 'You checked your e-mail?'

'What are you smirking for?'

'No reason,' he smirked. 'Tell me about the e-mail'

'Is my hair looking stupid?'

'No,' he said, stifling a giggle. 'Just tell me about the e-mail.'

'Someone read the article in *The Irish Times* and . . . ', he was still smiling. . . 'What is it?'

'Nothing. I'm sorry I'm smiling. I'm happy.'

'Right. Okay', I said, although I was still suspicious. Maybe I was being paranoid. I decided it was unsafe to eat any of the food in front of me in case it had been tampered with.

'Somebody read about us in *The Irish Times*. They've given us loads of business phone numbers for Dave Gormans. There's *Gorman Quigley Penrose* and the stockbroker we met on the first day, but also another stockbroker, *Intercontinental Cargo* and *Gorman Ceramics*. It's a good job we stayed an extra day.'

We checked out of the hotel and parked ourselves firmly in the bar – the place we'd agreed to meet our next Dave Gorman.

He was another stockbroker, which prompted yet more statistical analysis from Dave.

'This next one means that nine out of 41 of the Dave Gormans work in the financial sector you know. Over 20%. That's the most popular area of work for a Dave Gorman'.

'Really?' I said, flatly, and then, with sarcasm: 'Pray, do tell me, Dave, how many of them were wearing blue shirts?'

Dave started flicking through the polaroids once more.

'Let me see . . . well, that is *amazing*. Abso-bloodly-lutely amazing, Dan. Only two of them! You're not going to believe this – the other seven were all wearing *white* shirts!'

'Goodness. What's going on there, then?'

'I know! But I swear it's true! White shirts are the second most popular choice accounting for eleven out of 40, but seven of those eleven work in the financial sector!'

I didn't know what to say.

'I don't know what to say, Dave.'

'Now – glasses. If you remember from the other day we worked out that just over a quarter of Dave Gormans wear glasses. And yet, when we look at the Daves in the financial sector we find four out of nine wear glasses. Over 40%!'

'You're doing an awful lot of talking, Dave.'

'I'm just saying . . . this Dave who's on his way, right? If you had to guess what job he did, you'd probably guess that he worked in the financial sector because it's the most popular kind of job for a Dave Gorman.'

'But we don't *have* to guess – we *know* he's a stockbroker.'

'There you go. Proves my point. But if you were to guess what colour *shirt* he'll be wearing then you'd probably have said blue because that's the most popular colour shirt.'

'Right.'

'But, given that he works in the financial sector, he's much more likely to wear a *white* shirt. And while Daves are more likely to wear glasses than other people, on the whole it's still only around one in four, but within the financial sector it's much more likely.'

'So you're saying that he's likely to be wearing a white shirt and glasses?'

'Yeah. Well, actually, statistically he ought to be wearing a monocle, but yeah, I bet you a tenner that he's wearing a white shirt and glasses.'

'Alright, I'll bet you a tenner that he's wearing a *blue* shirt and *no* glasses.'

'You haven't really been listening to the maths, have you?'

'I have, Dave . . . but I've also been watching the door. I bet it's that bloke there.'

We met our 41st Dave Gorman and I gave Danny £10.00.

A short taxi drive in to the suburbs deposited us at the home of DG42, the man behind *Gorman Ceramics.*

He opened the front door wearing a t-shirt that declared he'd once been to Boston, and a pair of very, very short shorts. To be honest, he didn't look like a man who was expecting company.

'Are we early?' I asked

'No, not at all', said Dave, beckoning us in. 'Come on through. . .'

We walked into the living room and Dave asked the family's live-in Italian exchange student to make us all a cup of tea. The floor was awash with children's toys. I'm relieved to report that this wasn't because our latest Dave was a simpleton, but because he was the proud father of two angelic little daughters.

I watched my flatmate's face flash a look of disappointment when he heard their names and realised that neither was a Dave.

I tried to steer us through this encounter as swiftly as possible. The moment I saw that DG42 had a moustache I could sense some statistics were bubbling up inside Dave's head. I didn't want to subject this DG to that, so I kept the conversation moving quickly and efficiently, took the requisite photograph, and then steered Dave out of the door before he had a chance to start. As we walked up the drive his chance arrived.

'He was only the second Dave we've met with a moustache, you know. We've met four before, but that was with beard and 'tash combinations. But it's only him and French Dave who choose to wear a solo 'tash'.

Through the window of the taxi that took us to our next location I tried to count 42 people to see how many solo moustaches were amongst them. I think I saw three, which would still make Dave Gormans less moustachioed than a random sample of the Dublin public. That is assuming we didn't pass anyone with a false moustache.

We arrived at a large unit within Santry Industrial estate. We were unsure if this was the right place until we were shown through to the office of Dave Gorman. On the wall behind Dave was a large map of the world. On his desk was another map of the world and a couple of telephones. We were either in the lair of a low-rent Bond villain plotting to overthrow the world from this secret location, or we were in the offices of a Development Director for a freight and cargo company. The words 'Inter-Continental Cargo' written on the side of the building led me to believe that the second option was the more likely.

DG43 had the look of an army PT instructor about him. He had close-cropped greying hair, and the aura of a man who meant business. (Incidentally, he was wearing a white shirt, did not wear glasses and had no beard or moustache).

'So, what's all this about then?' he asked, which was fair enough.

'We're trying to meet 54 Dave Gormans', I said.

'54?'

'It was a bet. It's one for every card in the deck', I said by way of explanation.

'Including the jokers', added Dan.

'And what number am I?' asked DG43.

'You're DG43', I told him.

'You're doing quite well', he said, nodding his approval.

I felt we'd now won him over.

'I can show you pictures of the other 42 if you like?' I said, offering up the photo album.

Dave took the album and started to flick through it. He asked a few questions along the way. 'What does this fella do?' and 'where was this one?' – that sort of thing. And between us, over a cup of coffee and half an hour or so, Danny and I answered all his questions.

'Myself, I often use the Gaelic version of the name,' said Dave. 'Have you come across that often?'

'Not at all,' I said. 'What's that then?'

The answer sounded something like 'Darr-hee O'Gor-ha-mine'. I tried to repeat it: 'Docky O'Goramane'.

He shook his head.

'I'll write it down for you.' He took a business card from his desk drawer, and on the back pencilled the words 'Daithí ó Gormáin.'

'I'm none the wiser on the pronunciation, to be honest.'

For five minutes or so the two of us sat there while he coached me in the correct way of saying Daithí ó Gormáin. I can find no satisfactory way of writing it phonetically, so you're just going to have to trust me when I tell you that I am now able to render the words with relative success.

All this was very satisfying until I realised that maybe the man whose company I was enjoying so much wasn't actually a Dave Gorman. Maybe he was a Daithí ó Gormáin instead. It may be the Gaelic version of my name, but we weren't looking for *versions* of the name. We were looking for the name itself. Unless we actually shared a name I knew he wouldn't count.

'So, are you Dave or Daithí?', I asked, trying to sound casual.

'Well, both, I suppose,' said Dave. Or Daithí. Well, both.

'But which one is your actual name?' He looked slightly perplexed by my latest line of enquiry. I decided to be direct.

'What I mean is, are you a real, 100% Dave Gorman? It's important that we only collect *pure* namesakes.'

'Oh, I see. You're alright there, I'm a real Dave Gorman', said Dave. 'Look on this side here.'

He turned the business card over to reveal the printed side. And there it was; his name, my name, our name: Dave Gorman.

'I just started using Daithí ó Gormáin for my signature. Somebody unauthorised signed for a few things in my name if you know what I mean, so I changed my signature to something a bit harder to fake. That, and I'm proud of the history, you know.'

I was relieved to hear it.

'Oh, I'm a real Dave Gorman alright. In fact, I've a little lad called Dave as well. . .'

'I beg your pardon?'

'Yeah, my little boy's called Dave.'

I was stunned. I looked across at Danny. He was looking similarly taken aback. We'd been here for 50 minutes or so and now, after hearing all about the bet and the lengths we'd gone to, after all that, only now did he think to mention he was father to another Dave Gorman!

'We'd love to meet him.'

'Really?'

What did he mean, 'really?'? Of *course* we would!

'Of course. Every Dave Gorman counts.'

'He's only five.'

'It doesn't matter how old he is, if he's a Dave Gorman, we want to meet him. And if we meet your son, we only need ten more in all. . .'.

Before I knew it our 43rd Dave Gorman had picked up the phone and called his wife.

'Hello darling, listen . . . can you get Dave out of school?'

Ten minutes later we were in the back of his car, motoring through the Irish countryside at pace until we came to a small rural infants school. There to meet us was little five-year-old Dave Gorman, his mum and his gran.

Tiny Dave was sitting in the back of his mum's car and he wasn't keen on getting out to meet the two strange men.

'Brilliant, Dan! Look at him! He'll be our youngest yet! Five years old! Oh, Ireland, you're good to us. . .'

I nodded in agreement . . . but it was far from over yet. With just a look we shared the knowledge that being in the same car park did not constitute a proper meeting. Every Dave Gorman we had met so far had shaken Dave's hand – that was the standard to which we aspired. Anything else simply wouldn't do.

We stood by and watched hopelessly as two generations of Gormans tried and failed to lure our youngest Dave Gorman ever from out of the safe confines of his mother's car.

This was like Chinese water torture to a Dave Gorman-hunter. I could see him. I could hear him. He could see me. He could hear me. But he wasn't coming out to play.

'Aw, c'mon, now David. Don't be so silly,' said his mum gently. 'Come on out of the car, now. Mammy wants you to get out of the car.'

Little Dave's grandma smiled over at me as if to say 'aren't kids funny?'. I smiled back, but inside I was a nervous wreck. This little man didn't seem keen on meeting me at all.

'Come on now. Daddy wants you to get out of the car. I've some people for you to meet,' said his dad, our ally in this battle of wills.

Little Dave shook his head and remained firmly planted in the back seat of the car.

'Oh, no, Dan. I've got a bad feeling about this. Do I have to shake his hand? Would a wave not be just as good?'

'You know the rules, Dave. It's a handshake or nothing.'

Little Dave glanced out of his window while his gran tried to whisper into his ear.

I waved at him.

'Doesn't count, Dave.'

'I know! I was just waving!'

Little Dave's dad – hereafter known as Big Dave – shook his head and smiled.

'He's gone shy, lads. I'm sorry about that.'

'That's okay,' I said. 'If he's shy, he's shy.'

'He gets like that sometimes,' said Big Dave. 'Well, kids always do at that age, don't they? It's a pity I've not got a lollipop on me, or something. That might have worked wonders. . .'.

Of course! Bribery! If there's one thing my training as a three-times uncle has taught me it's that bribery almost never fails with a five-year-old.

I patted the sides of my parka. What did I have in there?

'Dan, check your pockets. See if you've got any sweets or anything.'

'Eh?'

'We'll bribe him out.'

'Hey, hang on, Dave. There must be something in the rules about bribery. . .'

'Shut up and look in your pockets.'

But it was no good. I had some receipts, a cracked cassette cover and about eleven pence in change. Which even a five-year-old would sneer at as a laughable bribe.

'We need to pool our resources. What have you got?'

'It's a pity I left those puppies back at the hotel,' said Dan. 'I've got nothing.'

Curses! Another perfectly good plan scotched.

But then I remembered something.

I asked Big Dave to open the boot of his car. I took out my rucksack. And there I found the solution to all our problems. Because, thanks to laziness and my need to get to a nightclub as soon as I could manage, I hadn't emptied it from the day before.

I crept closer to little Dave's window, and he eyed me with suspicion. Until, that is, I showed him a toy NYPD motorcycle, two sew-on Dekalb County Police badges, and an unnecessarily large bar of American chocolate.

I was more grateful than ever before for the gifts bestowed upon me by Detective Dave and, just as we had passed on the free brewery t-shirts from DG7 in Wolverhampton to DG14 in New York, it now seemed only right and proper for me to pass on the gifts from DG40 of Georgia to DG44 here in Ireland.

In the end I gave him everything except the chocolate.

It worked brilliantly. Little Dave – our five-year-old from Dublin – was clutching his brand new toys in one hand while shaking my flatmate's hand with the other. He signed his name on the polaroid in big, circular motions, and earned himself a smattering of delighted applause from all concerned.

We'd done it. We'd met him.

And there ended the three most remarkable days of Gorman-hunting yet.

Dublin had given us ten new Dave Gormans. Now we only needed ten more to complete our journey.

Chapter 16

ISRAEL – THE PROMISING LAND

It was good to be home. Even before we were back in the flat, it was good to be home. As soon as we were back in the East End, Dave wandered across the street to order two takeaway omelettes and I let some fresh air into the flat. I scanned the mail, put the kettle on, and checked the answerphone. The red light was blinking and there were two messages waiting.

One was from Hanne.

'Hi Dan. Look. I don't know where you are. Give me a call. Let's talk about things. I know you're nowhere near the end of this thing and I know you're not going to give up so we have to talk. Thank you for the flowers. Call me.'

The other wasn't from Hanne. It was from a man. A man with a Scottish accent.

'Hiya Dave! Listen, it was great to bump into you the other night – hope we can do it again sometime! I've still got visions of you trying to start that conga! Nice one. Okay, pal, love to Danny if he's there. . .'

Surely this couldn't be. . .

'Oh . . . it's Dave Gorman by the way! Ha ha, cheers mate, bye.'

I had never doubted my flatmate's honesty for a second.

I picked up the phone and dialled Hanne's number.

'Hanne, it's me.'

'Hello.'

She sounded distant, but I could win her over. I'd last seen her outside the theatre five days or so before, and in those five days we had come fourteen Dave Gormans closer to our target. Surely that was worth something?

'And it's partly because of you, Hanne . . .' I pleaded. 'I'm trying to get this finished as quickly as possible, for you.'

It was tough having responsibilities.

'So where have you been?'

'We just got back from Ireland. I left a message on your mobile. I tried to call you at home but you were out.'

'Yes. I've been going out more lately.'

I didn't like the sound of this.

'Right. Well . . . that's good. Who with?'

'Just people.'

I didn't like the sound of this at all.

'I just realised I needed to enjoy myself more. Seeing as you're having all this fun flying around the world visiting foreign countries.'

'We're not doing foreign countries any more – we gave that up, I promised you. It's just not productive enough.'

'What about Ireland?'

'That's not a foreign country.'

'What?'

'Don't be stupid Danny. Don't take me for a fool. You and Dave, the best of friends, travelling all around the place, getting drunk, meeting new people. It's no way to live.'

Dave walked into the flat, two takeaway boxes under his arm, sensed what was happening, and gave me a worried look.

'Hanne . . . just a little more time . . . please . . . we've met fourteen Dave Gormans since the last time I saw you. We only need ten more. Please . . . wait for me. I'm almost done. I've been working my arse off trying to get this thing done and dusted.'

'Whatever, Danny. I'm sick of hearing about it. Just give me a call when you're free and we'll see where we are.'

I listened to her put the phone down and glumly replaced my receiver. I hadn't needed this. What I'd needed was a bit of enthusiasm. A bit of energy to get me through the final mile. I didn't need guilt as a distraction.

But hey-ho, I still had my omelette. Life wasn't too bad. And Dave, of course, I still had Dave. My friend. The person with whom my troubles would be ended. I could count on him. We'd get through this together. We'd. . .

'What the hell is this?'

Dave was reading from a piece of creased, white, A4 paper.

'What the hell is what?'

'This . . . you git!'

'What? Why am I a git?'

He read from it.

'"Are You Danny Wallace?"'

Oh my Lord. Dave had found the e-mail from Ian that I'd printed out . . . the one about the Danny Wallace get-together that never happened. I hadn't given it to Hanne. I'd told her about it on the phone in the end, and just tucked the paper into an old cookbook. The cookbook Dave now had in his other hand.

'Dave. That's not real. It was a joke. From Ian.'

'A joke, was it? Are these real Danny Wallaces?'

'I think so. Ian says they are. Dave, what are you doing?'

He'd walked over to the phone and picked it up. He dialled the first number on the list and waited, his eyes wide and furious, his chest heaving. This was bad.

'Dave . . . don't be silly. You're over-reacting. . .'

Someone answered the phone and Dave suddenly became very polite.

'Hello? Is that the right number for Daniel Wallace? It is? Right, thank you. . .'

He slammed the phone down.

'You little bastard.'

'Dave . . . I can explain. . .'

'Dave Gormans not good enough for you, now, are they?'

'It's not that, mate, it's just that Ian and I were having a chat ages ago, and. . .'

'Danny, I need you focused! I need you alert! We're almost finished, and you're putting the whole thing at risk with your self-centred, egotistical namesake-pandering?'

'Hey . . . hang on a second. . .'

'Well what else would you call it Dan? Apart from . . . *betrayal*?'

'Dave. . .'

'I bet you had a great time, did you? Meeting all these Danny Wallaces? I bet you all want to move in with each other now.'

I thought, for a second, I saw a tear forming in the corner of his eye.

'Dave . . . no . . . *you're* my flatmate, mate. . .'

'I suppose they were *better* than Dave Gormans, were they?' he said, anger breaking over the sadness. It was like I had cheated on him.

'It's not like that, Dave. I didn't even go. I was with *you* meeting *your* namesakes. Honestly, I've never met another Danny Wallace in my life. . .'

'Really?', he said, a hopeful look in his eye. Maybe we could save this thing. 'You've not even met one?'

'Not even one, mate. I just wouldn't do that to you.'

He walked towards me and we shook hands. And then had a little hug. And then we coughed, remembered who we were, and ate our omelettes.

I checked my e-mails after dinner and found that new tip-offs hadn't been backwards in coming forwards.

The trouble was, the more Dave Gormans we were meeting, the less useful the tip-offs were becoming.

Three different people had taken it upon themselves to alert me to the fact that the Assistant Manager of East Fife Football Club goes by the name of Dave Gorman. One person, working at Legal & General, thought that there might be another one for us in the region of Eastbourne. Another person had found out about an expert on the Alexander Technique who now lived in France . . . though we should be careful, she warned us, as he was 'often to be found in the UK'.

But one e-mail in particular stood out from all the others. It was from someone who, having taken the oath in Edinburgh to do their utmost to find us a Dave Gorman, had performed above and beyond the call of duty. This man had uncovered five Dave Gormans, all in the same city, all just waiting to be met.

Five in one city. This was brilliant. If we worked hard, we could meet all of them in one day – imagine the satisfaction!

My new correspondent knew how thorough we had to be, and had even enclosed phone numbers for each of the David Gormans he'd uncovered.

But what made them unusual – and exciting – was that they all lived and worked in one very unlikely place indeed.

Tel Aviv. Israel.

Now I know that Danny and I had agreed that foreign travel was, with the exception of Ireland, out the window. I know that we had agreed that it just wasn't worth our while at this late stage in the game. But surely the fact that five Dave Gormans lived in Tel Aviv made the trip a worthwhile one? After all, it was only because we knew Dublin would hold more than one that we went there – and now we only had ten more to collect. Israel would halve our workload!

I called Dan into my room and told him what I'd found out. At first he was suspicious.

'But Gorman is hardly an Israeli name, is it?'

'I don't know. Isn't it? Maybe it's got different roots – it's just spelt the same.'

'Does that count?'

'Course it does.'

'It just doesn't sound very . . . *Jewish*.'

'It didn't sound very Norwegian, either, Dan. Or Italian. And remember – there was Jewish Dave in Chappaqua, New York. It can happen. . .'

'And you're sure there are five out there?'

'Yes! Look!'

I showed him the e-mail.

'Phone one of them,' he said. 'Phone one of them up now and check.'

I did. I phoned Israel. I spoke to a young woman. She told me that her landlord, David Gorman, wasn't in right now, but that this was indeed the correct number for him and she'd make sure he got my message. I phoned another number. It was for an attorney by the name of Gorman. I left a greeting on his machine and told him to expect my visit. I phoned another number and, finally, thankfully, spoke to a Dave Gorman in person. This one, it turned out, used to run a wafer factory and took great pleasure in the idea of meeting with Danny and myself.

'I have just got back from China,' he said. 'And I would welcome a visit from England!'

And so it was agreed. Danny was satisfied and I was excited. We arranged to fly out, meet this Dave Gorman, and then meet the rest of his Israeli namesakes.

We would fly out one night, work hard for most of the next day and then return first thing the next morning. Two days and five Dave Gormans and the end would be in sight.

What could possibly go wrong?

It was only when we got to the airport and discovered that the *El Al* check-in desks were positioned in a special, very isolated corner of the airport, where the policemen hang around with big guns and bullet proof vests, that I started to feel nervous.

Now, I doubt we were actually in any real danger, but if the authorities think that guns might be a necessary part of everyday life at this end of the airport, then it does tend to make me feel a tad uneasy.

Two huge queues of people snaked their way to the check-in desks. Dan and I joined the end of one of them, and waited for it to slowly disappear ahead of us. Once at the top of the queue, however, we were met by a man, smartly-dressed and wielding a clipboard, who blocked our path and smiled a dutiful smile. The smile soon melted into a stern, officious grimace. He held his hand out and indicated that now was the time to show him our tickets. We did. He read them and frowned. Then he asked us three questions.

They were all easy questions. I knew all the answers. Danny knew all the answers. By now, you should know all the answers. But the moment I heard the third of his questions I knew that there was going to be trouble.

Number one: 'Are you travelling together?'

Easy.

'Yes.'

Number two: 'How are you connected with each other?'

Easy.

'We're flatmates.'

And number three: 'What is the purpose of your visit?'

Arse.

Arse. This could be trouble. Dave was the one he was asking the questions, for a start, and that wasn't the wisest choice he could have made if he was looking for an easy life.

Lie, Dave. Please. Lie.

Now, I wasn't about to lie. There were policemen with guns around and this was all too official to risk messing around with untruths. But at the same time, I knew that the truth sounded more like a lie than anything I could possibly concoct. The truth really had become stranger than fiction.

'I'm going to meet some other people called David Gorman,' I said.

The official's frown didn't waver.

'What?'

'I'm going to Tel Aviv where I intend to meet some other people called David Gorman.'

This clearly wasn't making sense to him. I tried to clarify things.

'We're collecting them. We're trying to meet 54.'

He blinked at me. His frown remained where it was. The more of the story I gave him, the more unbelievable it seemed to be. He blinked again. He might just as well have set off a siren and yelled, 'I've got one!' for all the subtlety his expression could contain.

Finally, he spoke.

'Would you follow me please, sir?'

The official gestured to Dave to follow him, while summoning a colleague over for a word in his ear. Dave was now standing by a desk on the other side of the room from me, and we looked at each other and shrugged. The official returned to Dave while his colleague walked towards me. Apparently, I was *also* now in for a bit of a grilling.

'Are you two travelling together?'

Easy.

'Yes.'

'How do you know each other?'

Easy.

'We're flatmates.'

'And what is the purpose of your visit?'

Er. . .

Arse.

There followed a 40-minute interrogation which circled around the following exchanges of information too many times for it to have been mere forgetfulness.

'Why are you meeting these men?'

'I had a bet with my flatmate.'

'Gorman isn't a very Israeli sounding name . . . why do you think there will be any Dave Gormans in Tel Aviv?'

'Somebody sent me an e-mail with their phone numbers on.'

'Who sent you this e-mail?'

'A stranger.'

'Why?'

'They wanted to help me prove Danny wrong.'

'Why are you meeting these men?'

  'I had a bet with my flatmate.'

  'How do you know each other?'

  'We're flatmates.'

  'And why are you trying to meet these men?'

'What do you have in your bag?'

  'Some clothes, some toiletries, a polaroid camera and pho-
tographs of 44 Dave Gormans.'

  'Please show me these photos.'

  'Of course.'

  'So why did you meet these men?'

  'I had a bet with my flatmate.'

  And so on and on and on it went.

  Eventually, finally, thankfully, he seemed to have run out of
questions. Or he'd got bored with asking the same set over and
over again.

  'Stay here,' he said. 'I'm coming back.'

  I mopped my brow and looked across at Dan. He looked just as
sweaty and exasperated as me. We raised our eyebrows at each
other while our two interrogators met halfway between our tables
and compared notes to make sure that we had both told the same,
stupid story. They were scratching their heads, and shrugging
their shoulders, and looking back and forth between us. After a
few minutes, they returned to us and begrudgingly gave us a
bright green sticker each. We'd been questioned, searched, and – it
seemed – believed. We were finally allowed to check in.

'If at all possible, can I have an aisle seat?', I asked with my politest
face.

  'I'll see what I can do, but I can't guarantee anything. You should
have checked in an hour ago, you know.'

  I was being scolded by the girl behind the desk, a girl apparently
oblivious to the fact that were it not for her security team we'd have
done just that.

  When we finally checked in to the hotel we decided that it was still
too early in the morning to start ringing strangers. Our first appointment with a Dave Gorman was at 11am so it seemed sensible to grab
a couple of hours sleep before we got on with the business of the day.

At 10.20 I had arranged to ring our first Dave Gorman in order to get directions to his house.

'Shalom,' he said.

'Shalom. Is that Mr. David Gorman?'

'Yes it is. Is *that* Mr. David Gorman?'

'Yes it is.'

A hearty chuckle rang through my ear.

'I must say you have been very persistent in tracking me down.'

'Do you think so?' I was genuinely confused. This was only our second phone call.

'Telephone calls and messages everywhere . . . this is clearly very important to you, Mr. Gorman.'

There was a knock on my door.

'Come on – we have to go', said Dave. Oh, I forgot to tell you – it was Dave at the door.

'I'm ready when you are.'

'Well, I'm wearing trousers so I reckon I'm that bit more ready than you. Jesus, Dan, do you *ever* take those elk pants off? Come on.'

'Have you spoken to any of the others?' I asked, scrambling into my trousers.

'Sort of.'

'What does that mean? Have you spoken to the wafer factory guy?'

'Yeah.'

'Excellent. What about the lawyer?'

'Yep.'

'Well done, Davey. Any of the others?'

'All of them.'

'Blimey', I said. I was impressed, and rightly so. 'So what's the schedule; when are we meeting them?'

'At 11am.'

'And then?'

'No that's it. Just at 11am.'

'Dave, you are a bloody genius. Get them all together in one place. It's obvious. Brilliant. Ten minutes, bang, we've done all five of them. Off to the beach we go. We should have thought of this sooner. We can have a fantastic afternoon, it must be 30 degrees out there. . .'

'Um . . . Dan. The thing is . . . we *haven't* found five Dave Gormans.'

'Eh?'

'We've found one Dave Gorman.'

He paused.

'With five phones.'

Dave Gorman 45 laughed and laughed and coughed and laughed when I explained the story.

'So I am the *only* David Gorman in Israel!' he declared.

We met Israel's only David Gorman – a spritely 70-year-old – at his house on a quiet, shady street about a ten-minute walk from our hotel. He welcomed us in with open arms and immediately set about making us feel at home.

'You want some coffee?'

'Coffee would be great,' I said.

'Or water? Would you like water?'

'Water, yes, lovely,' said Dave.

'Or we have other things to drink . . . what would you like?'

'Anything's fine, really,' we assured him, in unison.

'I tell you what – I will get you water, and my wife will serve you with coffee.'

We were presented with an elegant, white-haired lady in a silk, Chinese dress, who moved with the grace and speed of a woman half her age – this was Mrs Gorman. She was just as keen to make us feel at home as her husband.

'What kind of coffee would you like? We have normal coffee, or what we call 'mud' coffee. . .'

'Normal coffee's great,' we said. To be honest, mud coffee didn't sound all that appetising. It would have been like Mr. Gorman fetching the water and offering us 'still' or 'cloudy'.

'I will bring you both and then you can choose.'

Their house had originally been a bungalow, but a growing family and a successful business had meant that the Gormans soon needed to put an extra storey on top. We sat in the cool and airy living room – a room sprinkled with the fruits of their travels. Mr and Mrs Gorman had been all over the world and had, as he'd indicated to us on the phone, just returned from a trip to China. Travelling is one of their greatest pleasures, and was something they were determined to do to make up for the time they'd spent bringing up their family and then, later, looking after their parents. Now they were out to enjoy life. They seemed to be making a good job of it.

David Gorman walked back into the room with a bottle of water which he proceeded to pour into two tall glasses for Dave and myself, while his wife clattered away in the kitchen, preparing a mass of coffee and cakes and getting the best cutlery ready.

'So, tell me about this crazy idea – where was it born?'

Dave and I were ashamed to tell him it was borne out of a night of drunken whimsy, but David Gorman was a man of the world and immediately got into the spirit of things.

'Let me have a look at these other David Gormans,' he said.

Dave handed him the photo album and began to tell the story. David Gorman looked amused.

'But tell me . . . who of them is Jew?'

We showed him the photo of New York's Jewish Dave Gorman.

David Gorman looked shocked.

'Only *one* is a Jew?'

'Uh-huh.'

David Gorman looked sad.

Mrs Gorman walked into the living room carrying a tray of delights just as her husband was making Danny and me laugh for what seemed like the hundredth time. This was such a good-natured, gentle, funny man – a man who filled me with hope that, if we really do share some genes some way down the line, I might one day be the kind of 70-year-old that now sat before me.

But he was just as interested in Danny's name as he was in ours.

'We were in London a few years ago,' he said. 'We saw The Wallace Collection. Very nice. So very nice. And there is *William* Wallace, too, is there not?'

'Yes,' said Dan. 'And a footballer called Wallace who played for Southampton and Manchester United in the 1980s.'

'Is that so?' said David Gorman, taking in the fact. 'Would anyone like more coffee?'

We spent perhaps two hours sitting with Mr and Mrs Gorman in their living room, during which time they showed, in the way that people who've been married for more years than you've

been alive always do, exactly how their marriage works; he the teasing joker, she the more sensible – but just as loving – side of the arrangement.

I felt such warmth towards them. So what if he wasn't five Dave Gormans? Perhaps this time it really was a case of quality being more important than quantity.

'I would like to take my two new friends on a little trip around Tel Aviv,' said David Gorman, suddenly standing up. 'And then I would like to invite them to have lunch with my wonderful wife and me in our favourite vegetarian restaurant.'

We were only too pleased to accept on both counts.

I climbed into the back seat of David Gorman's car and did my seatbelt up as the car moved out of its parking space and headed on down the road. For a split second it appeared that no one was driving it, until I realised that David was quite a short man, and even from the outside it would have looked like a pair of disembodied hands and some eyebrows were steering the car round the city.

Tel Aviv gets older the further south you travel, and David drove us north, south, east and west to prove it. We saw beaches, and churches, and the ancient port of Jaffa – once the second-largest city in Palestine and now pretty much nothing more than a town tacked onto the edge of Tel Aviv . . . the same Tel Aviv that was once a mere suburb of Jaffa itself.

We drove through markets teeming with shouting Moroccans, and past a queue of people waiting to board a bus that would take them to Cairo. On our way to the restaurant, we slowed down as we passed a mass of grey concrete which turned out to be a far more poignant sight than I've just made it sound. It was here, in 1995, in Kikar Yitzhak Rabin – then named Kikar HaMalkhei Yisra'el – that 150,000 Israelis showed their support of the Oslo Peace Accord. The same day, Yigal Amir, a right-wing extremist, shot Prime Minister Yitzhak Rabin dead. It was a black day for many of the country's people, because it signified so much more than a murder. In a country which, despite its obvious troubles, had always relied on at least a feeling of unity among Israeli Jews, it was unthinkable that one of their own would shoot dead their leader. We drove past slowly and in silence.

We picked up Mrs Gorman on the way and settled down to lunch – which was a real treat. We laughed. A lot. We talked about life, about politics, about religion, about everything. We swapped stories and compared notes on everywhere we'd been, and everywhere they thought we should go. We talked about Dave Gormans, about Danny Wallaces, and about Yiddish words that he thought we might know. Like *schlep* and *schmuck* and even *schlong* – which is quite a rude word for an old man to bring up at the dinner table. And we laughed some more.

When all this was just starting and Danny and I were on a train bound for East Fife to meet our very first Dave Gorman, I never for a moment could have guessed that one day I'd be sitting in a Tel Aviv restaurant discussing the word *schlong* with a 70-year-old Israeli Jew who shared my name. If we hadn't got drunk on the night of Danny's belated birthday celebration, there is no logical way in the world I would ever have met this man. Not that the way I had ended up meeting him was particularly logical either. But on the surface, we have nothing in common but our name – and that's not usually enough to convince one of you to travel thousands of miles to meet the other. But I was so, so pleased that this time it had.

After a two-hour lunch, we knew that the time had come to leave our latest Dave Gorman. He gave us a leisurely lift back to our hotel, and he and his wife stepped out of the car to shake hands and say goodbye properly.

'Dave and Danny, may I say this to you, please. . .'

He was working up to something, trying to remember something. He looked to his wife for encouragement, and she gave it to him in the form of a smile. He looked back at us.

'Gentlemen, you are exactly my cup of tea.'

A sweeter thing I have never heard.

A few hours later and we were checking our bags into Ben Gurion Airport.

We handed our passports over to a young female security guard, who flicked through them with speed and efficiency.

'Can I ask you what you were doing in Israel?'

'We came here to meet five men who share my name but it turned out to just be one man with five phones', said Dave.

A frown.

'Follow me, please, gentlemen. . .'

Chapter 17

AROUND THE WORLD IN MATEY DAVES

I walked back into the flat with mixed emotions. We'd had a marvellous time in Israel, with a marvellous man, and yet I just couldn't shake the disappointment that he'd been alone out there. He was one Dave Gorman. He wasn't five Dave Gormen.

I glanced at his polaroid and went over our meeting one more time in my head. English is his second language. He's 70 years of age. He's Jewish. We have nothing in common in our background either culturally or spiritually. And yet the fact that we shared a name, a mere label, was enough to bring us together for a day. And a very happy day, at that.

Nevertheless, the fact remained – we should have been at number 49 by now and instead we were at number 45. We still had nine more to go.

It was Danny's turn to get the omelettes, and I went through the post and checked the answerphone. There were a few official-looking envelopes, so I put them in the cutlery drawer with the others. There were three messages. They were all from Hanne. The third one left me shocked.

'Dave. It's Hanne. Call me.'

Crikey.

Dave appeared to be a little distracted as I removed the omelettes from their yellow styrofoam boxes and shovelled them onto two plates.

We ate in virtual silence. I made three or four attempts to start up a conversation but Dave might as well have been back in Israel. Which I guess is where his thoughts were, anyway.

'Well, I'm going to have a shower,' I said, standing. 'You know what it's like after a flight.'

Dave didn't answer. I left him alone with his thoughts.

The very moment I heard the shower start up, I rang Hanne.

'Hi Hanne, it's Dave.'

'Where's Danny?'

'In the shower, why?'

'Right, shut up. I'm talking. This thing is nearly over. We all want it to be over, right? Me included. Me possibly more than anyone. So I'm going to help you. Again. Danny told me that after today you would only need five more, right?'

'Ah. Now, that was bef. . .'

'I've found you three more. It's all organised for tomorrow. You're driving us to Manchester.'

'Us?'

'You, me and Danny. Then there will be two more to find; the bloody jokers that will complete your pack of cards. That won't be a problem, I am sure. But enough of the stupid travelling. From now on, you don't go anywhere overnight. Day trips only.'

'Okay, but the thing is. . .'

'No. No talking. I want you to bring Danny home at night. I am going to confiscate his passport to ensure you behave.'

'But. . .'

'No. No "buts".'

'But. . .'

'Ah ah ah. Now – is that okay?'

'Yeah. Except. . .'

'Ah ah. That is the same as a "but". Now, pick me up tomorrow morning at eight. Bye.'

Crikey.

The next day my worlds collided. The forces that had been pulling in wildly different directions with such success were suddenly working together towards one, shared goal. My flatmate, my girlfriend and I were all in a car hurtling towards Manchester on the hunt for Dave Gormans. It should have been a nightmare journey. As it was, it turned out to be rather jolly.

The only complication was in remembering who knew what. Dave had briefed me on his conversation with Hanne, and I learnt that as far as she was concerned, we were on our way to meet numbers 50, 51 and 52. But both Dave and I knew that, thanks to our less than successful trip to Israel, they were really only numbers 46, 47 and 48.

There was no way of telling Hanne that we were still some way off our target. She would explode and, being in a car with her, Dave and I would have nowhere to run.

I looked behind me to see her on the back seat studying the road atlas.

'What are you doing?' I asked.

'I'm checking that Dave drives the correct route to Manchester.'

'He knows the way,' I said. 'He used to live there.'

'I am in charge on this trip,' said Hanne, sternly. 'Nothing is going to go wrong. You two have been very sloppy so far. You need a Norwegian in charge. Or a woman. Or better still, a Norwegian woman.'

And there's not a lot you can say to that.

Our first Mancunian DG lived in Walkden, approximately ten miles to the north west of the city, so I headed out onto the orbital motorway – the M60.

'What on earth is that?'

The voice came from the back of the car, was female, and carried a slight accent, so I knew it wasn't Dan. Looming up ahead of us was the Trafford Centre, a huge and imposing building that feels like some kind of odd parody of elegance and classical design.

'That's the Trafford Centre,' I explained. 'When they built it, it was Europe's biggest shopping centre. It probably still is.'

'Take me there!' she screamed.

'No, we haven't got time for shopping, we have to go and meet Dave!'

Danny seized this opportunity to make his point.

'You see, Hanne!' he said. 'We don't have time for fun on these trips! We never do! You probably think we've been playing with kites on beaches, or riding around on horse and carts in Central Park, or dancing about in clubs in Dublin . . . but we haven't! There's no time for fun on these trips. We go there, get the job done, and go home. We haven't got time to go shopping.'

'But I'm not meeting your Dave Gormans,' said Hanne.

'It's Gor-men,' I said, sighing, although to be honest I didn't think my new pluralisation was going to catch on.

'Whatever. You are the idiots. I am just the director of operations. I can go shopping while you go and do . . . whatever it is that you go and do.'

Dave Gorman 46 is a stocky chap; short, muscular and with the look of an Action Man about him. His shoulders are as broad as his Mancunian accent, and he welcomed us into the house, introduced us to his girlfriend, cooed over his baby and then, in what I can only guess is a true sign of his character, invited us to take a quick walk to his local.

On the way there, he told us about his job (he's a bouncer), and about his hobby (he's a kickboxer). I got the impression that this particular Dave Gorman was a bit of a hard one.

We found ourselves a picnic bench in the beer garden and I soon came to the conclusion that he was actually even more than a bit of a hard one.

He told us of bar-room brawls in the kind of pubs where the sawdust on the floor was furniture the night before. He told us of gangsters, and of troublemakers, and of the best way to punch a man to make sure he doesn't get up again for a while. He showed us battlescars and bruises and a hole in his arm. His knuckles 'are like space dust', he told us, as he rubbed his thickly-bandaged hand, a rascal's sparkle never leaving his eye for a second.

But there were also stories of worldwide travel, of hitchiking alone through international troublespots, of taking care of stray Greek dogs, of the friends he'd made in various tribes of gentle rainforest people.

Granted, many of these stories involved vicious beatings and bullet wounds, but the others revealed a deeper, more thoughtful side to this Mancunian bouncer. This was a man who'd seen the world. A man who'd seen things that most of us would only ever see if David Attenborough pointed a camera at them – and a man who'd seen things that David Attenborough would only ever see if Quentin Tarantino pointed a camera at them.

We were both caught up in his stories of adventure and misadventure, and it soon became clear that so much had happened in this man's life that nothing he could possibly say could surprise me any more. But then he said something that did.

'Did you see them watercolours in the house?', he said. 'You know . . . of birds and flowers, and that?'

'Yes.'

'Well, I did them.'

My mobile phone rang. It was Hanne.

'Hello Dave, where are you now please?'

'We're still with Dave in Walkden.'

'You're still with number 50?'

'Er . . . yes', I white-lied.

'Well you should be on your way to number 51. Come on. It's no wonder you haven't completed this silly bet yet. You have no discipline. Chop the chop.'

'We'll get onto it right away.'

I finished the call with Hanne and looked up. DG46 gave me a quizzical look.

'Who was that?' he asked.

'That was our director of operations.'

Having parked the car in the centre of town we made our way to King Street – pedestrianised, stylish and lined with expensive shops selling designer gear.

'I imagine that if Posh visits Manchester when Becks is playing, this is the only street she'd shop on,' said Dave. 'But let's not tell Hanne about that, eh?'.

We were buzzed in through a discreet door, and a brief ride in a lift found us at the offices of our next DG, yet another stockbroker.

We approached the receptionist.

'Can I help you?' she asked.

'We're here to see Dave Gorman,' said Dave Gorman.

'And your name is?'

'Dave Gorman.'

She looked confused.

'And Danny Wallace,' I said.

She looked relieved, and picked up the phone. She was either dialling security or Dave Gorman.

'There are two gentlemen in reception for you,' she said. 'A Mr Danny Wallace and . . . another gentleman. . .'

She put the phone down.

'He won't be a minute, gentlemen. Do take a seat.'

We'd only just sat down when a smartly dressed and smiling Dave emerged and offered us both a hearty handshake.

He invited us through to a wood-panelled boardroom where a flask of coffee and a small plate of biscuits were promptly delivered by the same lady we'd confused moments earlier.

'Did you notice, Dan?' I asked.

'What?'

'Hard Dave was wearing a blue sweatshirt . . . this one, financial sector – white shirt.'

'Amazing.'

I sensed confusion emanating from our genial host. And who could blame him? We both smiled reassuringly in his direction.

'I once bumped into another Dave Gorman,' he said.

'Really?'

'Yeah. I was at a big conference . . . you know, everyone wears name badges, we just saw each other and, well, your own name leaps out at you, doesn't it?'

This was exciting. I passed him the photo album.

'Was he one of these ones?'

He started flicking through the various pictures.

'We only had a brief chat. It was a while ago now. But I don't think he's in here. No. No, I can't see him in here.'

Hearing that sentence lifted my spirits. It was a chink of light breaking through the darkness, evidence that another fresh Dave Gorman was still out there, waiting to be found.

My phone rang. The display told me it was Hanne. I looked at my watch and knew we had to be on our way.

'Hi Hanne,' I said. 'Where are you?'

'King Street. Why didn't you tell me about this place? Where are you?'

A 300-yard walk and we were at the offices of the *Manchester Evening News*. This was the workplace and agreed meeting point of our third Dave Gorman of the day.

Through the front door there was a small window on our left, behind which a couple of security guards were nursing mugs of tea. They noticed us peering in their direction and the window slid back.

'Hello,' I said. 'We're here to meet Dave Gorman?'

'Won't be a minute.'

The window slid shut. There was a pause. The window slid open.

'He's in a meeting.'

'Oh . . . but we've got an appointment. Can you tell him it's Dave Gorman here for him?'

Window slid shut. Pause. Window slid open.

'What did you say your name was?'

'Dave Gorman.'

Window slid shut. Pause. Muffled laughter. Pause. Window slid open.

'He says he won't be able to see you, I'm afraid. Meeting. Sorry.'

'I knew I should have come with you', said Hanne, as Dave motored down the M6.

'It wouldn't have made any difference', I said. 'We were on time for the appointment but he was in a meeting. Besides, you were bored of the whole thing before we even reached the first Dave Gorman, you didn't want to come with us.'

'I'm a girl. Not an obsessive-compulsive like you. Anyway, who was he meeting?'

'Don't know. We never got the chance to find out.'

'I expect he was in a meeting with Royal Leamington Spa Dave Gorman!' said Dave, his knuckles white on the steering wheel.

'Bastards!', said Hanne.

I was shocked. I think it was the rudest word I'd ever heard her use.

'Absolute fucking bastards.'

Until then.

On the way back we stopped at Watford Gap service station and grabbed a quick coffee. While Hanne went to the toilet, Danny and I took the opportunity to have a private chat.

'Are you staying at Hanne's tonight?' I asked.

'No.'

'Oh. I thought you'd. . .'

'Whatever you thought you were wrong,' said Dan, tersely. '*That's* been banned.'

'Oh.'

'Until this is over.'

'Ah.'

'So we have to get it finished as soon as we can. Oh, shit, Dave. What are we going to do?'

'What do you mean?'

'Well, now Hanne thinks we've met 51. She thinks we need three more. We need seven more. We can't keep hiding it from her. We're going to have to do something. And quickly. My girl-friend is sleeping with my passport but not me.'

'What?'

'I had to give her my passport this morning. She said she's going to keep it under her pillow. It's like I'm living in a police state. I've been tagged. I've got to ring her every evening so she knows I'm home. I'm not allowed to leave the country. It's all wrong, Dave – it's like Hanne is Big Brother.'

'That's very wrong indeed, Dan. You shouldn't go out with your big brother.'

We dropped Hanne off at her house in Kenton and continued our drive through London towards the flat.

'The thing is, Dave, what's happened here is you've just ended up adding more pressure to it all,' I said.

'How do you mean?'

'If you'd come clean to Hanne on the phone and told her we hadn't met the five Dave Gormans we thought we were going to, at least now she'd know the truth. She wouldn't be under the impression that we're only three away from completion. But we've got to find four more Dave Gormans, now, in secret. And that's only to get our story straight with her. We've got to meet three more after that! We're going to have to move quickly and secretly. Do you know how difficult that is, keeping a secret from her? She knows everything.'

'Except that we haven't met as many as she thinks we have,' said Dave.

'Well, yes, except that.'

'We can do it, Dan. I've got a lead. I've got another Dave Gorman up my sleeve that we can meet in the next couple of days or so. Someone sent me their address in an e-mail – I checked it out last night before bed and he's a real Dave Gorman.'

'Good. That takes care of one more. Where is he?'

'He's an Irishman.'

'Ireland, then? Well, that's fair enough – we'd rack up a few more there in no time, but I think you've forgotten. Hanne's banned foreign travel. I'd need my passport for that, and anyway, it'd be an overnighter. That's banned, too. No foreign travel, no overnight stays. Let's not make life too difficult, Dave. We've got to look local.'

'We've looked local. Believe me, if there were any more to be found locally, or even nationally, we'd be meeting them. But we're drying up, Dan. It's getting harder. Too hard to throw one away. We're going to have to meet him.'

'We can't, Dave. Ireland is a foreign country.'

'Relax. I didn't say it was Ireland, did I? I said he was Irish.'

'Well, good. So where is he?'

'Germany.'

I'll be honest. I had a job convincing Danny on this one. Whatever Hanne was – or wasn't – doing to him was obviously working.

I tried to tell him that Germany is really just around the corner. I tried to tell him that it was very possible to make it there and back in one day. I tried to tell him he wouldn't need his passport. But I think at that point he'd pretty much worked out I was making it all up as I went along for my own benefit.

'It's not possible, Dave. We can't. Hanne won't let me. She won't let you. Do you know how much trouble we'd be in if she found out? We'd be in very big trouble indeed.'

'She's only a girl, Danny.'

Danny flashed me a you-don't-know-what-you're-talking-about-on-this-one-at-all look – all wide eyes and quivering lips – and I had an idea of what he meant. Hanne could be feisty, to say the least.

Nevertheless, I continued to try and win him round.

'Look,' I said, back at the flat and in front of my computer. 'These are the tip-offs we've received lately. Tel Aviv . . . Dublin . . . Tottenham . . . Germany . . . Dublin again . . . East Fife . . . Dunstable . . . East Fife . . . East Fife . . . Braunston . . . Peterborough . . . and East Fife. And that's it. All the earlier ones are about Dave Gormans we've already met, or more about Dave Gorman the Assistant Manager of East Fife, or they're from helpful onlookers who want to know whether we've thought of looking in the phonebook yet.'

'That's not a bad idea.'

'We've looked! And we're still desperate for Dave Gormans! We have to meet Germany's Dave Gorman. He lives in Schlangenbad. It's about twenty minutes from Frankfurt. The flight to Frankfurt is about an hour and a half. So we can be there and back in a matter of hours, I promise you. Hanne need never know!'

'I still need my passport. That's at her house, under her pillow – I don't have keys.'

'We'll work something out,' I said. I had him now. We'd win this thing yet.

The door opened. We were looked up and down, with disgust.

'Hello Danny. Hello. . .' she paused, and then, with a sneer, '. . . Dave.'

'Hello Janne. Is Hanne in?'

'She's at work. She's always at work at this time. You know this. She's not like you two. She can't just sit around her flat watching *Lassie* and *Trisha* all day and then get in a car and drive places.'

'I know, poor thing,' I said. 'I'm just popping round to drop something off.'

'Okay. Give it to me and I'll make sure she gets it.'

'Er . . . no. It's a bit awkward. It's an ointment. For a condition.'

'It's deeply embarrassing,' added Dave. 'Hanne would prefer it if no one knew about it.'

'What, so *you* can know what it is, Dave? But I, her flatmate, am not allowed to know?'

'Dave *doesn't* know what it is,' I said.

'Yes I do. Danny tells me everything. I bet Hanne doesn't tell you everything.'

'She told me about that girl from Colchester.'

'What? How did she know about that? I only told Danny that.'

'I tell *Hanne* everything *too*,' I said.

'Well, you haven't told her about Germany!'

'What is this about Germany?' asked Janne.

'Shut up, Dave. Look. Can I please come in and put this ointment in her room?'

'What is this about Germany?'

'Er . . . Hanne's very gullible. I once told her that England beat Germany in the 1966 World Cup final and she believed me.' I followed up with a forced laugh.

'Oh,' said Janne, puzzled but not all that interested. Thank God she was Norwegian. Thank God she was a girl. And thank God she was just as gullible as Hanne.

'You won't tell her, will you? She'd be very upset with me.'

'Okay, whatever. Look, I can't stand around talking all day. If you have to drop something off, do it quickly, please.'

I ran into Hanne's room and rifled around until I found my passport. It was indeed under her pillow. I like that kind of thing about Hanne – less interesting people would have used 'it's going under my pillow' as a metaphor.

I ran back towards the door where Dave and Janne were still chatting.

'Listen, Janne,' I said. 'If for any reason I have to come back later, before Hanne gets home from work, and take that ointment away because I got the wrong one or something, you won't tell Hanne we were here, will you? She'd hate to know you knew about . . . you know.'

'Her condition,' said Dave.

'I am sure Hanne will tell me about it in her own good time,' said Janne.

'I'm sure you're right,' said Dave. 'In the meantime, make sure you have plenty of fresh towels, please, and I wouldn't let her sit on the sofa if you've just had it cleaned.'

Leaving Janne shocked and pale on her own doorstep, we got in the car and drove.

I'd promised Danny we'd be quick. I don't think he was prepared for how quick.

A flight, a taxi, a meeting. A taxi, a flight, a short drive to Kenton where Danny put his passport back, and we were done.

We had been to Germany and back in less time than it had taken us to visit Manchester two days before. DG48 was in the bag.

The adrenaline rush was superb.

Now, our editor, Jake, has informed us that it is customary in a book that involves foreign travel to discuss the countries visited, in order to try and give the reader a flavour of each location. We have told him how quick our trip to Schlangenbad was, but he has insisted. So here goes:

Frankfurt Airport is clean, and seems efficiently run. Our taxi driver had a moustache. He was polite, spoke little English, but enough for our purposes. The roads were not overburdened with traffic. Schlangenbad translates directly into English as 'snake bath'. That is all we discovered.

Happy, Jake?

Our trip to Germany had *indeed* been quick. Dave Gorman of Schlangenbad, and his wife, Frau Gorman, had laid on a little welcome breakfast for us, and Dave had even had a bottle of fizzy wine made from the grapes of Schlangenbad's vineyards ready and waiting.

He had a remarkable history, this Dave Gorman – an expert on hotel management, he'd worked all over the world. At one time he'd even been made the Honorary Consul of the Federal Republic of Germany in St Lucia.

We wanted to stay on and talk about it. But we couldn't. That wasn't the point any more. We'd met him. He was in the album. We were one closer to completion. We had to go.

We drank a traditional Schlangenbadian toast on the balcony of his spacious, airy house, and that was that. We had a taxi to jump into, a flight to catch, and a passport to return. And we managed it all with near-military precision.

The only downside was the phonecall I received that night.

'Danny, it's Hanne. Why did you come round to the house today? What is all this about my "condition"? How did your passport get from under my pillow to under yours? And why is there a boarding card tucked inside it which suggests you were in Germany today?'

'Would you like a word with Dave. . .?'

We were in trouble again.

We thought we'd been clever, and we thought we'd been fast. We even thought we'd get away with it. We were naughty little schoolboys who thought we'd got one over on Miss. We hadn't.

'I am prepared to forgive your deception,' Hanne had said, 'but only because that puts you at 53 Dave Gormans and the end is soon here now.'

It took me at my bravest to admit to her that we hadn't been entirely truthful to her on the way up to Manchester and that we were still to meet even a 49th Dave Gorman.

Well, actually, I first tried to lie, of course.

'We miscounted,' I tried. 'I'm not much good with numbers.'

'You're lying,' she said. 'You did a maths degree.'

'Ah, but I never finished it,' I said.

'So I suppose you left before the bit about counting?' she said.

It was too late. She knew, and she knew I'd tried to lie.

'Hanne, please, be reasonable. We had every right to believe that the trip to Israel would land us five Dave Gormans. It was virtually guaranteed! And c'mon . . . you can't be angry about Germany. We only did it because there was a Dave Gorman there. We're already back in the flat and it's not even 9pm. I'll make sure Danny's safely tucked up in bed by ten.'

'Dave, let's talk like adults. How long do you see this going on for.'

'Absolutely no longer than it takes to meet 54 Dave Gormans. But they need coaxing, and encouraging. They can't be rushed to come out of the woodwork. They can only be met when they're ready. We have to approach them cautiously, and on their own terms.'

'You talk about these Dave Gormans as if they are not human. As if they are urban foxes or something.'

'All I'm saying is I promise we'll rush but you never know where the next one is coming from.'

Hanne sighed. I sensed that she was almost beaten.

'And where is the next one coming from? Where are you meeting the final six?'

It was my turn to sigh.

'I don't know, Hanne. The source seems to have dried up. We had high times in Dublin, but it appears that we peaked too soon. The flow has become a dribble. I just don't know where we're going to go next.'

Hanne's voice became harder. More grown-up. More frightening.

'Then I am afraid the bet is over.'

'What?'

'I'm taking Danny off the bet.'

'You don't have the authority!'

'I'm his girlfriend, Dave. I have more authority than you know what to do with. I could have broken this bet anytime – and you with it – but I chose not to.'

This was all a bit too much like *The Godfather* for my liking, but I couldn't do anything about it – I was sucked in.

'Please . . . Hanne . . . just a little more time. If not for me. . .'

'It wouldn't be for you.'

'No, I'm saying, if you don't do it for me. . .'

'I wouldn't.'

'No, listen, hear me out. If not for me, then do it for Danny. He's invested so much in this. Don't break his little heart, Hanne, I beg you . . . just a little more time . . . for Danny.'

There was a long, long silence.

Eventually, slowly, she began to talk.

'You have 24 hours, Dave. 24 hours to come up with a plan. If by 9am tomorrow morning you have failed to come up with anything that will end this bet as quickly as possible, I am taking Danny away from you for good. He'll be off the bet. That'll be the end of it, Dave. No more fun for you. No more terrorising others with your ridiculous behaviour. 24 hours. And that is that. Think long and hard. I want assurance in the morning that you have found some more Dave Gormans and that you are going to meet them. Otherwise you are finished. Do I make myself clear?'

I shut my eyes and hung my head low.

'Yes.'

'Oh, and Dave?'

'Yes?'

'I've hidden his passport properly this time. . .'

I had just worked out that an anagram of 'David Gorman' is 'Mr Odd Vagina', when a sudden rush of cold water forced me out of the shower and onto the bathmat. Dave had turned on all the taps in the flat. It was his way of subtly telling me he needed a word.

There followed a loud banging on the door and a shout of 'Dan! I need a word!'

We sat in the living room and I quickly explained the situation. We needed a plan and we needed to come up with it quickly. I opened a bottle of rum and poured two large measures. This was, I imagined, how a managing director of a multi-national corporation would behave if he was calling a 'crisis meeting' with his lieutenant. I guess it should have been whiskey, and we should have been smoking cigars, and we should have been in an office somewhere, and Dan shouldn't have been wearing a dressing gown, but nobody's perfect.

'What about the Dave O'Gormans?' asked Dan, desperately trying to find a way through the mire.

It was unthinkable.

'No, Dan, the extra vowel would make me a liar. I'd be haunted by O's forever.'

'Going "oooo".'

'What?'

'I just thought that was the noise "O"s would make,' he said, blushing. 'You know. If they were haunting you. . .'

I stared at him and the sentence trailed off into nothingness. He wasn't taking this seriously, but a look was all it took. Silence. We sipped at our drinks for a while until Danny, again, spoke.

'What about Dave Gurman?'

'No, Dan.'

'Ormans?'

'What?'

'There could be someone out there called David G. Orman.'

Danny was starting to annoy me. He just wasn't taking this seriously at all. I tried desperately to control my temper. I stood up, turned my back on him, and walked to the window.

'What about David *Morgans*?'

'What about them?' I said through tight lips.

'Well they're anagrams of David Gorman . . . they could sort of count . . . we could meet, say, five David Morgans and a Mr Odd Vagina, and we're there.'

I looked down at my glass, flicked my wrist and swirled the golden, honey-coloured drink around. I focused my eyes on the centre of the sugary vortex shutting out the real world while I tried to tame the ire.

'Or we could get some animals? Goldfish: they're easy. We get six goldfish and we name them all Dave Gorman.'

There was nothing I could say. There was nothing I could do. I gripped my glass tighter and tried to shut out Dan's voice.

If we could complete the task we would have achieved something. It might be a futile something, but it would still be *something*. What was the point in Roger Bannister breaking the four-minute mile? What was the point in Edmund Hillary scaling Mount Everest? Where was the net benefit to mankind? There was none.

But did the world mock them for their achievements? No. If we didn't succeed we would be laughing stocks.

My name would be sullied forever. Other Dave Gormans would be affected. They would be mocked as they walked down the high streets. This wasn't just between Dan and me any more. I had a responsibility to all of them to get this thing finished. There's a fine line between success and failure, and I knew on which side of it I wanted to be.

And what was Dan suggesting? David Gurmans, David O'Gormans, David G. Ormans, anagrams, and goldfish! I could contain it no longer. I slugged back the rum and then in one fluid movement turned and hurled the glass in his direction.

'WHAT DO YOU MEAN, GOLDFISH?' I screamed.

He dove for the sofa, pulling a cushion in front of his face for protection as the glass smashed on the wall behind him.

'I just thought. . .'

He shut up. He had to, because I'd grabbed him by the throat.

'No you didn't Dan. You *didn't* think. You didn't think *at all*. We can't just *make* Dave Gormans! If animals counted we could have finished this months ago! If I'd come to you on day one with 54 goldfish called Dave Gorman, would you have accepted that? I don't think so, Dan, so don't take the piss. . .'.

My left forearm was across his throat, my right hand clenched in front of me. 'We can't just *make* Dave Gormans. . .'

'Yes we can', he said, pushing me away and nursing his throat. 'There *is* a way.'

And he was right.

There *was* a way.

Chapter 18

NAMEDROPPERS

'Hanne. . .'

'Who is it? What time is it?'

'It's 7.30, Hanne. It's Dave.'

'Dave? Why are you calling me now?'

'I wanted to make sure I told you before the 24-hour deadline was up. We've got a plan . . . Danny and I have got a plan. . .'

'And that would be. . .?'

'Some men are born Dave Gormans. Some men achieve Dave Gormanness. And some have Dave Gormanness thrust upon them . . . we'll call you later, bye!'

There *was* a way of *making* some Dave Gormans. When we'd taken the stage show to the Edinburgh Festival, and then onto the West End, thousands of people had come to hear our story. And seven of them had volunteered to change their names to Dave Gorman.

At the time, we'd politely taken down their details, but we had never suspected we'd need to call them. And we certainly didn't think that if we ever did, they'd go through with the change.

Now, it looked like they might be our only way forward.

In our quest to meet 54 Dave Gormans, the bizarre truth was that a Colin, a Graham, a Tom, a Dan, a Pascale, a Kelly and one David might be the answer we were looking for.

If they were still willing to proceed, they would take us to 55 Dave Gormans – more than fulfilling our needs.

Dave scurried off to his room to try and find the notebook containing the vital phone numbers. He returned with it in hand, and sat by the phone.

'This could do it, Dan. This could take us right to the end.'

I couldn't watch. My future hung in the balance. Everything was resting on Dave's phone manner and whether or not these ex-audience members would even remember offering to change their names just to help Dave prove me wrong.

I got jittery and went to my room.

'Good luck,' I said.

The first time anyone had said they would change their name was when I'd done the show in Hammersmith. The potential Dave in question was Colin Hurley. I dialled the number.

'Hello, is that Colin?', I asked.

'Yes, who's that?'

'It's Dave Gorman.'

'Oh.'

That wasn't a good 'oh'. That sounded like the kind of 'oh' people say when someone on the doorstep reveals that they are a policeman. I had some work to do. I tried to affect a casual air.

'Anyway . . . it's about this changing-your-name thing. . .'

'What?'

'You know . . . changing your name . . . to Dave Gorman.'

'Oh.'

'Well, we're quite keen to organise it pretty soon so we. . .'

'The thing is . . . my little lad . . . he's not keen.'

That did make things a bit more complicated. But I wasn't giving up. I had to try something, anything. I knew as the words fell from my mouth that I was talking complete nonsense, but I was desperate. And it had worked before.

'We've got t-shirts?'

'What?'

'Er . . . t-shirts?'

'Oh.'

It hadn't worked. It would have done in Norway. I decided it was time to seize the moral high ground.

'But you promised!' I said, full of affront.

'But it was. . .'

'You shook my hand', I added, 'in front of witnesses!'

'Yes, but. . .'

'That's a legally-binding contract as far as I'm concerned.'

'Oh.'
Colin was in. One down, six to go.

I heard a pop. Moments later Dave stormed into my room. He looked happier than I'd seen him for a long time. He was carrying two glasses of champagne. He left one glass on my desk and then waltzed out.

'Cheers!' I shouted.

But he was already gone.

I figured David Heffron would be the easiest of the seven to approach. After all, we were only asking him to change *one* of his names.

The phone was answered by a female voice.

'Hello, is David there?'

'Yes, I'll just get him. Can I say who's calling?'

'It's Dave.'

'Oh, you're a Dave as well!' She chuckled at the coincidence. Little did she know! 'I'll just fetch him.'

I was amazed to discover that Dave didn't need much persuading at all. In fact he didn't need any.

'Hi Dave, it's Dave Gorman here. . .'

'Excellent, when do you want me?'

Two down, five to go.

The door to my room opened and Dave was there. Dancing. Alone.

All the time singing, he danced in and then danced out. I don't think it's a dance I've ever seen performed solo, but I immediately recognised it. I think it was the words to the song that gave it away.

'Let's all do the conga. The conga's getting longer. La la la la, hoy! La la la la.'

If ever a conga wasn't getting longer it was that one. Still, it was a happy dance.

I was on a roll. I decided to ring Tom next. He should be easy enough.

When we'd met him in Edinburgh, he'd spoken with a pronounced lisp. His surname was Simpson. Surely a Tom Thimpthon would be keen on becoming a Dave Gorman? A less sibilant name would be hard to find.

'Hello, is Tom there?'

'And you are. . .?'

'Dave Gorman.'

'You want Tom, yeah?'

'Yeah.'

'Tom who?'

'Tom Simpson.'

'Oooh . . . *that* Tom. Er . . . I'm afraid he moved out a while ago. We don't know where he went.'

'You don't have a new phone number for him?'

'No. Not at all. No.'

'Oh. Well, if you see him. . .'

'We won't. We never do. He moved.'

'Are you sure. . .?'

'I'm abtholutely thertain. Bye.'

The phone went down. Hmmm. 2 – 1.

The music had stopped. In a gesture loaded with significance, Dave opened my door and took back the glass of champagne. I hoped nobody else refused him. I would have hated to have seen him take back the dance.

So Tom was no longer playing, but we had two on board and four more to go. If they all came in, we would still hit the target, we would still make 54.

There were four more to go, but there were only three more phone calls to make, because unless things had gone wrong since we'd first met them, Graham Cleminson and Pascale Noele were a couple. They were a *lovely* couple. But would they soon be a lovely couple of Dave Gormans?

I had to get this over with. I decided to ring them next. I spoke to Graham.

'Are you still offering the money?' he asked.

I'd forgotten about that. But if that's what it took.

'Count us in, then!'

Fantastic. The money had won them over. Just as well they needed it; they were planning a trip to Peru and the cash would come in handy. Plus, they'd have the added romantic extra of travelling on matching his 'n' hers Dave Gorman passports.

My mind started to race. Maybe one day they would marry!

We could end up with the world's first Mr and Mrs Dave and Dave Gorman-Gorman!

There was music. There was a conga. The champagne was topped-up and returned to my desk. I drank it quickly, fearing it might be withdrawn.

We had four Dave Gormen-in-waiting, including our first female – the soon-to-be-former Pascale Beatrice Noele. I was delirious with happiness. I just hoped she stayed true to her word. Well, her boyfriend's word.

But there was another girl to call. Kelly Scutts. No offence is meant to her parents, but if someone with a name as soft and lyrical as Pascale Beatrice Noele can be persuaded to change it, then surely a Kelly Scutts with its pair of alliterative, harsh 'k' sounds could also be persuaded?

'Hello . . . is that Kelly? It's Dave Gorman here.'

'Thank God. I was getting worried about you.'

'What?'

'Well, I was worried something had happened to you. I was expecting you to get in touch about this Dave Gorman thing and there was nothing, I kept thinking "he'll call tomorrow", but nothing. I started thinking you'd had a car crash or some- thing . . . anything could have happened.'

I felt like a fifteen-year-old who'd missed his 10 o'clock curfew and was now getting a harsh but loving telling off from his par- ents. All my instincts were to say, 'I'm sorry, we missed the last bus and no-one had 10p for the phone and it won't happen again' but I managed to remember where and who I was.

'I'm sorry about that. I'm fine.'

'Oh, what a relief . . . the panic.'

'We just got a bit busy. You know what it's like when you're travelling the world trying to meet Dave Gormans?'

'Not really.'

'No. I suppose not. Still, we were hoping you were still inter- ested in the opportunity to become a Dave Gorman. The offer is still open.'

'Oh yes!'

Oh yes!

5-1 to us. We were romping home. That would take us to 53 Dave Gormans. One more and we'd be home and dry.

Danny entered the room. He held up his empty champagne glass.

'Do you want this back or is it still mine?' he asked sarcastically.

'I'd top it up, but it might be premature,' I said. 'We've got Colin, David, Graham and Pascale and Kelly. Tom said "no". I'm about to ring Dan.'

'Oh no. I've got a bad feeling about this.'

'Do you?'

'Why would a Dan want to change his name?' asked Dan.

'Because he wants to help me. Because if he says "yes", this thing is as good as finished. Because if he says "yes", we know we're going to reach 54. That's it, that's the lot. We'd be finished!'

We stared at the phone in reverent silence. Just one more 'yes' and our journey would be over!

'Cross your fingers, Dan.'

He held up both hands to show me that he had taken my instruction seriously.

I picked up the receiver and dialled the number.

I heard a voice.

A female voice.

A female computer voice.

A female computer voice bearing bad news.

'The number you have dialled has not been recognised. Please check and try again.'

The day of the historic namechanging was soon upon us. If all went well, by the end of it, we would be up to 53 Dave Gormans. We both woke and rose from our respective beds early and nervous. I'd last felt like this the day of my last maths GCSE, and I'd positively revelled in the fact that I'd never have to feel like that again. And now here it was, in the pit of my stomach, like it had never been gone. And worse, much *much* worse, it was self-inflicted.

You see, I'd had my doubts in the night as to whether or not our brave volunteers would all go through with the change. It's a serious business, changing your name. There are forms. There are lawyers. There are repercussions. Especially, I suspect, if you're a girl changing your name to that of a boy. I became convinced that something was going to go wrong, and, over what little breakfast I could eat, I tried to relay my fears to Dave.

'I'm worried. This is such a big thing these people are doing for us. They're going to change their identities. They're going to change their lives. Should we really be forcing them to do this?'

'But we're not forcing anyone, Danny . . . these people are *willing* to change their names, voluntarily, just to help us. By the end of the day we'll be virtually there!'

'But what if we're not? Do you really expect to turn up at the solicitor's office and for Graham, Pascale, David, Colin and Kelly to be sitting there waiting for the opportunity to join the Dave Gorman Brotherhood? I don't think we're going to get to 53 by the end of today, Dave. I think we're setting ourselves up for a fall.'

'They'll turn up, Dan. You have to have faith in Dave Gormans.'

'They're not Dave Gormans!'

'Not *yet* they're not.'

We put our coats on and walked down the road to the tube station where we jumped onto the Central Line and were carried along to the middle of town. We were heading for Mayfair and, more specifically, for the offices of our agreed solicitor, Charles Gorman. At such short notice I'm afraid a Charles was the best we could do. If only his parents had had a little foresight, we might have had a chance of reaching 54 by the end of the day.

At a little before 11 o'clock we were standing on the stone steps outside his offices, scanning the road left and right for any approaching cars, taxis or bicycles bearing potential Dave Gormans. At one point we were passed by a pregnant woman, who I suppose technically *could* have been bearing a potential Dave Gorman, but we were too embarrassed to ask.

'They're not going to come, Dave. They probably thought it was all a big joke. Why the hell would they change their names, anyway? It's lunacy!'

'Shut up, Dan. They'll be here. They're going to take us right to the edge. They *have* to turn up.'

We waited a few more minutes. Nothing much happened. And then a black cab pulled up in front of us. The man in the back waved at us – a happy-faced, spiky-haired man. This was David Heffron – the keenest of our possible namechangers. A man so keen, in fact, that he'd just flown all the way down from Edinburgh to meet us and do the deed.

'Where do I sign?' he said, jumping out of the cab.

A moment later another cab pulled up. It contained Colin Hurley and his little boy.

'I don't suppose we can convince you, as well?' I asked the tiny, tracksuited lad.

'No!' said his father, protectively. 'Don't listen to the bad man, son.'

I sensed Colin wasn't as sure about what he was doing as he could have been.

Kelly Scutts was next. Danny looked amazed.

'She turned up! A girl! A girl who wants to be a Dave! These people are really going to go through with it,' he said, shaking his head. 'What have we done?'

Finally, Graham and Pascale came into view, walking down the street, studying the buildings, holding hands.

We had our set.

Our new Dave Gormans.

We were all here. We were going to make history.

Charles Gorman looked confused. A well-mannered, smart-suited young man with a plummy accent and very shiny shoes, he appeared not to want to ask too many questions, for fear of offending anyone.

'This is Colin, Graham, Pascale, David and Kelly,' said Dave. 'They'd all like to change their names to Dave Gorman, please.'

'Right. . .' said Charles, uncertainly. 'And . . . er . . . and what about you?'

'I'm already a Dave Gorman,' said Dave.

Charles looked to me.

'I'm Danny,' I said. 'And I'm staying that way.'

Charles took on the face of a very relieved man indeed.

'If you'd like to follow me, please. . . .'

We tailed Charles out of the reception area and up a grand old red-carpetted staircase. On the top floor, he ushered us into a boardroom and we all sat down around a long, mahogany table.

'I won't be a moment,' said Charles. 'Now, I *did* hear you correctly when you said that you all wish to be named . . . er . . . Dave Gorman?'

'Absolutely,' said Dave, and there were a few nods of agreement from around the table. Charles looked at me and shook his head before closing the door behind him. I shared his disbelief.

Here, in this Mayfair solicitor's office, sat five complete strangers. And yet they were about to begin to bond with each other totally and without question. It was a kind of bonding I'd seen happen just as instantly between Dave and nearly 50 other strangers in the past few months. These people were about to share a name. Never again in their lives would these five people struggle to find something with which to start a conversation with one another. These five people were about to become namesakes. That's one better than penpals. Two better than cousins. Just one below lovers. But who knew what excesses the emotions floating around this boardroom might muster before the day was out?

I was excited to be a part of it.

I was proud. Proud of what we were about to achieve. Proud that we were making a difference in people's lives. Granted, the difference might not actually make their lives any better, but it was a difference nevertheless and that's what counted.

The atmosphere around the table was jokey, but not exactly relaxed. I could see everyone eyeing each other up trying to work out why the others were doing it in the hope that in doing so they would discover why they themselves were there.

Charles Gorman walked back into the room with some official-looking documents under his arm and a rubber stamp in his hand.

'May I ask, if it's not being rude, how it is that you all came to decide that the name Dave Gorman, in particular, was one that you would all wish to take as your own?'

'It's for a bet,' I said, speaking for the group.

Charles nodded.

'Ah. Okay, then. Well, I suppose if you're all doing it for a bet, then. . .'

'Actually, the bet's between Danny and me. These kind people have just agreed to help out.'

Our solicitor friend blinked twice, then took his place at the head of the table, frowning.

'Well, let's begin,' he said. 'Let's see . . . right. David James Heffron. . .'

All of a sudden the atmosphere changed. The jokiness that existed beneath the surface tension evaporated completely. The formality of the surroundings, the earnestness with which Charles Gorman spoke, the legality of what was about to ensue struck everyone in the room. This was serious.

'That's me,' said David, nervously.
And so the madness began.

I watched with wide eyes as David Heffron stood up and approached Charles Gorman. Charles had, in the last few seconds, turned into a model of formality, dishing out long words willy-nilly and signing various forms in royal blue ink with a gold-tipped fountain pen.

'Is your name David James Heffron?' he asked.

'It is,' said David James Heffron.

'Repeat after me . . . I, David James Heffron. . .'

'I, David James Heffron. . .'

And I had to look away. I looked anywhere. I looked at my shoes. I looked at the wall. But most of all, I looked at the other four poor people we'd forced to come to this office to sign away something they'd had since birth and probably thought they'd have until death consigned it to a grave stone, or, in other cases, when marriage might replace it with something less familiar.

But I was surprised. They didn't look too uncomfortable. They didn't look too uncomfortable at all. They watched in calm concentration as David James Heffron signed his new name for the very first time. Charles Gorman signed his name beneath it with a sweeping gesture and more of that royal blue ink.

And with the slam of a rubber stamp a brand new Dave Gorman materialised in front of us.

There was a pause. Then applause. Slaps on backs. And the giddy laughter of my very giddy flatmate.

I hugged my new Dave Gorman. And he hugged me back. I felt like a parent. We had met a five-year-old Dave Gorman in Ireland, but now, here in my arms, was a fully-grown, adult Dave Gorman who was barely one minute old! I'd given birth to this man – this bonny, bouncing Dave Gorman standing in front of me. I felt like I'd been in labour for many months but that finally I was in line for an easy delivery.

I hugged him again and looked back at Danny.

'That's 49!' I said. '49 Dave Gormans!'

'Colin Thomas Michael Hurley?' said Charles Gorman.

The room fell silent. It was time to make another Dave Gorman.

Colin looked at his little lad and smiled, stood up, and walked towards Charles Gorman.

'Okay, let's do this, then,' he said. 'Why not?'

I watched Colin nod his way through Charles Gorman's questions, and then I studied the faces of the others as they prepared themselves mentally for what lay ahead. The reaction that the brand new Dave Gorman had received upon attaining his Dave Gormanness had been surprising, but lent the proceedings the kind of atmosphere it needed. It was an atmosphere of good-natured anticipation.

I studied the man formerly known as David Heffron. His cheeks were red and his eyes were glowing. I looked at my flatmate, next to him. His face was bright and happy. Colin, too, went through some kind of transformation at the hands of Charles Gorman – both in name and personality. As soon as the rubber stamp had confirmed his entry into the brotherhood, his mouth took on the broadest grin I have ever seen on a man with a normal-sized face. He was genuinely, deeply happy. Was there something about the name that was giving off these vibes? I tried to make sense of it all. But I started to feel something a little strange. I had a very odd urge indeed. It had crept up on me. But now it was growing by the second.

I looked to Danny, another new Dave Gorman in my arms, and shouted '50!'

He smiled at me and nodded . . . but there was something different about his smile. It was a smile that seemed to be hiding something – a smile plastered on to hide deep thought. He seemed to have lost his concentration. I wanted to ask him whether he was okay or not, but Charles Gorman had work to do. . .

'Graham Cleminson. . .'

I didn't know why I'd started to think the thoughts I had. The fact that I did worried me to the very core of my being – and worries me still. If the me of the day before, could have seen what the me sitting in that boardroom in Mayfair was now considering doing, I dare say emigration might then have seemed a very viable way forward in my life.

Graham Cleminson – now suddenly Dave Gorman number 51 – walked over to Dave to collect his hug.

'51!' yelled Dave. 'Dan! That's 51!'

Graham – sorry, Dave – sat back down next to his girlfriend, and I looked into his eyes. He was happy. Alive. He'd done something stupid and he was loving it. Maybe it was the moment and maybe it was the mood, but this man looked . . . fulfilled. Part of something. He looked like he belonged here, and he laughed out loud as he introduced himself to Dave, and Dave, and Dave.

I caught sight of my own reflection in the glass frame of the painting to my right.

I was becoming an outsider.

An outsider in my own adventure.

And I didn't like it.

We were now only three Dave Gormans away from our target. It was just Kelly, Pascale, and then one more Dave Gorman after that.

Who knows – maybe with the kind of atmosphere we were creating in this room, we could convince Charles Gorman to change his christian name to David! It just seemed to be that sort of day.

'Pascale Beatrice Noele?' said Charles, and Pascale raised her hand. The room was all smiles.

'Repeat after me, please. . .'

Right. I can't justify it properly, but this was the way my mind was working at that moment in time.

In just a few minutes time, we would have 53 Dave Gormans.

That would leave just one more to find.

Just one more Dave Gorman, anywhere in the country. The world, possibly.

If there were any more out there, that is. I mean, heaven knows we had to work hard just to get to this stage. And it wasn't as if there were Dave Gormans banging on our door any more, was it?

What if there weren't any more out there?

What if I'd been right all along?

What if we'd always go on needing one, final, elusive Dave Gorman?

But what if one more person were to change their name to Dave Gorman?

And what if that person . . . were me?

The Dave Gorman formerly known as Pascale Beatrice Noele – the first female Dave Gorman in the history of the world – sat back down in her chair and breathed a huge sigh of relief. But she was happy. I was happy. We were all very, very happy.

'Kelly Ann Scutts. . .' said Charles, and up stood Kelly. 'I take it this will be your 53rd, Mr Gorman?'

'That's right, Mr Gorman,' I said. 'Just one more after this. Just one more, Dan!'

The words were welling up in my throat, but I didn't know what they were. How would I explain what I was about to do to Hanne? To my parents? How would we cope in the flat as two Dave Gormans? How would we know whose mail we were opening?

Kelly Ann Scutts was transformed into Dave Gorman number 53 before my very eyes and I began to tremble.

'53, Dan!' shouted Dave, clinging onto his latest namesake. 'We've hit 53!'

One more and this will all be over. I was repeating the sentence in my head.

The Dave Gormans were standing now, shaking hands with each other, congratulating each other, laughing with each other. I remained sitting where I was.

Charles Gorman caught my eye. He had started to pack up his things but stopped when he saw me rise from my chair.

'I've got something to say,' I started, nervously, as I pushed the chair back behind me.

Everyone looked my way.

'Er . . . Dave?' I said, wondering how best to phrase my decision.

Silence.

Then a giggle.

'Yes?' said six people, all at once, before they fell about laughing.

'Nice one, Dan!' he chuckled. 'So what do you want to say?'

I blinked.

The spell had been broken.

'Nothing,' I said, and sat back down in my chair with a bump.

That was close.

Chapter 19

GORMAN AGHAST

'Dave, I have a confession.'

'What is it?'

'I don't quite know how to tell you.'

'Tell me what?'

'I suppose I can say now that we're almost finished.'

'Say what?'

'You know that first anonymous tip-off? The one that made you buy two tickets for New York?'

'Yes?'

'Well . . . that was me.'

'Oh.'

'Sorry.'

Chapter 20

DESPERATELY SEEKING DAVE

There was a real buzz in the air for the few days that followed the creation of our five new Dave Gormans. And I hadn't even been annoyed when Danny had revealed to me his little fact about New York. Why should I be? If we hadn't gone, we'd still be some way short of our target, and as it was, we only had one more to find.

But that made the pressure on us enormous. Just one more! We were nervous wrecks. On tenterhooks. Stressed. We were dropping things in the kitchen. And not for fun, either. We were nearly there, nearly at the conclusion to the insanity. Teetering on the brink of being able to give all this up and allow the rest of our lives to begin.

And yet there was nothing. Nothing to give us hope. Nothing to suggest a way forward. Nothing to lift the tension. Nothing for days.

E-mails were still arriving regularly, but they were usually just messages of support from interested members of the public, or tip-offs about DGs we already had under our belt.

I kept walking into my room and scouring my e-mail inbox. And I re-read every letter, every tip-off I'd scrawled on a scrap of paper, every doodle I'd done while on the phone to a Dave Gorman. I stared at my computer, willing it to bring me fresh news of a Dave Gorman. But it just didn't seem to want to any more.

I could hear Danny in the next room, on the phone to a 192 operator.

'Coventry,' he said, and there was a pause.

'Well . . . can you try Stoke, then? Yes, same name.'

Another pause.

'Right. None at all? Hmm. Can you try . . . Swansea? Yes, he moves around a lot, yes. . .'

I wandered through to the living room to join him.

'Durham? Can you try Durham? Oh. Okay. Bye.'

He replaced the receiver.

'Going back to basics, eh, Dan?'

'Thought I'd try a few places. You never know.'

'Just think. If we'd met just one more along the way we'd be done by now.'

'If only *Manchester Evening News* Dave Gorman had met us,' mused Dan, chewing on a pencil.

'Yes. Or Royal Leamington bloody Spa.'

'Bastard.'

'Or if only Tom Simpson had changed his name.'

'Bath-tard.'

I sat down on the sofa and Danny held his head in his hands. We were exhausted; deflated. We'd done everything we could. But it seemed as though all the work was to be in vain.

'I know!' said Dan, standing up. 'Let's have a cup of tea!'

'I'll make it,' I said, because there was nothing else to do.

The phone rang in the other room and Danny shouted that he'd get it. I finished making the tea and brought it through. Dan was in the middle of a chat with his mum.

'So are you still out and about finding these Dave Gormans?' she asked.

'Yes,' I said, slightly embarrassed. But mum didn't mind. She thought the whole thing sounded like fun.

'What a lot of places you've been! Your dad and I are a little jealous!'

'For every Venice there were ten Peterboroughs, mum. . .'

'Yes, I know, but it's nice to get out of the flat, isn't it? Your dad and I have just come back from Jersey – I told you we were going over there, didn't I?'

She probably had.

'Er, yes. How was it?'

'Well, the funniest thing happened. I told you we were going over with Mrs. Clarke, didn't I?'

Probably.

'Because you remember I told you about Mrs. Clarke having her nephew Tim out there? I told you about Tim, didn't I?'

She probably had.

'Well, I was just explaining to Tim what you'd been doing – he didn't really seem to understand the whole thing, but he said he'd read about you and Dave.'

'Really?'

I wasn't all that surprised, to be honest. Newspaper coverage had been widespread by this stage, but it was nice to know that the journalists were still doing their bit.

'Yes. In fact, Tim says he's even met that Dave Gorman, so maybe he should try and find 53 more of them as well! We couldn't stop laughing. . .'

'Yeah, maybe he . . . hang on. Which Dave Gorman has he met? *My* Dave Gorman?'

'No, no – he said he didn't like the sound of yours! No, he met the Dave Gorman you met in Jersey. At a cricket match or something.'

'Mum, we haven't met a Dave Gorman in Jersey. We haven't *been* to Jersey.'

'Oh, you must go, it's lovely at this time of year, and Hanne would love the. . .'

'What was this article he'd read? Was it just an appeal for Dave Gormans to come forward or was it. . .'

'No, no. There was a big picture of him in it.'

'Of who?'

'The Dave Gorman in Jersey. Tim found it. It was in *The Jersey Evening Post*. I'll send you a photocopy. . .'

'Have you got one?'

'Of course! I keep *all* your. . .'

'Mum – go and get it. I'm going to put you on speakerphone so Dave can hear you as well. . .'

'Hello Dave!'

'Not yet, mum.'

'Hello Dave!'

'Not yet – I'll put you on in a minute, go and get the article. . .'

I heard her put her phone down with a clunk and nearly trip over the cat as she moved off to find this most confusing of articles.

'What's going on?' asked Dave.

'I'm not sure,' I said. 'But I think we might be onto something. . .'

Danny's mum returned to the phone as we sipped at our tea in excitement.

'You there, mum?' asked Dan.

'Hello?' she said. Her heavy Swiss accent made her instantly recognisable. That, and the fact that Danny was calling her 'mum'.

'Hello Mrs Wallace!' I shouted.

'Hello Dave!' she shouted back. 'I've got the article. There's a big picture of this Dave Gorman and he's holding up a cutting from Page 3 of *The Sun* and pointing at it. They've covered up the naked lady. And he's smiling a lot, and it says "Jersey's Own David Gorman" underneath the picture.'

Oh my. Oh my oh my. This could be it. This could be our Dave Gorman – delivered unto us by Danny's mum. But what was he doing in the paper talking about our journey? Surely he'd only be in the paper if we'd already met him? If he was part of the story? I became certain that it was one of the 53 Dave Gormans we had in our album already – someone with a holiday home in Jersey and a penchant for publicity.

'What does he look like?' I asked.

'Well, he's smiling,' said Danny's mum. 'And he's got black hair. And a white shirt on.'

'Financial sector,' I said under my breath. 'Makes sense – Jersey.'

My mum read the story to us. I say 'story'. To call it that implies that it has some sort of news merit to it. But no. *The Jersey Evening Post* had decided to run a half-page article based around the fact that a man called Dave Gorman in Jersey had discovered that another man called Dave Gorman on the mainland was looking for men called Dave Gorman. And that was their story.

It wasn't that we'd met him. It wasn't that we were *going* to meet him. It was that we were looking for men with his name.

And at no point had he thought to get in touch with us. He'd got in touch with *The Jersey Evening Post* to tell them that we were looking for him, but he hadn't thought to speak to *us*. And at no point had the journalist gone, 'Tell you what, here's an idea for an even *better* story. . .'. Journalism seems to be lacking essential skills in the Channel Islands.

We thanked Danny's mum from the bottom of our hearts, and told her we needed to phone Directory Enquiries as quickly as we could.

First, though, we danced around the flat. This could be it – this could really be it! We babbled excitedly about a trip to Jersey – possibly the last trip we'd have to make before the bet was at an end!

We called Directory Enquiries. And they gave us a number for a David Gorman in Jersey.

Danny handed it to me.

'Here you go,' he said. 'Let's just hope he's up for it. . .'

'He's got to be. He's the final one. He's all we need.'

I studied the piece of paper in his hand, and repeated the number quietly to myself, as if it were a prayer.

'What if he doesn't meet us, Dave? I don't think I could take that sort of rejection.'

'I know, Dan. We'll just have to dust ourselves down and keep looking. We shouldn't get our hopes up too far. Look at what's happened in the past. We have to accept that he might be another B. David Gorman waiting to happen.'

'Just call him. Call him now, please. Let's get this over with.'

I left the phone on speakerphone so that we could both hear this most historic of moments take place, or both share in the disappointment it could just as easily bring. I dialled the number and we waited as, somewhere in Jersey, a telephone was ringing . . . and ringing . . . and ringing. . .

And then. . .

'Hello, David Gorman speaking.'

Bingo!

It was a posh voice. We both instinctively stood up straight. It felt more polite. Like he'd be more willing to meet with us if our backs were straight.

'Er . . . hello, David Gorman. Um . . . my name is *also* David Gorman, and. . .'

'Ah. Hello there. I've been waiting for you to call. About bloody time. . .'

This was it. David Gorman of Jersey *did* want to meet us. It was all arranged. And it seems he did like the publicity.

'When are you planning on coming?' he'd said.

'As soon as we can,' replied Dave.

'What, so we're talking . . . this weekend?'

'Well . . . what are you doing this afternoon?'

'This afternoon? Well . . . that doesn't leave me very much time to notify the press, but . . . yes . . . this afternoon it is!'

London City Airport was just a fifteen-minute ride from our flat. We had twenty minutes before we needed to be at our gate, and I took a seat in the lounge while Dave wandered off to find a toilet.

In the rush to buy tickets and get to the airport, I hadn't had time to think . . . but now I realised: this really would be our last journey together. At least on *this* mission. And it *had* been a mission. It was like for the last six months we'd been colleagues, working together on a seemingly impossible job and now our contracts were about to expire. I didn't know how it would be for us to go back to being unemployed. To not have that excitement any more. To face an altogether more predictable existence. To have lost the one thing that had put an edge on life: the chase.

We'd done so much together, these last six months. I knew everything about this man now. I could accurately predict, looking at his mood and what he'd had for breakfast, which sandwich he would pick from any given list for lunch. I knew his roots, his tastes in music, films, girls, art and clothes. I knew about his mum, his dad, his brothers, his cousins. I even knew what he wanted to call his first son. David. (His second choice, he says, if he couldn't meet a girl willing to raise another David, would be Norman. . .)

And he knew everything about me, too. Far more than I did.

I tried to think back to what we'd done before all this began. How we'd spent our days in the flat with nothing as specific as the hunt for Dave Gormans to fuel our little chats. I wondered how we'd ever found the promise of yet another episode of *3-2-1* or *Karaoke Challenge* as exciting as we had, and tried to add up all the cups of tea we must have drunk while laughing about nothing in particular. What had we talked about back then?

I'm not saying they were wasted days; they weren't. They were cosy, and blokey and important. I'm just saying that, as you approach the end of any big adventure, you've got to worry about how you're going to spend your time once it's just a memory; once you have to move on.

Early on, one of the Dave Gormans we'd met had said he envied our freedom. The fact that we could just get up in the morning and drive anywhere we wanted around the whole country. To Swindon, or to Warminster, or to Bromsgrove, or Manchester, or Dunstable. That we could just hop on a train and a few hours later be in Edinburgh with no thought of the consequences. That we could jump on a flight to Marseille without having to organise the family, or cancel the milk, or even care if we'd forgotten to cancel the milk. They hadn't seemed to worry that there was no discernable purpose to the thing, that there was no real reason to be doing it. That's what I'd been looking for all along – something to justify it all. But they didn't need convincing like me. They'd just enjoyed the stupidity, the carelessness and the freedom of the thing. And so had Dave. But it was a freedom that would be hard to replicate. After today, it might be gone.

I thought of Hanne and suddenly missed her very much. She knew where Dave and I were going today and why, and had responded with a clap of her hands and a 'thank God!'. She'd waited – patiently much of the time, not so patiently the rest – for her boyfriend and his flatmate to finish what they'd started, to get it out of their systems, and it was finally about to pay off.

The last six months would represent as intense a flatshare as I think it's possible to get. But maybe it would also come to signify a peak in our friendship. We were as close as two friends could be, and we'd always have it . . . but would we ever have anything else?

'You ready to go?' said Dave, suddenly there, interrupting my thoughts.

'Eh? Sorry, mate, I was miles away.'

'You ready to move on?'

'Yes,' I said. And it was true. 'I think I almost am.'

We climbed into a little plane and pushed our coats into the overhead locker. Danny was being quite quiet, and it had started to rub off on me. Usually, I'd have tried to cheer him up, to start a singsong, or suggest a game.

But not today.

Because as we flew to Jersey I suddenly found myself becoming more introspective. The finishing post was now in sight. Soon it would all be over. I felt displaced. The one thing I had been striving for, for so long, was about to be over. Then what would I do?

In the white heat of our quest I had thought of nothing else. I had only ever looked forward as far as the next Dave Gorman we would meet. Now I found myself looking back over our travels and asking myself what it had all been for.

A lot of people who travel the world say that they 'found themselves'. I had travelled the world and I had found myself over and over again. Or had I? I'd found my namesakes, but what had I actually learnt about *myself*?

Before all this started I was Dave Gorman. Now, I was only *a* Dave Gorman. Those two words that had once defined me now merely defined a subset to which I belonged. I was one of many. It seemed I had spent the last few months slowly diluting my own sense of self.

Throughout that time I had woken up with one thought on my mind: where will we find the next Dave Gorman? But in completing the task, I would rob myself of this sense of purpose. Tomorrow I would wake up and do . . . what? I didn't know. Other Dave Gormans would spend the next day driving lorries, flying planes, trading stocks, managing surgeries, investigating crime, fitting carpets, going to school or any one of many different activities.

What did Dave Gorman do? Anything. Who was Dave Gorman? Anyone. Where did Dave Gorman live? Anywhere. My name meant everything and nothing. How would I face the future? What would I do? Who was I?

Under an hour later and we were beginning our descent into Jersey. We watched the neat, little houses shoot by beneath us, and the tiny cars as they negotiated their way around the fun-sized island.

Once we'd landed, Dave and I spoke only a few words to each other. We were excited, but we were subdued. We didn't know why. Or, at least, that's what we told each other. I was pretty sure we both knew.

We walked through Jersey airport – empty apart from the fifteen other people who'd travelled with us, who, with meetings to go to, were now all scurrying quickly away through automatic doors and into waiting taxis.

'Where did you say we'd meet him?'

'He said he'd be in the airport. He'd look out for us, he said.'

We turned a corner and saw our man. He was with two other men.

'That's them!' he said, and one of his companions started to take pictures of us. His friend wrote furiously into a notebook.

'Dave Gorman?' said Dave.

'That's me!' said David Gorman.

The photographer kept click-clicking away.

'I'm Carl. We're from *The Jersey Evening Post*,' said the man with the notebook.

'Ah,' I said. 'Now, *this* is a "story", eh?', but he looked at me oddly and didn't write it down.

'I would've got a TV crew down here, as well,' said Dave Gorman number 54, apologetically. 'But a tanker went down in the sea and I think they're all over there, covering that.'

Clearly, the Jersey media was yet to get its priorities straight.

'But Jersey Radio are coming down later on to do an interview with me. They might want to speak with you as well, if that's okay. . .'

'Fine by us, Dave,' said Dave.

'So where have you been so far?' asked Carl.

'Oh, everywhere, really,' said DG54. 'I read all about it. You've been to Italy, Norway, France . . .'

'. . . Germany, Israel, America. . .' said Dave.

'. . . Dunstable. . .' I added. I was just trying to join in, really.

'And where are you planning on going next?' he asked. 'Where's the next one?'

Dave looked at me. I nodded.

'Well, that's it, now. We've completed the bet. We were trying to get to 54. And this man here . . . well . . . he's Dave Gorman number 54.'

DG54 looked incredibly proud.

'I'm it, am I?'. He shook his head in disbelief. 'I'm it!'

'Dave,' I said. 'There's one thing you have to do before you've met him properly . . . it's tradition. . .'

Dave nodded and extended his right hand. David Gorman took it and shook it furiously.

'Pleased to meet you, Dave Gorman 54 . . . we never thought we would. . .'

Chapter 21

THE END OF THE GORMAN CONQUESTS

For the rest of that day, I couldn't shake the feeling that I should have been happier than I was.

We'd completed our task. I'd proved Danny wrong. There *were* 'loads' of Dave Gormans in the world, and we'd met 'loads' of them to prove it. One for every card in the deck, in fact, including the jokers.

Dave Gorman 54 had seemed proud and honoured to have been the conclusion to such a noble quest – so much so that he'd taken it upon himself to introduce us around the island, take us to a local hotel facing the seafront for a posh slap-up meal, and even driven us back to his place to collect an expensive bottle of champagne to help celebrate the completion of our task. We drank it on the beach. It was bittersweet. Because while we'd succeeded, it meant that the adventure was over.

The radio journalist Dave Gorman 54 had summoned arrived soon after, and asked us how it felt to have completed our journey. We couldn't answer her. It was too soon to tell.

Danny phoned Hanne to tell her we'd finished. My namesake and I sat and smiled as we heard her screams of delight spilling out of his mobile.

And then I realised. We should be happy too. We'd achieved something. Something pointless, maybe. But something, nevertheless.

I raised my champagne glass and clinked it with Danny's, and we both did the same to DG54.

I would love to be able to say that the sun was setting, or that a rainbow suddenly burst out from behind a cloud, but I can't. You'll just have to believe me when I say that the fact that the three of us – me, Danny, and the final Dave Gorman – were sitting on this beach, in Jersey, slightly chilly, but toasting the end of an adventure with a glass of champagne, is more than enough for me. For the first time in months, I was content. For the first time in months, I was satisfied. I was at peace with myself.

Hanne met us at the airport with a small and rather pathetic looking *'Congratulations!'* balloon, and the three of us shared a black cab into town, where we first had a curry, then a few drinks, then enough drinks to convince us that dancing was a good idea. We ended up in a karaoke bar in Shoreditch. Dave sang 'It's Raining Daves', his own subtle reworking of the Weathergirls classic. I sang 'It's The End Of The World As We Know It'. Hanne didn't sing anything at all. But we were happy, the three of us. Things were back to normal. Back to normal between Dave and me. Back to normal between Hanne and me. And – though I never thought I'd see it – back to normal between Hanne and Dave.

We had a great night. A night without pressure. I knew that in the morning, I didn't have to go anywhere, didn't have to *be* anywhere. I could sleep in. No one would wake me, there'd be no need to jump into a Vauxhall Corsa bound for Luton Airport or somewhere just as glamorous. A weight had been lifted from my shoulders. Dave, too, was more relaxed than I'd seen him in weeks. Months, even.

We stumbled home with a batch of bagels we'd collected from the 24-hour bakery on Brick Lane, and slept for a very, very long time indeed.

When we woke up it would all just be something we'd done, once. Not something we were doing. It would be in the past. My head hit the pillow wondering how that would make me feel. But I fell asleep before I could work it out.

The fortnight that followed saw our lives slowly returning to normal. We used the time wisely – catching up with friends, staring in disbelief at bank statements, working out what to do with our afternoons.

But the emptiness that existed now that the search was over made me more aware than ever of quite how all-consuming our quest had been. During those two weeks, time passed far slower than it had ever seemed to before . . . and yet, what were we doing differently? Life hadn't felt like this in the past. Something had changed. I'm the first to admit that our quest had been completely and utterly pointless. But now it wasn't even that. We didn't even have a *pointless* point to prove.

I took a quick trip up to Manchester to meet up with a few old mates. While I was there, I realised that a life-changing decision would soon be forced on me.

I was bored.

I'd been bored for a few days, now. And I'd also had a gnawing worry in the pit of my stomach, about Dave and me. I knew that we'd always be friends – always close friends, at that. But something had shifted and I wanted it back in place. I had a small, stupid plan at the back of my mind, only half worked out, and now seemed like a good time to try it.

We were sitting in the living room drinking tea and watching *Gloria Hunniford's Open House* on Channel 5. Gloria was interviewing a man at great length about the best place in the house to put an aspidistra, or some such nonsense. We had the windows open and the sun was streaming in.

'Is there anything else on?' I asked.

'Just snooker,' said Dave.

'What time is *Psychic Livetime* on?'

'6 o'clock.'

I tapped the sides of my chair and yawned.

'D'you fancy a kickabout?' asked Dave.

'Mmm . . . no,' I said. 'Maybe later.'

'Another cup of tea, then?'

'No . . . but . . . actually . . . do you fancy a tequila?' said Danny.

'It's 3 o'clock! And I thought you said you'd never drink tequila again?'

'I did say that, yes, but it's your birthday.'

'It's not.'

I was confused.

'You know the rules of the house,' said Dan. 'If your present arrives, it's your birthday.'

I was still confused.

'But I haven't got a present.'

'Yes you have', said Dan, 'I got it for you.'

'What? What is it?'

'It's a bottle of tequila!'

I poured two ample shots into some mugs and handed Dave his. I'd already prepared the lemon and salt, and brought these out on a small tray.

One, two, three . . . lick of salt, slug of tequila, bite of bitter lemon.

We were ready. We weren't drunk yet but we were ready to be.

'Right,' I said, looking around the room for inspiration. 'I . . . bet . . . you. . .'

Dave flashed me a look. Suddenly he knew what was going on, and his eyes widened with excitement. A smile of anticipation crept across his face.

'Yeah? You bet me what?' he said.

'I . . . bet . . . you . . . that . . . er . . . that you can't get a fridge magnet from 26 towns, each town beginning with a different letter of the alphabet!'

It was rubbish.

Dave sat back in his chair.

There was a pause and I poured two more shots.

'Hey!' I said. 'You know the Eurovision Song Contest? Well, I bet you couldn't go to Norway and sing a song with every Norwegian performer to have scored *nul point* in the competition's illustrious fifty year history. I bet you couldn't do that!'

'Riiiight,' said Dan. 'And . . . what would be the point of that?'

'I dunno. Do you want some more tequila?'

'No. I dunno what the point of that is, either. What's the point in any of this?'

We both knew that it wasn't the same. Perhaps it never would be. These things just have to . . . *happen*.

The problem was, could we really afford them just to happen? How could either of us go to the pub opposite the flat ever again without worrying that the next six months of our lives might be about to go up in smoke as we trek along the Himalayas collecting goats just because one of us said we'd never manage it?

Ours was a dangerous friendship. A dangerous flatshare.

'Dan,' I said, managing to interrupt his thoughts and surprise myself at what I was about to tell him. 'I met up with the tenants of my flat in Manchester the other day. They told me they're moving out. It makes sense to put the flat on the market. You know . . . move down to London permanently.'

'Oh,' said Dan. 'Only, I've been thinking. . .'

'Thing is . . . I ought to *buy* somewhere down here. But I wasn't sure . . . should I be looking at *one* bedroom places, or *two* bedroom places? I mean . . . what do *you* reckon?'

'Thing is, Dave . . . me and Hanne. We've been thinking of getting a place together and . . . well . . . you know.'

'Oh. Right. Yeah. Of course.'

'Not for a little while, though, you know.'

'Well, I'll be looking for a buyer first, obviously.'

'Yeah. Where were you thinking of looking?'

'Where were you? You and Hanne?'

'Around here, I think. I like it.'

'Yeah. Me too.'

'Around here, then?'

'Yeah. Around here.'

And so it was decided. We'd move out. Not yet. But soon.

'Dan?'

'Yeah?'

'I bet you can't meet 54 Danny Wallaces.'

EPILOGUE

Since their adventure ended, Dave and Danny have continued to eat lunch together most days, though they now technically live over one mile apart. They are slowly adjusting to the long-distance friendship.

In November 2000, Dave and Danny organised a party and invited all the Dave Gormans they knew. They also invited brand new Dave Gormans that they'd heard about since ending the quest.

Fifty Dave Gormans attended.

They were all made to wear name badges.

Nineteen of them were brand new Dave Gormans – taking the total of Dave Gormans actually met to 73 by the end of the day.

The popular lecture, 'Are You Dave Gorman?', has been taken around the world to cities such as Aspen and Melbourne, and new Dave Gormans have regularly attended.

Dave and Danny got back in touch with the television executive Myfanwy Moore after the bet had ended, and the story was made into a six-part BBC2 series called *The Dave Gorman Collection*, which Dave and Danny wrote and produced as best they could.

A researcher from *The Guinness Book of Records* got in touch with the boys with a view to including them in the next edition. It was thought they would be eligible for two categories. Dave, under *Most Namesakes Met*, and Danny, under *Most Of Someone Else's Namesakes Met*.

Someone recently appeared in the background of an episode of the sitcom *Friends*, wearing an 'I Am Not Dave Gorman – Are You?' badge.

A story appeared in *The Sun* soon after the boys stopped looking, about a Scottish Dave Gorman who works in waste disposal and had been shot by an air rifle.

Three dogs, two cats, an unspecified number of goldfish and a van have all been named Dave Gorman by members of the public.

Dave and Danny were sent another book written by another Dave Gorman. This one is an expert on dating, is known as The Love Doctor, and has appeared on *Oprah*. He lives in Arizona and his book is entitled *Have I Got A Match For You?*
    Which is odd, because he does.

More American Dave Gormans continue to be brought to Dave and Danny's attention. A Dave Gorman who works as a lawyer for US retail giant Walmart appeared in an episode of American TV news show *60 Minutes*. A Dave Gorman in Washington DC is a spokesman for the Disabled American Veterans. Another, living in San Francisco, is married to a man called Kevin. Yet another plays lead guitar in Boston heavy metal band Vicious Cirkill.

A punk band have renamed themselves The Dave Gorman Project.

A nightclub in Nottingham recently offered free entry to anyone by the name of Dave Gorman.

When The Spice Girls hosted a special episode of Channel 4's *TFI Friday*, someone had planted a sign in the background of the set reading 'Are You Dave Gorman?'
    The show was recorded at The Riverside Studios, Hammersmith.

Eleven more people have offered to change their name by deed poll to Dave Gorman. Only one of them is a girl.

The producers of a major Australian drama series, *Something In The Air*, heard about the story. They immediately got in touch to say they were introducing a new character to the show . . . and calling him Dave Gorman.

A character on page 186 of the Irvine Welsh novel *Filth* is called David Gorman.

There's a Dave Gorman who's a professional boxing manager. At one point he was managing Tyson.

Darryl Tyson.

A Mrs Rebecca Whiting paid £80 to register a star under the name Dave Gorman. She wrote to Dave and Danny saying simply, 'I hope this helps.'

Dave Gorman of Royal Leamington Spa remains unmet.

While they are no longer actively trying to meet Dave Gormans, Dave Gormans seem to be seeking the boys out. The current total of Dave Gormans met is somewhere in the nineties.

They have yet to meet anyone else called Danny Wallace.